This Victorian Life

This Victorian Life

Modern Adventures in Nineteenth-Century Culture, Cooking, Fashion, and Technology

Sarah A. Chrisman

Skyhorse Publishing, Inc.

Skyhorse Publishing books may be purchased in bulk at special discounts for sales promotion, corporate gifts, fund-raising, or educational purposes. Special editions can also be created to specifications. For details, contact the Special Sales Department, Skyhorse Publishing, 307 West 36th Street, 11th Floor, New York, NY 10018 or info@skyhorsepublishing.com.

Skyhorse® and Skyhorse Publishing® are registered trademarks of Skyhorse Publishing, Inc.®, a Delaware corporation.

Visit our website at www.skyhorsepublishing.com.

10 9 8 7 6 5 4 3 2 1

Library of Congress Cataloging-in-Publication Data is available on file.

Cover design by Erin Seaward-Hiatte
Cover photo credit Hyo Gyung Choi, Mary Studio

Print ISBN: 978-1-63450-237-5
Ebook ISBN: 978-1-5107-0073-4

Printed in the United States of America

*To every "man in the arena"—those who understand
why it is not the critic who counts.*

Table of Contents

Author's Note   *xi*

Introduction: The Angels in the Details   *xiii*

CHAPTER 1: A Home of a Distinct Form   1

CHAPTER 2: Thanksgiving   15

CHAPTER 3: Settling In   21

CHAPTER 4: Our New/Old City   27

CHAPTER 5: The House—And Furnishing It   33

CHAPTER 6: Maligned Plumbing, a Beautiful Toilette Set, and a Surprise Visit from a Daughter of Arachne   63

CHAPTER 7: A Detail as Fine as a Hair   75

CHAPTER 8: The Brackens   81

CHAPTER 9: Ghost Stories   89

CHAPTER 10: Writing   109

CHAPTER 11: The Book of Household Management   125

CHAPTER 12: An Exotic Flavor   137

CHAPTER 13: Our Daily Bread   141

CHAPTER 14: Chestnut Shrapnel, "Pure Evil," and a Few Sweet Delights   149

CHAPTER 15: A Problem That Didn't Exist in the Nineteenth Century, and a Treat That Did   163

CHAPTER 16: Portrait   171

CHAPTER 17: Communication Parallels   179

CHAPTER 18: Chatelaine   183

CHAPTER 19: Watches   195

CHAPTER 20: Science Matters and Outdoor Outings   203

CHAPTER 21: Strength and How to Obtain It   219

CHAPTER 22: An Ordinary Bicycle   225

CHAPTER 23: Woman's Cycle   231

CHAPTER 24: My First Adventure in Cycle Touring   241

CHAPTER 25: Wheeling   263

CHAPTER 26: A Typical Day   277

Epilogue   *287*

Acknowledgments   *289*

End Notes   *291*

Resources   *301*

"Webster says, 'History is a continuous narrative of events,' but I include in mine many private thoughts."
—James Eagleson, 1884[1]

Author's Note

A careful reader of these pages will notice that the events described are not always recounted in strict chronological sequence. (For example, more than a year passed between the day Gabriel gave me my vasculum and our fossil hunting expedition, but it was logical to relate them in the same chapter.) This is intended to aid in readability of the text. Life does not always occur in neatly grouped subject headings, but a neatly organized book is a more enjoyable read than the randomly lumped stream of consciousness that generally constitutes daily life. Of course, the very subject of this book will alert its audience that my nature inclines me to take liberties with temporal chronology.

The events in this narrative are all true and as accurately depicted as my memory can make them.

Introduction

The Angels in the Details

All creatures surround themselves with the things that make them most comfortable. In the case of my husband and myself, we just happen to be most comfortable with surroundings more of a nineteenth-century nature than of a twenty-first-century one. In technical terms, our life is a long-term experiential study in temporal diversity of culture and nineteenth-century technology. We study the late Victorian era the way avid linguists study foreign languages: by interacting with our subject as much as possible. There is no passport for traveling through time, but we do our best.

It started with our clothes. When Gabriel gave me a corset on my twenty-ninth birthday, I had no idea how that simple garment would capture my imagination and ultimately lead me into a different world from the one I had been born into—a world of ticking clocks and rustling silk, scented by kerosene and paraffin and inks pressed from the fragrant petals of flowers. It is a world that the modern era is separated from, yet touched by. As historian Vaclav Smil says in *Creating the Twentieth Century*, "[T]he fundamental means to realize nearly all of the 20th-century accomplishments were put in place even before the century began, mostly during the three closing decades of the 19th century and in the years preceding WWI."[2] The nineteenth century birthed the twentieth—and, by extension, the twenty-first.

My husband and I have both always loved history in general and the Victorian era in particular. It often seems to us as though everything worth inventing—everything that made the modern world what it is (for good or ill)—came into being in the last few decades of the nineteenth century. When I started wearing Victorian clothing on a regular basis and we realized how much insight this provided into the everyday lives of the past, we started wondering what other windows were waiting to be opened through the exploration of more elements of the Victorian experience.

When we first resolved upon this life, we tried to find other people like us, individuals who viewed the past as a different culture and wanted to comprehend it. Too many academic historians view the past as a dead thing to be dissected and then encased in glass. Collectors often focus on specific items rather than the big picture of the culture that gave those items context. There are certainly some very impressive collections in the world, and we enjoy seeing them when they pertain to our interests, but we have broader goals than collecting for its own sake.

The people we find truly anathema are the ones who reduce the past to caricature and distort it to fit their own bigoted stereotypes. We've gone to events that claimed to be historic fashion shows but turned out to be gaudy polyester parades with no shadow of reality behind them. As we heard our ancestors mocked and bigoted stereotypes presented as facts, we felt like we had gone to an event advertised as an NAACP convention only to discover it was actually a minstrel show featuring actors in blackface. Some so-called "living history" events really are that bigoted.

When we object to history being degraded this way, the guilty parties shout that they are "just having fun." What they are really doing is attacking a past that cannot defend itself. Perhaps they *are* having fun, but it is the sort of fun a schoolyard brute has at the expense of a child who goes home bruised and weeping. It's time someone stood up for the past.

I have always hated bullies. The instinct to attack difference can be seen in every social species, but if humans truly desire to rise above barbarism, then we must cease acting like beasts. The human race may have been born in mud and ignorance, but we are blessed with minds sufficiently powerful to shape our behavior. Personal choices form the lives of individuals; the sum of all interactions determine the nature of societies.

At present, it is politically fashionable in America to tolerate limited diversity based around race, religion, and sexual orientation, yet following a trend does not equate with being truly open-minded. There are people who proudly proclaim they support women's rights, yet have an appallingly limited definition of what those rights entail. (Currently, fashionable privileges are voting, working outside the home, and easy divorce; some people would be dumbfounded at the idea that creating beautiful things, working inside the home, and marriage are equally desirable rights for many women.) In the eighteenth century, Voltaire declared, "I disagree with what you say but I will fight to the death for your right to say it."[3] Many modern Americans seem to have perverted this to, "I will fight to the death for your right to agree with what I say."

When we stand up for history, we are in our way standing up for all true diversity. When we question stereotypes and fight ignorance about the past, we force people to question ignorance in general.

Our embrace of historic culture came at a crossroads in our lives, and we found ourselves contemplating the ways in which surroundings affect lives at a time when we were also seeking a new home for ourselves. My husband had recently graduated with a master's degree in library science from the University of Washington in Seattle. A disastrous—and very brief—move to Washington, DC (when Gabriel accepted a contract job at the Library of Congress) so strongly impressed the importance of community and surroundings upon us that we practically left skid marks across the country getting back to the Pacific Northwest. The result was that we took a leap—partly a leap of faith in our own determination but also a leap of hope for what we could accomplish together. We bought an 1888 house in Port Townsend (Washington's Victorian seaport and long our favorite place) and proceeded to see how Victorian a life we could truly carve out for ourselves in the twenty-first-century world.

An enormous amount of the infrastructure that supported society and people's everyday lives in the nineteenth century has vanished. Some disappearances happened long ago, others are more recent than most people realize. The culture of the past—like any culture—was based on complicated economies and relationships among millions of individuals. Expecting two people to bring back multiple industries that supported millions would be patently ridiculous. Certain exigencies must be accepted because we live in the world as it is, not as we would wish it to be.

We are not playing a role, but living a real life, and a lot of that involves working out ways to exist in the world without sacrificing our principles. In this, we are no different from anyone else with strong convictions.

I have a degree in international studies and, four years into this endeavor, our household reminds me of the many homes of immigrants I have visited throughout the years. Whether they are the homes of expats abroad or the US households of fresh entries into the American melting pot, settler domiciles always show the cultural identities of those who inhabit them, alongside the inescapable reminders that one has not actually traveled very far. Our personal histories assert themselves, no matter where we are. We all do what we can with what we have to make our dreams come true. Completely shifting our home to embody the ultimate incarnation of our dreams is a lifelong endeavor that we recognize may never be finished, but we continue to move along that long and winding path, and each step we have taken has taught us something about the world that has been, the world that is, and—perhaps—the world that is yet to come. The longer we do this and the deeper we delve into the minutiae of nineteenth-century life, the more I see its reflections in the world around me, even outside my home. Traveling through different countries and studying their peoples helped me to see their influence everywhere I turned in my own country when I returned to America. So, too, our investigations through time have brought greater clarity to the echoing refrains of history still ringing in the modern world.

People say the devil is in the details, but I contend that a great many angels reside there as well. For one thing, details distinguish cultures from one another and allow us to revel in the great diversity that the human race can manifest. All people have the same basic needs of shelter, food, and companionship, yet the ways we define and realize these things vary widely. One's specific outlines of their needs define not only their culture, but increasingly specific subsets thereof, narrowing down to the identity that is truly their own. Shelter can be any structure from a palace to a yurt; food may range from raw seaweed to roast ortolan. As for companionship, it might take an entire network of acquaintances to stave off loneliness from one person, while another is happy nested within a large family or cuddled close to the heart of one person who means the world to them. For some, all it takes is a pet or a single cherished book. These differences are details, it's true, but they are details that define us and that we, in turn, define through our own choices and resources.

What distinguishes a Victorian home from a modern one? The answer is the same as if one had asked what distinguishes any culture from another: details. These details are too numerous to list and most, on their own, might seem small to an outside observer. Yet each has a lesson to teach us, just as each individual is a living part of his or her society.

Just as hosting an exchange student teaches lessons about another culture, interacting with an artifact from history provides insights into another time. The effect is amplified when exposure intensifies. Many artifacts were designed to function within a specific context and interact with other objects and infrastructure contemporary to themselves. The more one can reinstate an artifact's context, the better it functions and the more sense it makes. (Imagine trying to analyze a remote control without access to its corresponding device or the power sources of either.)

One of my favorite quotes about cultural meanings came from my first French professor on the very first day of class. "French people," she told the students, "don't say something in French because they mean it in English and just don't know any better. French people say something in French because they mean it in French!" To truly comprehend the meaning of something, understanding its context is vital.

Traveling to a foreign country is the best way to learn about its culture or language because it places the student in the context of the subject. They are exposed to all the details of life and witness how infinite factors compound each other to form the complex equation of a functioning society. We can't travel to the past, but we can surround ourselves with its details.

From the time my husband and I first envisioned this project, we knew that this form of historical education would be the slow and steady work of a lifetime. Someone who is born into a culture emerges into a time and place already surrounded by its details. We would have to slowly reinstate them when this was possible and compare and debate modern equivalents when it wasn't. For example, no publisher on Earth will accept a handwritten manuscript any more. I keep my daily diary by hand, as well as all my notes, and even draft my manuscripts that way, but when it's time to submit things to my editor, I have to transcribe all that I've written and submit an electronic version. The world is a complicated place. Anyone with a lifestyle that deviates at all from the mainstream must find ways to survive within the existing systems. The key is to not lose sight of one's philosophies in the process, to not lose track of ways those compromises can accord with the ideal.

When contemplating the past, many people think only of what it didn't have and consider that temporal difference only means cutting things out. In some ways, this would be easy, but it is the polar opposite of the task that Gabriel and I set for ourselves. Our job, as we saw it, was to put historical elements *into* our lives so that we could learn from them. Oil lamps, writing tools, period recipes, furniture, advice manuals . . . We knew all these things had lessons to teach us; the catch was we would have to acquire them first. Just getting hold of something from the nineteenth century often constitutes more than half the struggle to use it. Before bringing even small, quotidian elements of the past into our lives, we must always deal first with challenges of money, time, and the quirky twists of fate.

No one pays us to live as we do or sponsors us in any way. Nor are we even remotely wealthy. Everything we gather is something we've saved for, in many cases for a very long while. Since the items we can afford are not

Gabriel and me. Image courtesy Matt Choi, Mary Studio.

always in the best condition, they often require repairs just to be serviceable. Just learning how to repair them (or finding someone who can) requires research, which, of course, takes time. The things we can make from scratch take time, as well. I make all my own clothes and most take months or even years of work.

Even if some beneficent sponsor were to sweep in and shower us with funds, there would still be the quirks of fate to consider. Some items are just hard to find now, period—even if they were common in the past. Ironically, the most common items often become the rarest over time because no one thinks them worthy of preservation. These are the sorts of things it takes patience and luck to find, and we must be quick on our feet about snatching them when they come up.

These are all challenges (in some cases very difficult ones), but we never consider them hardships. Seeking out quotidian items from the nineteenth century and learning how to interact with them properly constitute some of our favorite joys. Gabriel and I both love to learn, and we enjoy hunting together for an ever-deepening knowledge of a period that fascinates us.

The late nineteenth century was an incredibly dynamic time. We focus on the decades of the 1880s and '90s because they seem pivotal. People were dealing with technologies like telephones and ultra-fast mail for the first time and asking each other for advice about situations modern people still find challenging. The period is a goldmine of advice for issues that remain relevant today.

We focused our lens of inquiry upon the late nineteenth century and began gathering objects to aid our inquiries and be our teachers. The story that follows recounts just a few of our adventures from the first four years of this quest for knowledge and what we've learned.

1

A Home of a Distinct Form

Illustration from *The Wheelman* cycling magazine, June 1883.

"Residential buildings profoundly shape the behavior of people.
Individuals who live in homes of distinct forms and contents internalize
a spectrum of spatial and social rules regarding appropriate activities
there. They become socialized via cultural norms and kin to be sure, but
also through interactions with their furnishings and built surroundings."
—Jeanne E. Arnold, et al, 2012[4]

I've always loved electrical outages, even as a child. For me, these failures in
technology represented not inconvenience or hardship, but much-longed-for

peace. Growing up in a household where the television was never silent, even while we slept, and always growled in the background, I yearned for quiet. Power outages silenced the television and put the vulturine eyes of all the myriad blinking devices to sleep. What bliss that quiet brought! The gentle glow of lamplight or candle flame seemed almost holy in the solace it offered.

I never stopped yearning for that balance between sacred light and velvet darkness, and when I matured, I married a man who understood my sympathies in that quarter. Throughout the early winters of our marriage, we would celebrate the coming of the winter solstice by forgoing electric lights altogether for the weeks between December's first day and the official coming of winter on the solstice. While the pale radiance of our northern latitude grew rarer, and all our friends and neighbors fought the ever-increasing nighttime blackness with blinking strings and streamers of light, we eschewed electric illumination and faced the darkness.

The first year we did this, I was deeply struck by the psychological impact of the night. I had not been expecting to be hit so profoundly by the darkness—after all, I had grown up in the Pacific Northwest. A map places Seattle at 47.6 degrees northern latitude: farther north than Maine. Differences in geographical features mean we have less snow than many other locations, but the only US state with longer nights is Alaska. In some ways, the lack of snow seems to make Seattle winters even darker; there is nothing to reflect the sallow moonlight on those long nights, and gray rain clouds hide the wan sun throughout the ever-shortening days. Even when one or the other of those celestial orbs appears through a crack in the slate ceiling that covers us through all those long months, no crystals refract their light. It drowns in the puddles and is swallowed up by the mud.

I had understood these things about the light on an intellectual level, and, of course, discussions about seasonal affective disorder (SAD) and full-spectrum lighting are such popular topics of conversation in Seattle that they grow wearisome. On one of the coldest, rainiest days of winter, a text message received by one of my husband's colleagues ran, "Sitting under sunlamp. Gun to head." The Northwest does that to people.

Yet, I had never truly appreciated the stark difference between night and day when I could simply toggle a switch to convert one to the other. During our first several years of marriage—and thus of this particular tradition—we lived not in the city but in a rural location hemmed in by fir trees, so no metropolitan light intruded upon our self-imposed blackness. In those long weeks of darkness, I caught a glimpse into the minds of our ancestors. The death of the light grows very obvious as one nears the winter solstice in high latitudes.

With powerful electric bulbs destroying all distinction between night and day, it is easy to overlook the dying of the sun, simple to dismiss religious light festivals as mere superstition. But when the fallacy of electric light is banished and one must face the truth of the darkness as humans have done for thousands of years, with only flame between our mortal frames and the night, every lost minute of sun is mourned. The nights grow ever longer as the light dies, and the most stalwart logic cannot completely banish the primal doubt that creeps through the back door of the soul: will the sun truly return? As we sit through lengthening hours of darkness awaiting an ever-enfeebled dawn, the evidence contradicts our logical argument of a detached notion of planet rotation. The light is not coming back. Winter has given it a mortal blow, and nothing shall ever be bright again.

Then solstice passes. The days grow longer. Can words possibly express the absolute bliss of the soul as light returns to the landscape, the relief brought with brightness as logic is affirmed and celestial bodies proven to be turning in their proper orbits? Never! As humans, we can analyze the phenomenon, we can discuss it, but we can never truly understand it in our souls until we have lived it. We must confront the darkness to know the value of the light.

Darkness lends itself well to retrospection. Even while Gabriel and I lived through those powerless nights of winter holidays, we recognized how limited the experience was. "Imagine," we would tell each other, "what it would be like without any electricity at all. No noisy fridge humming, no modern inconveniences." The idea excited us.

Time and again, we came back to the topic and had variants on the same discussion. It was inevitable that conversation should lead to the extreme conclusion of the idea.

"What if we went all the way?" Gabriel asked. "Not just for a specified time, but always? What if we got rid of all the extra modern stuff we don't really need and went back to how people used to live?"

"I always did want to live in the nineteenth century," I said dreamily. "When I was a little girl and my mom took me to the Flavel House Museum in Astoria, I begged her to leave me there." I smiled into the darkness, my imagination split between memories of a girl younger than myself and visions of a century older than my time. "I used to dream about what it would be like to live there amidst all that beauty, what it would have been like when the house was new."

The Flavel House was the nineteenth-century home of a wealthy Victorian family, now converted to a museum, all its rooms filled with period artifacts as though it truly were still a bygone era and the family had simply stepped away for a short time. I wanted to stay there—to live there—more desperately than I had ever wanted to be anywhere else.

"I spent all my allowance on a little scented soap in one of the nearby shops, and after we went home I used to lie in that old fiberglass bathtub in the house where I grew up, closing my eyes and breathing in the scent of that soap. I would imagine I was in the bathroom of the Flavel House and the smell of the soap was the ocean air coming through the window. Then I would dream about being out in the rose garden with that same ocean scent all around me. I spent hours thinking about it." I sighed and looked over at my husband.

He smiled at me. "Wouldn't it be nice?"

"To go back in time? Of course it would." I shrugged in a fatalistic way. "Not gonna happen, though."

"Why not?"

I laughed at the illogical question.

"I mean—" he specified, "what I was saying before. Why couldn't we just incorporate as much as we can of the past into our lives? Bring back as much of it as we could?"

"Okay," I responded flippantly. "I'll stop driving and we'll both give up cell phones."

Now it was Gabriel's turn to laugh. The joke, of course, was that I have never possessed a driver's license and neither of us have ever owned a mobile telephone. As an adolescent, then later in college, I had never had the money to buy or maintain an automobile so there seemed very little point in learning to drive one. By the time I could theoretically have afforded a car, I understood how easy it was to do without one. I saw no reason to devote a large portion of my income to a machine whose role seemed to consist of fouling the air, eliminating exercise, and occasionally murdering squirrels and pussycats. I also admit that there was a certain degree of mulish stubbornness at work. Every time yet another person heard I didn't have a license and responded that of course I *had* to learn to drive, I became all the more determined to prove it is possible for an American to be a fully functioning adult without an internally combusting toy.

The story behind our lack of cell phones is a similar one. When they were initially introduced, they were expensive, and when they became cheaper and virtually ubiquitous, society's insistence that they were necessary made me want to prove that this was not the case. Human beings survived quite happily throughout the vast majority of our history with neither motorized vehicles nor mobile phones. They lived, prospered, procreated, and died without the slightest intimation that such things would ever exist. Large numbers of people covering huge swaths of the globe *still* live without such things. Why so many modern Americans have come to consider them as essential as oxygen is a mystery to me.

"Just because other people live a certain way doesn't mean we have to," Gabriel continued. It was an affirmation of the sentiment that lay behind my last sarcastic comment and, at the same time, a support of the larger idea he was arguing.

Suddenly, our refrigerator started its customary howling. It had a malfunctioning compression coil that went off with increasing frequency to split the air with a warbling shriek like a ghost in a low-budget horror movie. Profoundly irritating though this was, it didn't affect the cooling apparatus and we had grown accustomed to it. We calmly covered our ears until it finished.

Once we could hear each other again, Gabriel gestured toward the appliance. "Wouldn't it be nice to do without all that?"

"Or, we could just buy a new refrigerator," I suggested.

"They're expensive."

"So are your bicycles," I told him.

Gabriel worked at a bike shop and had a penchant for flashy models.

"Not nearly as expensive as a fridge," he argued.

"But maybe a little more practical?" I ventured.

"That depends on your point of view. Bikes take you places. It's not like you can ride a fridge."

I rolled my eyes at him.

"I'm not just talking about the fridge though," Gabriel went on. "I'm talking about everything. I'm talking about getting rid of all the modern stuff, all the modern inconveniences, and stripping it down to just what we really need."

"It's not exactly practical," I mused.

"Yes, it is! Honestly, what could be more practical than deciding what we really need and just going with that?" He kissed my cheek and took my hand, stroking the skin at the back of my wrist. "Think about it: wouldn't you love to live those old dreams you had as a kid, actually see those old fantasies become real?"

"I don't think that's possible."

He wrapped me in his arms. "But what if it *were*?"

It took a number of years for those old buds of thought to blossom and bear fruit. Life intervened, as it has a way of doing, and its obstacles led us in roundabout paths. I had an opportunity to work in Japan and I took it, spending a year teaching English in a small city on the northwest coast of Honshu. Meanwhile, Gabriel went back to university and earned a degree in history, and then at about the time I was returning from abroad, he started pursuing a master's degree in library science.

I had returned from Asia with a much-deepened perspective on culture and the influence of human environments on the lifestyles of individuals and societies. Gabriel had been enhancing his knowledge of a past that had always interested us, then honing his skills in research and learning to glean forgotten information from primary-source materials.*

Traveling along different routes, my husband and I were converging at the crossroads of those former discussions: the idea of setting up our lives in such a way that we could choose our culture—not based merely on the gilt embossing on the covers of our passports, but on the entirety of the lives we wished to follow. There were a number of detours along the way, but glossing over the larger part of these brings this story to its interesting bits.

It almost seemed as though Mother Nature approved of our choice to journey backwards in time and was helping us along with it, while at the same time reinforcing any doubts about exactly how difficult the path we had chosen was going to be. Snowstorms are rare in the Seattle area in the twenty-first century. Before global warming settled over the planet, they used to be more common: the biggest snowstorm of Seattle's recorded history happened in January 1880, when five days of steady snow drifted into piles six feet deep in some places.[5] Now, though, a few inches of white crystals on the ground in January or February are sufficient to make news stations interrupt regularly scheduled programming with reports so sensationalized that they might seem better suited

---

*Anyone who listens to me prattle on for any length of time will hear the term "primary source" a lot, so I should define it early in this narrative: a primary source is something directly connected to the subject under study; e.g., an antique nineteenth-century dress; a brass microscope from 1880; or a novel by Mark Twain are all examples of primary sources of information about the Victorian era since they all originate in that time period. A modern book written about any of these things would be considered a secondary source since it exists at one level of removal from the origin of the data.

to avalanches than to a bit of slush barely adequate to making a snow-fetus, let alone a snowman. Snow in November is virtually unheard of, yet here it was: a whirling, frosty delight. Gazing out the window, I reflected that this touch of nature could in a certain way be a metaphor for the nineteenth century, which is always so much in my mind: both are either beautiful or troublesome depending on one's perspective. My own attitude gives them the former description.

It was two days before Thanksgiving 2010, and I was relishing the weather. "Could there be any more Victorian weather than snow?" I asked Gabriel, who was watching through eyeglasses ground to his own prescription but framed by antique rims more than a century old.

My husband started to shake his head, then reflected. "Fog," he replied, smiling.

I gave him a peck on the cheek. "I do love fog," I said, pulling his arms around me in a hug. "But we get that all the time around here. This is far more unique and special." I gazed out the window at the cascading lace draping the world.

We were at my mother-in-law's house and she broke into our reverie. "Are you sure you guys want to go up there in *this*?" Barbara asked, putting emphasis on the last word and peering out into the storm.

We wanted very badly to spend a cozy Thanksgiving in our new house as soon as the realtor's paperwork went through, so we were spending some preholiday time at my mother-in-law's to make up for not being with her on Thanksgiving itself. "They're telling people to stay off the roads if they don't have to be out." She frowned, squinting first at the radio, then at the damp Pacific Northwest snow.

"It'll be fine, Mom," Gabriel reassured her. Around us, the lights blinked as the weight of snow on the area's power lines threatened to knock out the region's electricity.

Gabriel and I grinned at each other. "Go out! Go out, go out!" I jeered at the electricity in a quiet but excited whisper while my mother-in-law's back was turned. Gabriel smirked at me and gave the dimming of the lights an approving thumbs-up. Like me, he has long taken a delight in power outages that most of our compatriots would probably consider perverse.

Dusk settled and, as the natural illumination disappeared, the electrical lights, which had been blinking all day, finally went out. We retired to the guest room that Gabriel and his two siblings share in rotation when any of them happen to be visiting their mother. Surrounded by an odd hodgepodge of doll paraphernalia left behind by Gabriel's grown sister and musical miscellany stowed by his brother (the middle sibling, a professional hammer-dulcimer player who is almost perpetually on tour), we tucked ourselves snugly into bed and dreamed about a future based on the past.

In the morning, we awoke to a cold, hushed world. The power was still out, but a different sort of electricity was in the air—that empowering adrenaline rush that flows through animals' blood when we realize we are experiencing the eye of a storm. The sky outside was a clear, topaz blue so bright it almost reflected its color upon the snow on the ground, but no birds sang. When Gabriel and I ventured, shivering, out of the bedroom where we had slept, a battery-operated radio on the dining room table announced that more heavy weather was on its way and repeated the advisory to stay off the roads.

"Have there been any calls from the mortgage company or the realtors?" Gabriel asked, as eager as I was. We were anxious to get to our new home, but to be legal about it, we had to make sure all the paperwork cleared first. There hadn't been any calls yet, so we watched the telephone as a cat watches a mouse hole.

Our anxious wait slowed down time. Our nerves were as tight as over-wound clocks from anticipation, and beyond this our skin could feel the shifting barometric pressures in the air from the other half of the storm, which was still on its way. The radio station, tuned in on the little battery-operated device on the table, kept interrupting their programs to give updates on storm damage throughout the region and to warn that the situation would get much worse after the eye passed and the second half of the storm hit.

The phone calls telling us the paperwork had cleared came through just after lunch, and we immediately rushed to leave before the weather could get worse again. The storm was still tensing to strike, but we had no idea how long it would hold off and truly no concept of what the situation would be in Port Townsend. (The radio gave detailed descriptions of conditions in Seattle and each of its suburbs, but our new and future home was part of the consolidated category of "further north" where it was said conditions were stormier.) We wanted to get as many miles behind us as possible while the weather was still restraining itself and hopefully be in our new home by the time the winds and snow descended once more.

While I bundled up in my antique mink coat, Barbara rushed around her little house gathering impromptu emergency supplies in case we got stuck somewhere. Into a paper sack, she put some bottles of water, a box of crackers, and a large Cadbury's chocolate bar. I smiled when I saw this last item, thinking how appropriate it was. The Cadbury Company traces its origins to a nutritious chocolate drink sold in a tea and coffee shop started by John Cadbury in 1824, and chocolate bars came into vogue at the very end of the Victorian era.[6]

Barbara hugged us both and warned us to be careful. She gave Gabriel a few last pieces of advice about driving the vehicle we were borrowing from her. Then we were off, with a beautiful azure sky overhead and a new life awaiting us.

The roads were almost entirely coated in ice, churned up in places by the passage of vehicles with chains. Creeping along these paths like something out of a Zamboni's nightmare, we passed dozens of abandoned vehicles that had skidded off the side of roads, including a large Comcast truck with chains on its tires. Every block-length of road we covered seemed to have at least one obviously abandoned car on its shoulder, pitched at a weird angle.

We passed through the eye of the storm and met its other side near Port Gamble, a picture-postcard of a town. Like our destination and new home, it had also been founded in the nineteenth century. I squinted through the window for its trim houses and sturdy general store but saw only snow. Huge crystals fell with a steady swiftness, shrouding the road. I shivered and pulled my fur coat tighter around myself.

The white blanket over the earth and sifting lace in the atmosphere added an epic sense of unreality to the journey. Through the darkness of sunset and thick snow, I glimpsed Port Gamble's church steeple and the barest impression of gingerbread trim on its houses. Then those were gone, blanketed in fog and snow. I could almost imagine we truly were traveling backwards in time.

We soon reached that glorious Victorian seaport, Port Townsend, Washington. The nineteenth-century courthouse with its elaborate clock tower rose proudly on the hill, and all around the town lay still and serene while the snow turned the landscape into a steel-plate engraving from a Dickensian novel.

Arriving at our house, we were greeted by a chorus of tiny birds in the front yard, while in the backyard bunny tracks crisscrossed a clean field of white crystals. Admittedly, this idyll was somewhat spoiled by the mountain of trash also in the backyard, left by the house's previous owner. The building had been completely empty for more than a year before we'd bought it and before that it was rented out by absentee landlords for more than a decade. I considered that an entire year was an excessively long time to leave a massive heap of trash lying about but I tried not to let it spoil my enjoyment of the moment.

The journey to our new home had been a long one and I hurried to the downstairs bathroom—the older of the house's two lavatory facilities. My first rather urgent gaze was for the toilet, but what I saw when my eyes fell on it in the gathering dusk stopped me in my tracks. "You've got to be kidding me!"

I squinted. No, my eyes weren't mistaken. I wouldn't have even thought what I was seeing would be possible in the normally temperate climate of the Pacific Northwest. I knew I was cold, but—seriously? "You've got to be kidding me!" I repeated, louder this time.

"What?" asked Gabriel from the adjoining kitchen.

I shook my head in disbelief, bending over the incredible sight. "The water in the toilet bowl is frozen," I called through the bathroom door. "Solid!" I added, lifting up the seat and seeing the white starburst core within the ice. I removed the lid from the tank in the rear. "And there's . . ." I tapped the hefty tile of ice within with the ceramic lid, judging thickness, "at least two inches of ice in the tank at the back of the toilet!"

"Try the upstairs bathroom!" suggested Gabriel.

The tiny upstairs water closet was created in the 1940s by the simple expedient of walling off one corner of a bedroom and cramming in as much rerouted plumbing as would fit in a space equal to the average broom closet. I ran upstairs in a sort of dancing jog, hopping crookedly as I ascended. Reaching the newer loo, I found the upstairs toilet in exactly the same condition as its fellow on the ground floor.

"It's frozen, too!" I shouted, my panic rising. I hop-jogged back down the stairs, biological urgency taking its toll on rational thought.

"Well, it sure is cold in here!" Gabriel greeted me cheerfully back in the kitchen. He had heard my report of the upstairs status but clearly considered my predicament to be far more amusing than I did, and he smirked when he saw my unorthodox dance steps. "You could go in the back yard," he suggested merrily.

I glared at him, hopping up and down. "I am not," I told him firmly, "introducing myself to our new neighbors by flashing them my derriere in the middle of a snowstorm!"

Gabriel chuckled as I rushed back into the downstairs bathroom again.

After dealing with the emergency, I moved to the bathroom sink to wash my hands. *It's freezing in here!* I thought, shivering.

There was a six-inch icicle dangling from the faucet. Staring at it, I appended an adjective to my last thought:—*literally!* I disliked the current fad of misusing that particular adjective, but I realized it was appropriate in this case.

We had expected the heat to be off—the house had been empty for more than a year, after all—but it seemed the entire inside of the home was exactly the same temperature as the ambient air outside in the snowstorm. Looking up, I saw why.

The toilet in the downstairs bathroom faces the window, and as the urgency of one problem resolved itself and I could pay attention to my own shivering again, I clenched my shaking fingers into a fist. "They left the window open!" I shouted through chattering teeth.

I had initially been too preoccupied with water—frozen and otherwise—to take note of the wind gushing through the window that had been specifically bolted into an open position. Whoever had done it had wrenched the wing nut down so tightly that I had difficulty loosening it to shut the aperture, but my determination won out at last. The window slammed shut in the wind and I bolted it again in the closed position, then looked down to where the cast-iron claw-foot bathtub had filled with autumn leaves.

"It's November!" I told Gabriel, overstating the obvious as I came out of the bathroom. "The end of November, and we're in the middle of a snowstorm! No wonder it's so cold in here. What kind of people leave a window open in the middle of a snowstorm?"

Gabriel was staring at the kitchen faucet with a worried expression. He had pushed it to the farthest range of its "hot" position but not even a drop of water was emerging. He traced a line above it with his eyes, as if trying to X-ray it. "Let's hope the plumbing's okay inside the walls."

I moved to turn off the nonfunctional faucet but he stopped me. "Leave it on! If there's ice in there, we want to melt it."

I raised one eyebrow in an expression that was half-frown, half quizzical squint. "What if the pipes are damaged?"

Gabriel blew out a deep breath but smiled in an optimistic way. "Then the sooner we find out, the better. We've got to thaw all this out. Come on, let's get it warmed up in here."

That was certainly a sentiment I could support! I was shivering despite my mink coat and wool skirt. I looked longingly over to where there would have once been a woodstove and up at the blocked-off place in the wall where the old chimney had been sealed over by the absentee landlords (for whom I was compiling an increasingly long list of multilingual curses).

Back in the nineteenth century, the kitchen would have been the heart of this home and the warmest room in the house. Since the woodstove had been long discarded by the old landlords (the same ones who had filled the backyard with garbage and left a window open in a snowstorm), it was frigid in the extreme. I cranked the pathetic little electric range to its highest setting and left its oven door hanging open.

The house had a single heat source of its own: a decrepit propane heater from the 1970s, whose many failings we were to learn shortly. It had been turned off (of course) and Gabriel had some trouble relighting the pilot light. The chamber for the flames was completely sealed so it couldn't be lit with a match and the button that was supposed to electrically ignite the gas refused to spark. While my husband worked on the problem, I wandered over to inspect the fern and flower patterns of frost crystals on the parlor window, laughing in a sort of wry amusement at the steam clouds of my own breath circling me. There is, of course, nothing physically comfortable in a parlor whose room temperature could produce ice cream, and yet the whole experience and atmosphere was one of thrilling adventure.

After Gabriel had been struggling to light the stove's pilot flame for a while, I wondered if the propane might be switched off at the tank. I went outside to check, and when I returned he finally had it lit. We cranked the heat control to its highest setting and left it there. (The process of thawing the house and bringing it up to a relatively balmy fifty-eight degrees Fahrenheit would burn through two-thirds of our propane tank's capacity in the next three days.)

Gabriel slapped his hands together to wipe off some of the copious dust he had picked up while working on the stove. "Well," he said, looking at the suboptimal appliance with a wary optimism. "Let's hope that helps."

We started carrying the few things we had brought with us inside the house, but soon the world outside started growing dark from a combination of sunset and storm clouds. With the temperature plummeting and the wind picking up, I told Gabriel carrying in the rest of the stuff could wait. Whatever supplies we wanted had best be acquired now, before the sky started shoveling snow on us again.

Our main priorities were food and kerosene. It had been kind of Gabriel's mother to provide us with Cadbury's chocolate, but we had a natural desire for a slightly more substantial dinner. The kerosene was for an antique heater Gabriel had purchased through the mail. I had some trepidation about the safety of such an item but the severe cold was encouraging me to keep an open mind about any source of warmth. Besides, when I lived in Japan, I knew plenty of people who warmed their homes with kerosene heaters, and it's not as though the laws of physics vary on different continents. If something was safe in Japan, there was no reason for it to be otherwise here. I realized that my prejudice against kerosene heaters was a very American one—as well as very modern.

Getting warmth from our heater would take more than an open mind, though: it would take kerosene. The hardware store was sold out. At least we were able to procure a mop, broom, and soap. The house desperately wanted all of these, so the trip wasn't wasted.

After making our purchases, we hurried from the hardware store and held our breath up the steep and icy hill back to Uptown Port Townsend. Fat flakes of snow were falling swiftly and reflections from all the ice in the air were giving odd angles to the scanty red light pressed from the last of the sunset by heavy storm clouds.

A feeling of immense security settled over us as we gained the top of the hill. Uptown Port Townsend is like a citadel: on the landward side it overlooks fertile earth, and seaward it has clear, sweeping trajectories toward the straits between the Pacific Ocean and Puget Sound.

A few blocks from our new home, we stopped at Aldrich's, a small grocery store that has been in continuous operation since 1895. Sadly, the original building had burned to the ground a handful of years previously, but the business itself rose from the ashes. I would later spend time reading through the framed newspaper articles chronicling the store's history and resurrection that hung from the walls in the upstairs gallery, but at that moment our rumbling stomachs took priority. From the deli counter in the back of the store, we chose a small mushroom pie for me and a sandwich for Gabriel: hearty, autumnal Victorian food.

The bedroom had even more ferns painted in frost on the windows than the parlor. It was far too cold to sleep in, so we made a cozy little nest of blankets downstairs by the stove. One of the house's former renters would eventually make a habit of telling us how hazardous the 1970s-era propane stove in the parlor was due to the large quantities of carbon monoxide it pumped out. However, with the original woodstove gone and no kerosene for our space heater, we had little choice. Quite frankly, given that there were cracks and gaps around various doors sizable enough for snow to waft in and gather in dainty little fairy piles, I doubted that anything as volatile as a gas would see much point in staying inside a structure possessed of so many convenient exits.

Most of our belongings were being shipped in a large container a few days hence, so the little bedding we had with us was borrowed from Gabriel's mother. There was only one sleeping bag—not a particularly large one—but we managed to squeeze in it together and cover it with two sheets doubled over on themselves and a blanket, likewise doubled over. The result was slightly claustrophobic and our breath turned to steam in the cold air around us, but our mammalian sardine impression generated enough heat to keep our teeth from chattering. Eventually we drifted off to sleep, happy in the knowledge that we were at last on the road to achieving our dreams, however preliminary our steps on that road might be at the moment.

2

Thanksgiving

Picture from an advertisement in *The Cottage Hearth*, February 1888.

"And so on this Thanksgiving Day, the sunlight fell in blessing through
the many-paned windows of the old dining-room of the corner house,
where two sat together for the first time at their own table. In other
years, in other days, their friends should be bidden, this day seemed for
them alone in their thankfulness."

—Olive E. Dana, 1888[7]

The snowstorm and our icy entrance into our new home took place on the day
before Thanksgiving. As my husband and I snuggled together that first night in

our nineteenth-century house, with the storm howling outside and our hopes spreading out in our dreaming minds like the fractal patterns on the parlor window, it was hard to imagine a more appropriate holiday to welcome us into our Victorian home. We were incredibly thankful for the blessing of this momentous step toward our dreams of exploring the nineteenth century. Beyond this symbolism, there is a very real connection between the Victorian era and the origins of Thanksgiving as a national occasion.

Most modern Americans tend to associate the feast with the seventeenth century and pilgrims, but the celebration of the holiday was limited to New England until well into the nineteenth century. The concept of a festal celebration of thanks is an old one but it took a Victorian lady to institutionalize it. Specifically, it took the editress of one of my favorite magazines, *Godey's Lady's Book*, Sarah Josepha Hale.

Interestingly, Hale's conviction that we should have a national day of thanks played a part (although admittedly a small one) in landing her the job at *Godey's*. Hale began her writing career with a novel entitled *Northwood; or, Life North and South: Showing the Character of Both*, and her conviction about Thanksgiving enters into the book in a manner somewhat resembling a Socratic dialogue:

"Is Thanksgiving Day universally observed in America?" inquired Mr. Frankford.

"Not yet; but I trust it will become so. We have too few holidays. Thanksgiving, like the Fourth of July, should be considered a national festival, and observed by all our people."

"I see no particular reason for such an observance," remarked Frankford.

"I do," returned the Squire. "We want it as the exponent of our Republican institutions, which are based on the acknowledgement that God is our Lord, and that, as a nation, we derive our privileges and blessings from Him. You will hear this doctrine set forth in the sermon tomorrow."

"I thought you had no national religion."

"No established religion, you mean. Our people do not need compulsion to support the gospel. But to return to our Thanksgiving festival. When it shall be observed, on the same day, throughout all the states and territories, it will be a grand spectacle of moral power and human happiness, such as the world has never yet witnessed."[8]

Northwood . . . was an instant success—which was lucky for Hale, since she wrote the book after her husband died and she suddenly found herself a single mother with children to support, including a brand-new baby. Less than a month after the book was published, Hale received a job offer for the editorship of a new "ladies' magazine." She would move on from that project to *Godey's*, which became one of the most important periodicals in nineteenth-century America. It is now primarily remembered for its fashion plates and craft articles, but the magazine covered social issues as well.

Throughout her publishing career, Hale continued to champion her pet cause of turning Thanksgiving into a holiday shared by *all* people, not just New England Protestants: ". . . [C]ould not every Christian nation and every Jewish family in the world join us in this Thanksgiving, on the last Thursday in November?"[9]

Hale took the case for Thanksgiving to the highest authority in America— all the way to President Lincoln. In a letter to Lincoln dated September 28, 1863, Hale directed her perpetual request to the country's commander in chief. Given that the Civil War was raging and September's 174 battles had resulted in 35,499 casualties[10] (including Lincoln's own brother-in-law, Brigadier General Benjamin Hardin Helms, killed in the Battle of Chickamauga on September 21[11]), one might consider that the president of the divided United States had weightier matters on his mind than a holiday proposal by the editor of a domestic magazine. However, he clearly read Hale's letter and seemed to think her cause a worthy one—or at least, that it was politically savvy. (Declaring a day of thanks is, after all, politically somewhat analogous to kissing babies: easy to do and few people object.)

On October 3, 1863, President Lincoln proclaimed that the last Thursday in November would be a national Thanksgiving, exactly as Hale had proposed.[12] Personally, the part of this story I find the most impressive is its timing: President Lincoln's proclamation came less than one week after Hale had written her letter! Given the condition of the twenty-first-century postal system, I have difficulty imagining a modern American president even *receiving* a physical letter in less than a week, let alone acting on it!

Lincoln's presidential proclamation (which was a one-time deal, for a Thanksgiving in 1863 alone) still wasn't enough for Hale. She requested another Thanksgiving the following year and it was again granted by presidential decree. By this time, the country was getting used to the idea, and on April 8, 1865, the citizens of New York sent President Lincoln a thirty-one-page petition containing approximately 870 signatures requesting a national day of Thanksgiving.[13]

After Lincoln's assassination, later presidents continued the tradition and appointed yearly Thankgivings at the end of every November. Still not satisfied (and by now slightly obsessed), Hale's magazine urged not just the president, but Congress as well, to recognize her pet holiday. In 1874, when Hale was in her late eighties, an Editor's Table piece in *Godey's* pled for Congressional recognition of Thanksgiving and was accompanied by a hymn to the holiday—written by its strongest advocate.[14] Why, exactly, old Mrs. Hale felt such a driving need to keep fighting a battle that was already won is unclear. Perhaps she had just gotten used to fighting it. Unfortunately, she didn't live to see the Congressional chapter of Thanksgiving's story (which would finally take place in 1941).[15] However, she had certainly achieved her goal as far as the public was concerned. By the 1870s, Thanksgiving was already such a part of America's subconscious that the book *Thanksgiving: Memories of the Day . . .* refers to the holiday as if its origins had been lost to the annals of time:

> The bare mention of the word, the Old Thanksgiving Day—what a power it has to revive the pleasant reminiscences, and recall the brightest scenes of other days in many hearts! It transports them to the homes of their childhood. It takes them at once into the presence of the father and mother who, it may be, for many years have been sleeping in the grave. It recalls their smiles of affectionate greeting, their tones of cheerful welcome; tones and smiles such as none but they could give. Every image of peace, contentment, competence, abundance and joy, comes back spontaneously on each return of the grateful festival.[16]

The national holiday had become exactly what Mrs. Hale had envisioned, and what it remains to this day: a celebration of home and hearth and the blessings for which we are grateful.

The construction of our house began in 1888 and finished in 1889. In the very months when builders were putting up the walls that would one day be our home, *Good Housekeeping* printed an article about a young couple entering their own new home on Thanksgiving. "Isn't it old-fashioned and home-like and dear?" the wife asks as they enter the long-empty building. ". . . Any house for a home to grow in would be a great deal to us, but this is so good! I can't make it real!"

"But it is," her husband tells her. ". . . Do you remember, dear, how a year ago, you tried to cheer me, one day when things were more deeply, darkly blue than common? You said there would be a way. Our home would come to us, or we to it, in time . . . if we but worked and waited and hoped meanwhile."[17]

When I read the piece more than a century later, the sentiments it expressed were so familiar to me that my heartstrings thrummed in recognition of its themes.

It's true that our entry to our new-old home was significantly more barren than the one in the story. In the *Good Housekeeping* piece, the house in Old Hill Town is given as a present—furnishings, appliances, and all—to the young couple by a rich judge and his wife. The benefactors had seen that the couple were good and deserving people, and, displaying the generosity common in Victorian fiction, wished to help them into a new situation. In our case, the absentee landlords who had previously owned the house had actually traveled from a different state to pry up and carry off items that had been nailed down less than a week before the paperwork transferring ownership cleared. This booty included the kitchen shelves—and even the mailbox!

Then again, the *G.H.* piece was fiction, after all. Real life has precious few of the generous benefactors who act as *deus ex machinas* in stories. We had only ourselves, our wits, our hearts, and nerves and sinews. We knew that in many ways it would be more complicated to reconstruct elements of the nineteenth century, its culture and technology, than simply to live through it would have been. It wasn't just a matter of cutting things out but of resurrecting technologies that had existed and finding the most appropriate equivalents to infrastructures now gone forever. When I came across an 1889 poem, I felt its moral to be wonderfully apt for our situation:

> . . . There's much of truth we can surely find
> In her homely words, I wot.
> They are these, "Before you cook a hare,
> The hare must first be caught."
>
> And all through life, this simple rule,
> To every thing applies.
> It will even fit so simple a thing
> As the making of berry pies . . .[18]

Life in any society is supported by the entire infrastructure of that particular civilization; many of the quotidian elements of the nineteenth century have

long since disappeared. There are no icemen or milkmen in twenty-first century Port Townsend, although they would have once been a familiar sight to
virtually every home in America. The skilled artisans who could be relied on to
produce and maintain life's necessities are now often equally endangered species. Supplies that would have once been available at the many stores in town
have become extraordinarily challenging to find. We knew we had a lot of work
ahead of us. We also knew that it would be a great and educational adventure
and that we would love every minute of it—even the frustrating parts.

3

Settling In

Our home. Image courtesy Estar Hyo Gyung Choi, Mary Studio.

"Whether one 'boards,' and is changing lodgings, or is going into a new house, or over the hills to the poor house, [moving] involves discomfort that varies in amount merely, never in quality. . . . Above all, when the, at best, troublesome moving time comes, one should pray on bended knees for sweetness of temper. It oils the wheels of the domestic machinery in a truly miraculous way."

—Dinah Sturgis, 1889[19]

By our second day in Port Townsend, our new domicile was slowly turning from a house-sized freezer into a very large refrigerator. This represented progress we very much appreciated, although I continued to wear my coat indoors. By midday, the parlor was a relatively warm fifty degrees Fahrenheit and entering the bedroom no longer required me to wear my fur muff to keep my hands from going numb. An upstairs room with hole-riddled window frames was the one part of the house that still had frost on the glass. This was unsurprising, since I could poke my fingers through rotted portions of the wooden frames and touch the air of the outside world.

Chilled as we were, the fact that the frost had melted from most of the other windows told us the temperature inside the house was no longer freezing in the literal sense. The plumbing should have been working—but it was not. Gabriel walked around the house's outside perimeter and crawled under the structure, looking for the water meter. It proved oddly elusive, although he did manage to find the main water valves and made sure they were all turned to the open position.

While Gabriel was engaged in "The Case of the Missing Water Meter," I wandered around inside our four walls, reflecting both on how many childhood dreams this day represented and how much work we had ahead of us. I peered into an extra room downstairs that had been a particularly important part of our decision to buy this specific house. I'm a licensed massage practitioner and this room would make a perfect massage studio. I thought of our plans to put up pressed tin wainscoting—the sort that appeared in some spas in the late nineteenth century when massage was referred to as "the movement cure."*

Further explorations of the house brought additional delights. When I discovered a sweet little iron doorstopper with acorn accents attached to the back door, I cooed to myself over how special it was. Acorns were popular motifs in art of the Eastlake Movement, so it fit very well with the house's Eastlake architecture. There was a deeper significance to this detail than mere aesthetics, however.

"Mighty oaks from little acorns grow" is a maxim I have often repeated to myself and reminded Gabriel of. On our previous anniversary, when I'd had so little money that I couldn't afford a gift for him, I had gathered the most perfect acorns I could find, wrapped them as beautifully as I could, and gave them to him with a letter describing how they represented our dreams, and how with time and perseverance the acorns of our hopes would grow into the oaks of our goals.

Oaks are deeply sacred in Celtic tradition, representing all that is strong and wise. The Victorian artists and designers who made use of oak and acorn

---

*The term *Swedish massage* is a nineteenth-century one as well: It honors Pehr Ling, a Swede who promoted the idea of health through motion and helped massage become accepted by mainstream medicine in the early 1800s.

motifs knew these traditions very well, and they used the designs so freely because they (and their customers) esteemed the oak's significance so highly. There is a great value in symbolic reminders of strength and wisdom. Tied into these same ideas are the virtues of hard work triumphing humble beginnings. "Mighty oaks from little acorns grow"; from the children's stories of Frances Hodgson Burnett to the works of Charles Dickens, it was a philosophy dear to the Victorian heart—and my own. I touched a gentle and wonder-filled hand to the little iron acorn by our back door. Patience and fortitude grew these little seeds into the mightiest of giants, and these assets would likewise grow our dreams into our goals.

Admittedly, oaks do grow notoriously slowly and it was going to require a rather large quantity of patience and fortitude to get the state of things in our house where we wanted it to be. I assessed cleaning projects around our much-beloved new-old house: the bathtub was full of storm debris that had blown in through the open window. A layer of combined years of dirt, grit, and various detritus coated all the windowsills and floors. The floor of the pantry was covered in rat droppings. Various plaster on walls throughout the house was cracked at best or falling off in large sheets at worst. One room was completely filled with garbage left by the sellers, and the kitchen sink smelled like something had died in it—something that had not lived a salubrious existence before expiring.

As I shook my head over these various things, Gabriel eventually found the water meter. Bracing himself against the ground, he wrenched the meter to the "on" position and inside the house the water finally started flowing. It was the color and consistency of a bad case of dysentery, but at least it was running.

Gabriel went out to get supplies, including food for our Thanksgiving dinner, while I stayed at home to watch the water slowly convert to a more potable clarity. This took so long that by the time I judged the pipes clear enough to close the taps, thick-falling snow had filled in Gabriel's tracks in the yard.

Looking around, I reflected that, from the outside, it would be very difficult for anyone to tell that residents had moved in to the long-empty house. As I've mentioned, the house had been devoid of humans for well over a year before we bought it, and sporadically rented out by absentee landlords for the decade preceding that. Our new neighbors told us the building had been empty so long that they thought only ghosts would ever live there, and they were delighted to see people moving in—especially a young couple with the fortitude to move in at a time when most families in the area were sequestering themselves from a temporary spot of freakish weather.

The neighbors' jocular comments about only ghosts inhabiting our lovely house were echoed in a less lighthearted way by my mother when I called to let her know we had arrived safely through the snowstorm. She had never seen the house, yet was utterly convinced that any building of its age must, by necessity, be filled from floor to rafters with supernatural residents. "Aren't you afraid to sleep in that spooky old house?" she asked. "It might have ghosts in it!"

I have, in my various travels, fended off an Algerian thug in the Paris Metro, kept my wallet safe from pickpockets in Barcelona, and come to no harm from various four-legged predators while hiking in the Washington woods (although I've encountered bobcats, coyotes, and close evidence of a bear). I assured my mother that ghosts were not really high on my list of concerns.

When the water pipes started producing relatively clean fluid, I realized there were a few things missing from Gabriel's foraging list. Moreover, my growling belly reminded me that I had no idea when my husband was returning with the food. I bundled myself warmly and set out to get a snack.

This is probably an appropriate place in the narrative to explain that my love of the Victorian era extends to my wardrobe. I had been wearing a corset on a daily basis for nearly two years at that point, and my clothes as I left the house (perfectly normal, everyday wear for me) consisted of a white shirtwaist, ankle-length wool skirt padded by numerous petticoats, a Victorian-style broad-brimmed hat, an antique fur coat, and a muff. As I struggled with the fidgety old lock and the parlor door, out of the corner of my eye, I noticed someone staring at me.

To be perfectly honest, being stared at is not a novelty for me, although familiarity never does render it any less annoying to be gawked at. It is a common enough occurrence that I paid it no mind but concentrated instead on getting the troublesome old lock to catch on the door. I kept on ignoring the vacant stare and the eyes growing ever wider, the jaw dropping, as the latch finally caught and I leaned against the door to make sure it was locked. I slipped both hands into my muff, shivered at the cold, and stepped off the porch onto clean snow, still ignoring the staring eyes goggling at me.

I kept on ignoring the gaping features of the woman at the gate until I reached her position and wanted past. (She was blocking the exit.) *Well, I'll have to meet her eventually,* I reasoned, so I gave her the best smile possible under the circumstances.

"Good morning," I said, wriggling the fingers of my right hand to warm them inside my muff before I removed the hand and offered it to be shaken. "I'm Sarah—I just moved in."

The woman finally blinked, her jaw snapped shut, and she started breathing again. I'm not sure she had inhaled a single breath the entire time she had been watching me. "I—thought—" she stammered slowly, gasping. "You—were—a—ghost!"

Thus was the manner in which I met one of my new neighbors.

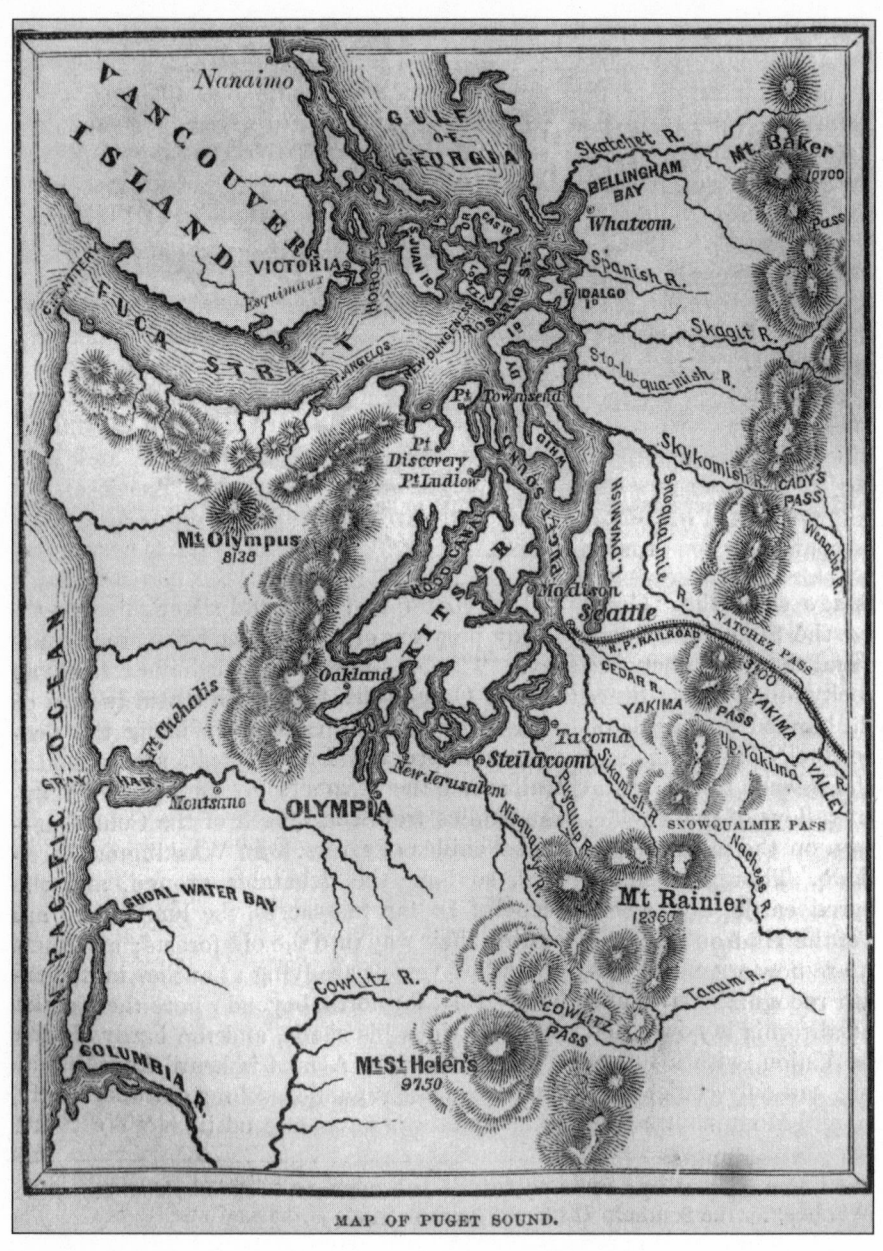

MAP OF PUGET SOUND.

Map of Puget Sound, taken from *Harper's New Monthly Magazine*, September, 1870, p. 482. Port Townsend is in the upper third of the map, near the center.

4

Our New/Old City

"A foreign language can always be best attained
in the country where it is the vernacular."
— *The Woman's Book*, 1894[20]

A few words might be in order as to why we considered Port Townsend such a promised land of Victoriana. Back in the mid-nineteenth century, the community that would ultimately be known around the world as Seattle was still a soggy trading post on a mud flat, situated on a section of Puget Sound too far inland for optimal importance to America at large. Port Townsend, in contrast, was placed so perfectly that it seemed destined for greatness to anyone with a cartographic view of the Pacific Northwest.

The Sound provides water access to the cities of Olympia (the state capital), Seattle, and Tacoma, but to get to any of these, a ship has to turn the corner from the Strait of Juan de Fuca—and sail directly past Port Townsend. Its placement is perfect for a customs port, and that was exactly what it became in 1854.[21] Formerly, ships had been required to travel all the way down to Olympia—at the base of Puget Sound—to declare their goods, which was rather inconvenient since it meant sailing past all the major cities, declaring goods, then sailing north again to actually conduct any business. A person can certainly imagine that various ships' captains must have been sorely tempted to cut out the tax-collecting middlemen who were far from being in the middle of their route.

Port Townsend had even more to recommend it to settlers than simply being a fantastic location for shipping—the soil of the region was fertile for farming; game, fish, and shellfish were all plentiful; and the supply of timber must have seemed limitless. By the late 1880s, everyone foresaw Port Townsend taking its rightful place as the thriving metropolis of the Northwest. (This role would eventually be filled by Seattle, but at this time the future Emerald City was still a muck-mired mill town populated by drunken loggers. By then they'd succeeded in driving off most of the tribes who had used the area as a trading hub since time immemorial, but one wouldn't necessarily say that civilization had arrived.)

In 1870, a journalist for *Harper's New Monthly Magazine* wrote:

> Bills may be proposed and defeated, particular schemes may be discussed and delayed; but let any one take a look at the position and contour of the northwestern corner of our country, and he will be convinced of its importance, and foresee its manifest destiny . . . If ocean steam is ever to become on the Pacific what it has been on the Atlantic—if our relations with Eastern Asia are ever to be what they have been with Western Europe (and why should they not?)—the Puget Sound must become one of the centres of the world's commerce. . . .[22]

The first edition of the *Morning Leader* newspaper (a publication still in business) on October 2, 1889, declared Port Townsend THE KEY CITY OF PUGET SOUND—the way to unlock the treasures of the region.[23] The newspaper went on to extol the many virtues of this paradise on Earth:

> The summers are cool and pleasant and far more enjoyable than those of Oakland, Los Angeles, San Diego, Ilwaco or Newport. Winters are usually mild, healthful and more agreeable than in any of the states of the East, Middle-West, or the Willamette valley of Oregon, the garden spot of the Northwest . . . Port Townsend possesses a diversity of lucrative business interests seldom met with in districts that have forced phenomenal city populations into the hundreds of thousands of active, aggressive, business men, intelligent citizens and prosperous working men. . . .[24]

An advertisement sponsored by the chamber of commerce and taking up a quarter sheet of newsprint on page eight of the same paper extols the community's virtues more succinctly (although in significantly larger typeface and even larger capital letters):

PORT TOWNSEND

THE

FUTURE COMMERCIAL METROPOLIS

OF THE

PACIFIC COAST

Assets of the city cited in the article included its safe, commodious harbor; its advantages for a leading port of wheat, lumber, coal, fish, and the tea shipped to this coast from China and Japan; "the most beautiful location and salubrious climate enjoyed by any city on the American continent"; and, of course, the absolute certainty that it would become the terminus of a transcontinental railroad system.[25]

With ships coming in from one direction, it seemed natural that trains would come to meet them from the other. By the late nineteenth century, more railroads were proliferating all the time, and what more natural terminus could there possibly be for a rail line than the location of the customs port? All that was wanted was some track, and those were being laid across America at such a pace that an industrial deity with a view of the proceedings might compare them to the rapid-fire lines of needlework pumped out by one of the new sewing machines. It was only natural that the shipping lanes would be joined to the railroad lines. Greatness seemed destined to result. Real estate surged in value and the building trade flourished as houses and shops sprang up to provide homes and services to the hordes of people who would surge into town.

Clearly, if the newspapers and pamphlets were to be believed, a person would surely be a fool if they didn't buy up land in the Key City as quickly as possible! *Not* buying property in Port Townsend in the 1880s would be like not buying real estate in America in the early 2000s.

Then the bubble burst.

The railroad didn't come through after all. An economic depression hit the country and the housing bubble popped. The economy crashed, and took everyone's dreams with it. The collapse in the nation's fiscal status meant jobs suddenly withered and disappeared, like crops slain by a surprise blizzard. People flooded away from Port Townsend—not toward it as everyone had expected. All those beautiful buildings lay vacant for decades. Denuded of inhabitants who would care for it, the city (like the castle of the Sleeping Beauty in the Grimms' tale) went dormant and was overrun by thorns and wild beasts.

People whose dreams have been shattered don't like to see reminders of how high their hopes once were. At worst, the buildings were torn down altogether—or mutilated. Even buildings that escaped an executioner's hand would often fall victim to the architectural equivalent of a barber surgeon. Entire wings or multiple upper stories were shorn off. In 2012, I was invited to tour a mansion where the customs inspector had once lived, an amazingly situated building with sweeping views of Admiralty Inlet and Puget Sound. The current owner had explained that the three-story home had once consisted of four stories, and the top floor was occupied by a ballroom where loving couples could enjoy that panoramic view by starlight. In the early twentieth century, though, that entire top story had been torn off. Ghastly as that amputation was, it wasn't the end of the poor house's degradations. It was lovely when I toured it in the second decade of the twenty-first century, but I was meeting the victim after a long recovery period.

I've known many families who kept an entire bookshelf of scrapbooks devoted to documentation of their children's growth. This family's bookshelf of scrapbooks, though, was a collection of documentation about the decades-long process they had undertaken to restore their home to livable condition. The owner had a right to be proud of her handiwork as she showed me all the labor they had undertaken to restore the house—and the photographs of the appallingly disgraceful condition it had been in when they took possession of it. One of her many horrific stories was of having to replace the wooden floor in the parlor because a former owner had driven motorcycles into the best room in the house so that he could do oil changes and mechanical work inside—in the parlor!

A walk around town shows a large number of buildings to be missing stories. Even City Hall lacks its top layers from the nineteenth century. However, many buildings did remain intact. In other cities, as fashions varied, codes changed, and human desires altered, old buildings were torn down and new ones erected to suit current whims. In Port Townsend, though, there were simply too few people left around to bother demolishing everything. In New York or Seattle, creating a new building virtually requires tearing down an old one because real estate is at such a premium. In Port Townsend, there was plenty of room and not much reason to build new structures, since there were so few people. In an odd sort of way, the sudden bust in Port Townsend's economy in the 1890s proved to be the ultimate salvation of a large part of its architecture. It simply wasn't worth the trouble of tearing things down if no one was itching for space to be cleared. Consequently, many of the old buildings remained in place, simply waiting. In the shape of one of these, we found our home.

We came here not through luck or foolhardiness, but through determination. When we reached that crossroads in our lives when we decided to start incorporating as much Victorian history into our lives as possible, I had just become certified as a massage practitioner in the state of Washington, and my husband had completed a master's degree in library science at the UW. Gabriel's first job offer was contract work at the Library of Congress in Washington, DC, but a few short months there enabled us to realize that it was not the appropriate place to pursue our dreams. We had realized that people's lives are intimately influenced by their surroundings. This was, of course, a huge part of the reason we wanted to surround ourselves with Victorian artifacts, but it was even more fundamental to place ourselves in Victorian geography. We wanted to be in a place where the late nineteenth century—our favorite era—had been the formative period.

This decision involved sacrifice. People often tell us we're lucky to be able to live as we do, but there was no luck involved. To come here, Gabriel gave up his work at the Library of Congress in DC and returned to his old position of managing a bicycle shop on the West Coast. This difficult choice enabled us to create a life where we wanted to be.

Even if the future the boosters dreamed of isn't here, our own future is.

Photo courtesy Estar Hyo-Gyung Choi.

"Any person who looks for furniture as he looks for friends,
because of a sincere value, must gather his treasures out of a mass
of false and gaudy styles, made to attract the crowd."[26]

—Helena Rowe, 1888

5

The House—And Furnishing It

"Furnishing a House is a matter upon which so much could be said that it would be impossible to give in this chapter much advice to the mistress of a household who has to undertake that duty. A very great deal depends upon the house itself; but there are certain things, and very many things of actual necessity in every house, and we would advise that if there is to be a limit to the expenditure in this respect, that all these necessaries should first be bought, and then, if there should not be enough left for all that is desired, that she should get these by degrees, keeping a good look out for pretty things which can often be bought far cheaper here and there than by ordering them all of one upholsterer. One great advantage of this plan is that one often lights upon something far prettier and more suitable than we had thought of before, while there is a great charm in adding constantly to the beauty or convenience of our rooms which we lose if we put in all they will hold at once."

—Mrs. Beeton, 1861[27]

After a lengthy and very thorough cleaning of our entire home (including an entire day spent on my hands and knees cleaning up rat droppings and sanitizing the pantry floor), we planned out things we could do—little and big—to help return our house to proper Victorian splendor. If life were a movie and we had the budget of the BBC or a Hollywood studio at our disposal, it might have seemed easy to accomplish this transformation the way it is invariably shown in television or movies: in a few humorous and/or photogenic scenes, accompanied by a fast-tempo soundtrack, and requiring no more than thirty seconds of screen time. Fact, however, is exponentially more time-intensive than fiction.

It was difficult to situate things with very little furniture, but I did my best. One of the townspeople, after inviting herself into our home, told everyone who would listen that our parlor was "bare." When I lamented about this to a friend, she put her hands on her hips on my behalf. "You don't say someone's parlor is bare!" she declared indignantly. "That's like telling a woman she's barren!" Her support was balm to my wounded pride and I swelled with gratitude for her validation.

I would later take a sort of "misery loves company" comfort when I read an 1889 *Good Housekeeping* article about a woman subjected to a treatment similar to the one I received by a caller who visits with the express goal of finding fault.[28] Some things never change!

Once the hardware store was re-supplied with fuel oils, we stocked up on both paraffin oil and kerosene. Standing in the warehouse-like store and squinting at the various containers, I frowned at the higher price tag of the paraffin oil and asked Gabriel if we really needed both.

"The paraffin's for the lamps," Gabriel explained. (Ever the researcher, he had been reading up on fuels.) "The kerosene is for the Perfection-brand heater." He enjoyed reciting the entire copyrighted name of our heater, although the patent had long since expired. I thought this was cute, even if it did make my husband sound a little like a commercial or like one of the salesmen who had sold these heaters off the backs of oil wagons in the late nineteenth and early twentieth centuries. The Perfection-brand heater is an appliance made of thin sheet metal, roughly tubular. Its top sits a little taller than my knee, and its width is roughly the same as the length of my forearm. A reservoir sits in the bottom of this shell and holds about a gallon of kerosene, which is soaked up and burned by a large round wick about the size and shape of an athletic sock with the foot cut off. The design remained unchanged for decades.

"Couldn't we burn kerosene in the lamps, too?" I asked Gabriel, my penny-pinching mind doing sums in a voice like the ghost of my Depression-era grandmother.

"Well," he said, hesitating. "Paraffin oil was what they used in the upper-class houses. It doesn't have a smell like kerosene and it burns a lot cleaner. You'll wind up cleaning the lamp chimneys a lot more if we burn kerosene in them."

Expressed that way, paraffin oil seemed like a good idea, so I agreed to Gabriel's suggestion regarding the fuel for our lamps. Life in general is a complicated proposition, and we knew the task we had set ourselves was not an easy

What You Can Do With This Oil Heater

With a Perfection Oil Heater you can heat a cold bedroom, make a sick-room more comfortable, warm a chilly hallway, heat water quickly, and do many things better than can be done with any other stove no matter what fuel it burns. There is no handier oil heater made for general household use. Can be used in any part of the house;—downstairs, upstairs, in rooms, hallways, or in whatever part of the house warmth is required. Makes warm and cozy the rooms not heated by other stoves or furnace. The superiority of the

PERFECTION
Oil Heater
(Equipped with Smokeless Device)

lies in the fact that it generates intense heat without smoke or smell. The oil fount and the wick carrier are made of brass throughout, which insures durability. Gives great heat at small cost. Fount has oil indicator and handle. Heater can be easily carried about. Absolutely safe and simple —wick cannot be turned too high or too low. Operated as easily as a lamp. All parts easily cleaned. Two finishes—nickel and japan. Every heater warranted. There need not be one cold spot in your house so long as you own a Perfection Oil Heater. If not at your dealer's write our nearest agency for descriptive circular.

Perfection heater advertisement, 1907.

A quiet afternoon with the Perfection heater. Image courtesy Estar Hyo Gyung Choi, Mary Studio.

one. It made sense to avail ourselves of the labor-saving resources available to people of our class in our period of focus, the late 1880s. (Our house was built in 1888–89, and we chose that as our rough target for reconstructing our surroundings.) Time travel is one thing; descending the social ladder is something else altogether. One of the driving ideals of Victorian life was the idea of self-betterment, so if we as middle-class people had the means to adopt a luxury of the upper classes, all the better for us.

I would come to appreciate Gabriel's research into the appropriate uses of various oils. At first, I thought the paraffin oil in our lamps was burning just as hot as the kerosene in our heater, and I attributed the difference in radiance to the vastly disparate size of the heater's wick versus those of the dainty lamps. My first opportunity to really compare the two fuel oils fairly came a couple Christmases in the future. I had been complaining about walking in the dark on cold winter evenings, so as a holiday present Gabriel had managed to find an antique railroad lantern I could carry to light my path when I went out at night.

The paraffin oil we used in our parlor and bedroom lamps was perfect for that function, but putting it in a railroad lantern would have been a bit like putting the fanciest, highest grade of gasoline in a beat-up old pickup truck. The lantern had always been intended to burn kerosene, and so that was what we used to fill its rather substantial reservoir. I placed one of our house lamps in front of a mirror (doubling its glow) so I could see what I was doing and struck a match to light the lantern for a test burn. The thick glass dome that would prevent the flame from being blown out once it was lit created the unfortunate side effect of making it fiendishly hard to get at the wick, and I snuffed several matches in the attempt. Once I had gotten the wick lit, though, the contrast between the paraffin-fueled flame behind me and the kerosene glow in front of me was extreme. Kerosene burns with a much more orange—and much brighter—flame than the white glow provided by paraffin oil and, as Gabriel predicted, does create more soot. However, the heat it produces is quite impressive. Paraffin oil versus kerosene is a give-and-take situation with advantages and disadvantages to both sides. Choosing which was preferred in a given household was (and in our home is) the prerogative of the woman of the house. After some debate with myself, I've stayed with our original choice of paraffin oil for the lamps and kerosene for the heater and lantern.

Back on the occasion of that first hardware store visit, since Gabriel had been so considerate in researching the optimally clean oil for our lamps, I didn't bother my husband about candles, even though I sorely wanted some. Over the next few days, I did a great deal of groping my way between various rooms in our house. Sundown comes early in northern latitudes in the winter, and the northern edge of the Olympic Peninsula is the farthest place north in the continental United States. At the end of November, it was getting dark by four-thirty in the afternoon, which is a bit early for bed no matter how one is living.

We had a lovely oil lamp in our parlor that was designed specifically to cast enough light for sewing, and its illumination was more than adequate for reading—even with small print common in the nineteenth century. (Paper was more expensive in the 1800s than now, so books and magazines made more efficient use of their page space.) However, it was too large to carry around, so once I blew it out, I would find myself in the middle of a rather profound darkness. This was where a candle would have come in very handy. A fingerlamp would be even better, but that, too, was waiting on a future purchase.

I didn't want to turn on the electric lights, which still had their modern bulbs in them left behind by the sellers. This disinclination of mine was two-fold, and each of my motivations was equal in strength. I couldn't bear to cast the garish glow of modern light on my beautiful Victorian surroundings like some nonsense bit of circuitry pointlessly glued to a precious antique. Also, I didn't want to get into the habit of flipping a switch for light. A major motivation for our move to these surroundings was the desire to train ourselves out of such actions, and I wanted to begin our new life properly.

We would eventually get period lightbulbs: replicas of the earliest lightbulb patents (one by Edison, the rest associated with Nikola Tesla) carefully made from hand-blown glass. We try to save these for use when we have company; beyond being an appropriate period use of electric lights for the late nineteenth century, this makes them last an extremely long time. (In the four years since we installed period light bulbs throughout our house, only two of them have burned out.)

When there is no company to show off our electric lights to, Gabriel and I tend to just use our oil lamps. Our original two oil lamps (one upstairs, one downstairs) have gained a number of illuminating companions; we've bought more antique oil lamps and someone gave us a few modern ones. The difference between the antique lamps and the modern ones is really rather remarkable. The technology seems simple at first glance, but when a nineteenth-century oil lamp and a modern one are filled with identical oil and identical wicks, then lit and placed in a dark room together, the difference between them is extremely obvious. Modern oil lamps tend to be made for cheap ambience; even in electrical outages, people are often discouraged from using them because of liability concerns. However, when they were used on a regular basis for ordinary lighting, people paid a lot of attention to how effectively they lit a space. The burners on the antique lamps were designed with more effective airflow (to provide an optimal amount of oxygen to the burning wick) and better flame spreaders. These details mean that they cast notably brighter light. We have antique cast-iron sconces mounted in the walls to hold the lamps, and the mirrors so prevalent in Victorian furniture reflect and magnify their light. The wall sconce in the parlor has a mercury-glass reflector (a curved, mirrored surface) at its back to magnify and focus its lamp's flame. For light when moving between rooms, we have fingerlamps—small lamps with a loop built in to secure a finger and make them easily portable.

And yes, we have even acquired candles.

For the first few days, however, we had none of these things, and I developed a rather intimate knowledge of my house's interior as I groped my way over every inch of parlor, staircase, and bedroom to find my way to sleep at night.

In our skid marks-across-America move, we had jettisoned most of our mundane modern possessions. The majority of households contain quite large numbers of utilitarian objects that have accumulated over the years because they were conveniently available at the time they were first desired. I don't really care for lemon yellow as a color, yet formerly we'd had both a polyester-bristled broom and a plastic dustpan in that garish shade simply because they had been the cheapest option when we had set up our first house. They clung to us for years. Brooms and dustpans don't wear out very quickly, so I had never considered myself as having sufficient justification for replacing them, unattractive though they were. Numerous other items had followed this same pattern of being bought for frugality then retained for functionality, whether we actually enjoyed the sight of them or not. Two rapid-fire moves (to DC, then back to the Northwest) had finally provided me with an excuse to eliminate things that didn't fit in with our Victorian aesthetic.

Collection maintenance (what to keep versus what to throw away) is an issue that has been with the human race since the first nomadic hunter-gatherers decamped. Our species probably didn't even have proper language yet, but if we did, it's tempting to imagine the conversation between Caveman Ug and his mate, Ughina:

Ug: No need stick!
Ughina: Is best stick hold meat fire! Good stick—never find stick so good again! (Pointing.) No need rock!
Ug: Is best rock break bones! No other man have rock so good!
And so on . . .

I'm sure that when the End of Days comes, the final heroes will be hmm-ing and haw-ing over what to bring to Valhalla.

Gabriel likes to point out that professional archivists don't get paid to save things; archivists get paid to throw things away. When a collection (whether it's a museum library, corporation, or a vast private collection such as the legacies of Paul Allen) hires a professional archivist, the whole point of the operation is to put the decisions about what to throw away in capable hands.

Households have archivists, too, although they may not recognize themselves as such—and they probably don't get paid for maintaining their family's private collection of materials. It is nonetheless a vital role in the workings of any home. Otherwise we would all spend our days blundering through endless heaps of garbage and never be able to locate our necessary items among the trash.

Due to a convergence of a rising middle class and the increasing availability of cheap, mass-market products, Victorians of the late nineteenth century saw themselves facing unprecedented challenges regarding what to keep and what to eliminate from their domestic lives. Because these decisions revolved around the household, they were solidly in the sphere (i.e., the control) of the feminine half of society. Middle-class women's magazines of the 1880s and '90s go back and forth on the issue in a way that seems poignantly familiar to modern people facing the same challenges—now on an even vaster scale thanks to quotidian objects becoming even cheaper and more disposable.

Clearly, to make sense of things, some sort of system is necessary. Victorian philosopher William Morris said, "Have nothing in your houses that you do not know to be useful, or believe to be beautiful."[29] The implication is that it is best for them to possess both these virtues together.

We are ephemeral creatures with but a short time upon this Earth; the decision to fill our days with ugliness or beauty rests in our own hands whenever we take something into our lives. We must have objects of use to meet our daily needs; why not choose examples that delight our senses at the same time? The Victorians believed very strongly that beauty inspires goodness. Teachers were urged to fill their classrooms with beautiful items to

> inspire the holiest, loftiest and noblest ambition . . . the aquarium, the trailing vine, the blossom and the specimens of natural history should adorn the teacher's desk and the windows, while handsome pictures should embellish the walls . . . [T]he pupils should be surrounded with such an array of beauty as will constantly inspire them to higher and nobler achievements.

All people were advised,

> The love of the beautiful ever leads to the higher, the grander, the better. Guided by its impulses, we pass out of the hut into the larger and better

house; into the charming and elegantly-adorned mansion. Actuated by its influence, we convert the lumbering railway carriage into a palace-car, the swamp into a garden, and the desolate place into a park, in which we wander amid the trees, the streams of limpid water, and the fragrance of beautiful flowers.[30]

Gabriel and I love our antique artifacts because they were crafted in a time when beauty and its elevating effects were still appreciated. We enjoy incorporating as many elements of the beautiful into our lives as possible because, like the people who made them, we too feel that they lift the spirit and inspire those who are surrounded by them to ever better ideals.

Giving away as many reminders of modernity as we could possibly part with had felt extremely liberating. Replacing them with more Victorian counterparts, however, was often a bit challenging. It would have been far easier to accomplish if this were still the nineteenth century, of course. In the actual nineteenth century, we could have gone into one of the local stores and any given object on the shelves would, naturally, have been authentically Victorian. Finding Victorian items amid a marketplace cluttered with newfangled paraphernalia was far more complicated.

We were lucky to have a few antiques from Gabriel's family. Our rug, for example, fulfilled a prediction written in *Good Housekeeping* back in the year our house was finished: "An unusually fine [rug] . . . will do service to the third and fourth generation."[31] As we positioned our rug in the parlor, I thought of the story behind it. It is a gorgeous, nineteenth-century Chinese rug we inherited from Gabriel's grandmother, Gogi. (Her real name was Miriam, but everyone in the family called her by the nickname, which, like the rug, had been passed down to us through a few generations.)

Gogi had been a classic New England blue-blood of impeccable stock. She had distinct ideas about taste. All her friends had antique Persian carpets, so she considered these a bit passé. She preferred antique Chinese carpets, and since she had the economic means to go to China and acquire them in person, that was precisely what she did. The one that eventually came into our possession shows a calm sea woven in cobalt blue wool, dotted with ships under sail. The only land in this scene—a pair of twin islands—is the one place where the carpet is threadbare. "That," Gogi had explained when she gave us the carpet "—was where Queen Hatshepsut sat. She lived to be twenty years old—a quite venerable age for a cat!"

That story had been told on our wedding day and now, years later, I reminded Gabriel of it as we rolled out the carpet. We laughed about the housecat who refused to sit in water—even the pictorial water of a carpet— and insisted on always sleeping on the woven islands for so many years that she wore a bare space in the warp and weft. The mark the kitty left decreased the carpet's fiscal value to any collector, but it increased its sentimental value for us because it told a story. Most things in life that are truly used eventually gain little stories like this, and those tales are the very reason Gabriel and I prefer antiques to reproductions. Travel is often more about the journey than the destination, and researching history through primary sources is the closest we can come to traveling through time. Objects are often better time-travelers than people, since the well-made varieties often survive their human owners. The indelible marks left on them over the years are their souvenirs of temporal travel.

"As a third of our life is spent in bed, it behooves all home-makers to expend their best energies in the selection and equipment of the first essential of a sleeping chamber—the bed."
—Lida Rose McCabe, 1894[32]

Our storytelling time travelers seldom encounter us as quickly as we would like them to. Even when they do arrive, they often make demands. It took us three years to find a bed frame that would fit in with the rest of our house, and it was admittedly sans mattresses when we got it.

For the first three years in our Eastlake home, dreams of a perfect bed danced through our heads at night—while we were sleeping on a futon. This had never been our ideal sleeping platform, but it had been cheap and convenient while Gabriel was in graduate school and we lived in a small apartment behind a futon importer. Many people deal with such circumstances that fate foists upon them, but if any of us would ever attain our dreams, we must never forget our aspirations.

Even before we could acquire an antique bed, we were able to tuck some very Victorian accessories in with us at night: hot water bottles. In our chilly house, we were incredibly grateful for these very efficient methods of keeping ourselves warm. A large number of items go unappreciated in this world for no other reason than that people don't understand how to use them. When a rubber bottle starts out cold and is filled with hot water, a good deal of the heat goes into equalizing the temperature between the bottle and its contents. The key is to treat the bottle the same way the Japanese and the British do their teapots: it should be filled with hot water to warm the container, emptied, then immediately refilled with equally hot water. A rubber bottle filled in this way will stay warm all through the night. When we have overnight houseguests, they often remark on how surprised they have been to wake up and find their hot water bottle still warm. I sewed cloth slipcovers for all of them so the rubber isn't directly against our skin, and they've always been nice and cozy—even when we were still grudgingly sleeping on a futon and continued searching for a real bed.

As often happens, we spent several years eyeing options we coveted (but couldn't afford) and dismissing possibilities within our budget but not to our taste. Some of these were too modern, others too broken. In some cases, they were simply too shockingly hideous. Victorians had individual tastes that varied widely from person to person, as people in any culture do. Merely because something is from the nineteenth century, it should not be assumed that my husband and I are obligated to fall desperately in love with that specific item. To assume this is as misguided as believing that the desires of *any* people in a given culture could ever possibly be uniformly homogeneous.

We tolerated the futon, tucked away money in the bank dollar by dollar, and reminded ourselves that things come along in their own time. In this case, the time proved to be an overcast day in early October while I was walking to the corner grocery store to buy some milk. Fate happened to place a garage sale directly in my path, and curiosity slowed my steps a little. I stopped outright when I saw—not the bed we'd been saving for—but the rocking chair of my dreams.

When we first moved to Port Townsend, Gabriel and I had sat down together and written a list of things we wanted, separated into three separate categories: Acquire Soon, Acquire Later, and Someday. Looking at bare floors and walls in those days, we had to prioritize.

Daily needs of life came first, so candles, kerosene, and a garbage can all went under the category of Acquire Soon, as did various items associated with setting up my massage business. Most of the furniture we wanted for our own use in private areas of the house went under the heading Acquire Later. The bed we wanted was on this list. The Someday list was for items that weren't, strictly speaking, necessary, but that it couldn't hurt us to dream about. Gabriel wanted a high wheel bicycle and I wanted a rocking chair.

A rocking chair is one of life's little luxuries, the sort of charming detail that turns a mere shelter into a home and makes it all the cozier. It is not necessary for survival, but it helps make life sweet. When Gabriel and I were newly married, his mother passed along a rocking chair to me that she had found at a yard sale, and I stubbornly clung to it through six changes of domicile. Every time we moved and therefore had to reevaluate our possessions, I told Gabriel, "If the rocking chair doesn't fit in the truck/storage unit/new apartment/shipping crate, etc., it'll be the first thing we jettison." It was expendable.

I sure did like rocking chairs, though, even if mine was just a chintzy one from the 1980s. It still symbolized calm comfort and a place to read. So through all our moves, I always managed to squeeze it into the very last spot available, no matter how tightly our possessions became packed.

As we slowly were able to replace a growing percentage of our possessions with their Victorian equivalents, Gabriel kept eyeing my pastel-blue chintz rocker, looking increasingly anachronistic against the backdrop of our other goods. "Don't you think it might be time to get rid of that?" he would ask, casting a baleful eye at the rocker. It clashed so violently against his grandmother's antique writing desk that one felt obligated to rub their eyes after seeing the juxtaposition.

"It still works," I would insist. "It's not broken."

"But—" and he would look back at the rocker, standing out against our Victorian belongings like a plastic kazoo in a Stradivarius string section. "It really doesn't go."

"But I sit in it!" I would insist. "I use it! The Victorians had rocking chairs— it's not like the idea of it is anachronistic."

"But I want to buy you a *nice* rocking chair," my sweet husband would insist, tempting me.

At this point in the oft-repeated conversation, I inevitably felt obligated to point out that there was a whole array of other things that pressed with more immediate urgency on our limited resources: a bed, books for our research, ongoing repairs to our shoes that we were always wearing holes through . . . My husband's romantic generosity and my grudging pragmatism (for I did want a prettier rocker, of course) would thus reach a stalemate, and we would put the discussion aside—until the next time. The conversation would be repeated any time the odd juxtaposition rubbed another sore spot in Gabriel's ocular nerve or when we went to an antiques store and saw a rocker for sale.

Part of the problem was that I had gotten spoiled. The rocking chair that offended Gabriel's eye so much he wished to pluck it out was a glider rocker, and I'd gotten fond of it. I had been willing to trade it in for a simple willow or maple chair on two curved bows—until I saw that the late nineteenth century High Victorians had their own version of a glider. I made the discovery one day in a dusty antiques store empty of customers but packed with furnishings.

"This is amazing!" I declared as I rocked back and forth, back and forth in a plush velvet armchair mounted on pivoting springs above a hardwood base. I looked over my shoulder and saw more carved hardwood framing the velvet that cushioned my head. "You can just leave me here for the next—oh, forever," I told Gabriel. I ran my hands along the length of the luxuriantly upholstered armrests until my hands gripped the ornate cherry wood at their ends. "Just leave me here," I repeated dreamily, closing my eyes. *Back and forth, back and forth.* "I'm so happy!" I purred.

Gabriel assessed the carvings on the chair. "Eastlake style—1890s." I could hear the approving nod in his tone. "It would fit right in with the house."

I opened my eyes. "We came here to look for a kitchen table," I reminded him. (This was still quite early in our residence. We'd been setting our dishes on cardboard boxes for weeks.)

"We've got to get these things when we find them!" My husband beamed at me cheerfully. "They don't come up very often!"

I stood up from The Glorious Chair of Ultimate Comfort. "A kitchen table is more pressing," I said firmly. I sought out the chair's price tag. "We can save up for—" I found the tag, gulped, and stepped away from the rocker. "—a bed. We can save up for a bed. When we've got that and a few other things that take higher priority, *then* we can think about—" I looked at the price tag again. "—a cheaper rocking chair. Things like this are above our station."

Gabriel tried to dispute this, but I cut him off. "I think a simple chair that's just on wooden rockers is a more realistic goal for us," I told my husband. The words of a nineteenth-century advice book whispered at the edge of my brain: *If in moderate circumstances, do not be over ambitious to make an expensive display in your rooms . . .*[33]

Gabriel inspected the price tag. "Well, how much were you expecting to spend?" he asked.

"With everything else the house needs?"

More nineteenth-century advice ran through my mind. *"As a general thing . . . women have common sense . . . Be careful that you do not estimate your husband solely by his ability to make display. The nature of his employment, in comparison with others, may not be favorable for fine show, but that should matter not. The superior qualities of mind and heart alone will bring permanent happiness."*[34]

I calculated, sighed, and named a particularly low figure.

Gabriel looked dubious. "You'll have a hard time finding even a simple rocker for that."

"Well," I said resignedly, "other things take priority—like a bed."

Three years passed between that day and the one when I came across my neighbor's yard sale on a gray October day. In all that time, I had visited more antiques stores than I could venture to count and seen a grand total of three 1890s spring-mounted rockers. As Gabriel had said, they don't come up very often. Suddenly though, outside in the open air, I was seeing a fourth.

The Chair of Ultimate Comfort! I approached it tentatively, in a sort of awed reverence. Overhead, the clouds grew thicker. I cast a cautious look upward. *It must not rain on THAT chair!* I told myself, horrified at the very thought. *I wonder—Do you suppose they'd mind—if, if I just sat in it, very gently, for just a minute?*

It was early in the day, and there weren't many people at the sale yet. I looked around and then, tentatively, gingerly, perched on the edge of The Glorious Chair. Silently, I sighed with happiness. I let my eyes close halfway and smiled.

"Found your chair?" A friendly voice broke into my reverie.

I jumped up, embarrassed as a cat found with her mouth full of feathers. *Me? I? Er, nothing to see here . . .* "I, uh—" I stammered awkwardly. "It's a really nice chair." I looked down at the velvet plush and at the Eastlake carvings that matched our other furniture with an uncanny exactitude, as if they'd all been an original set together. I thought of our bank account for the household budget, and a question pressed at my mind I was afraid to ask. "How much—" I began quietly, dubious but unable to resist. "How much do you think you'd want for it?"

The man—incredibly—quoted me a slightly lower price than I'd told Gabriel I would be willing to pay for an inferior rocker.

My eyes grew wide. I blinked. My jaw dropped. I forced it shut again, then swallowed the toad-sized lump that had suddenly appeared in my throat. I ripped open my purse and gave the man all my milk money. "Can you please take this as a down payment and hold it for me just ten minutes while I run to the bank? I'll be *right back*!"

While the man laughed at my enthusiasm and promised to hold the chair, I set off on a full-out sprint, petticoats flying. I'm not naturally a fast runner, but on this occasion I sent so much wind through my hair that I nearly lost my hat.

I arrived back at the yard sale out of breath and terrified that someone else would have snatched up the rocker with a more lucrative offer in my absence. When I saw that it was still there, I could have danced for joy. I paid the man, then hugged close my Glorious Chair and lifted it to carry it home.

I am five feet, nine inches tall. The Chair is three-foot-three. I don't care to disclose my own broadest dimension, but I will say that The Chair takes up a significantly larger ground space than I do. It has an approximately two-and-a-half foot by two-and-a-half-foot square footprint. Also, being set on springs on a wooden base, it has a perpetually shifting center of gravity while in motion. I wouldn't exactly call it easy to carry. Luckily, it doesn't weigh much (less than forty pounds) and I wasn't going far.

"Do you want help loading that?" someone behind me asked.

"Hmm?" I asked dreamily, half-drunk on the glory of my Chair. "Oh, no. I'm not loading it into any vehicle. I'm just carrying it home. I only live at the top of the hill, about five blocks that way—" I pointed in the direction of my house, which was slightly out of sight.

Some incredulity was expressed at the idea of carrying any furniture that far, but I simply laughed and had a merry walk home, clutching my beautiful (and somewhat large) Chair.

I carried The Chair home with only a couple of pauses to set it down and massage my biceps. I received more than a couple of strange looks from passersby in cars. Once I arrived at my house, I moved the chintz anachronism to the room with the broken windows for temporary storage and carried The Chair up the narrow staircase and settled it in our bedroom. After some misty-eyed moments admiring it, I ventured out again on my original errand—pursuit of milk.

When I came to the yard sale once more, I stopped to thank the man hosting it and to tell him of how long I had been dreaming of a chair just like that one.

He smiled at me. "Well, you know—" He looked off to the side. "We've got some other stuff we just haven't brought out yet because we were afraid it might rain. I don't suppose you need a bed, do you?"

Another sprint followed.

This time, the kind man and his brother helped me carry home my purchase: a full-sized wooden bed frame, complete with its original box springs. Astonished at my luck, I brought out the oil soap and had the old wood polished and gleaming by the time Gabriel arrived home. He was delighted when he saw our new acquisition.

Part Eastlake, part Renaissance-revival, the bed has square edges framing a towering headboard carved with the face of Hera, Goddess of Marriage, and a high footboard featuring carvings of harvest fruits—grapes, a ripe peach, and a pomegranate. The fact that the wooden frame still had its original steel box spring was a bit of a coup where antique furniture is concerned: box springs tend not to have survived very well through the metal drives of the two world wars. The only element the bed was lacking were mattresses—and I rather approved of this particular absence.

Since we'd been planning out a bed purchase for so long, Gabriel and I had had a great deal of discussion over the subject of mattresses. Every time he brought up the idea of buying a used mattress, I refused his suggestion as adamantly as possible. I brought my foot down as hard on the subject as if I'd been stamping out a metaphorical cockroach.

"But new mattresses are expensive," he told me repeatedly.

"I don't care!" I always replied in a tone that I meant should brook no argument. "I have been reading too many articles in my nineteenth-century *Good Housekeeping* magazines about how to get rid of bedbugs and other pests to ever sleep easy on a used mattress! Do you have any idea how many letters women used to write in to the magazine about the subject? Do you have any idea how many people *still* deal with this?" I set my jaw. "In our period, *Good Housekeeping* held a whole contest for half a year challenging people for the best bedbug remedies! Some people wrote in saying that the only way to kill them was to *drench—drench*, mind you—their word, not mine, their italics, not mine!—drench the whole mattress in gasoline and keep lamps out of the room until the fumes had dissipated. Can you even imagine the sort of desperation that speaks to? And quite frankly, I'm not crazy about the modern toxic chemical solutions, either! After all our painstaking care to neutralize pH and maintain the best archival conditions we possibly can for all our precious antiques, can you imagine turning an exterminator loose on them with his pharmacopeia of chemicals?" I crossed my arms in front of me. "I shudder to think!"

"We don't have bedbugs here," my husband pointed out in a calm tone several decibel levels below my shrieks.

"Plenty of places in America still do! I've heard New York City even has billboards warning people about bedbugs—and this is present day, modern times we're talking about! Not old news, not nineteenth century, but twenty-first century, now! It's in the news all the time! Chicago has them, too, along with a lot of other places! And if you buy a used mattress, there are absolutely no guarantees about where it's been!"

Incidentally—and very lamentably—Gabriel's assertion about the Seattle area not being prey to bedbugs is no longer true. Orkin's 2013 list for the worst US cities regarding bedbugs ranks the Seattle/Tacoma area at number 18 out of 50 metropolitan areas ranked. New York—ranked at number 17 by Orkin—placed just above Seattle, and Chicago topped the list as the current worst modern city for the pests.[35] If it's any consolation to inhabitants of the Windy City, a list by CBS News places Chicago down at number five on their bedbug list. Unfortunately, New Yorkers might not like the CBS list as much—their city came in first for that ranking.[36]

"Besides—" I continued my refusal of the used mattress concept. "Just—" I wordlessly screwed up my face into an expression of absolute disgust. "Eeeww!" I knew I was more or less using up my monthly quota of exclamation points in a single conversation, but I wanted to make it clear that, as far as I was concerned, a used mattress was not an option.

"But a modern mattress won't fit an antique bed," Gabriel reminded me placidly.

Uniform sizing of beds was a concept contrived in the twentieth century; Victorian beds tended to be smaller than modern ones. I had, however, given this point plenty of careful thought.

"I'll make one!"

"Make a mattress?"

"Why not?" I calmed down. "That's what most people in our class would have done in the nineteenth century. The letters I was reading from nineteenth-century women dealing with bedbugs tended to be from parson's wives who had to move a lot and always had the bedding in their homes provided by their parishioners. No one likes a used mattress if they have a better option. Middle-class women would have made new ones when they needed them—even farm-wives did that. A mattress tick is just a rectangular cube; it's nowhere near as complicated as a dress."

"What would you fill it with?" Gabriel asked curiously.

I shrugged. "They would fill it with whatever was on hand, depending on their means and what was around. Cotton, if they were in cotton country. I've heard of the poorest classes using dried corn husks in corn country."

Gabriel laughed. "That would be a little noisy."

"Yeah, probably not our style," I agreed. "Besides, we're in the wrong place geographically for that. I've heard of some women around here stuffing their menstrual rags with moss in the earliest pioneer days, but I'm not sure I could find enough to stuff a mattress with. Besides, in that much moss, I'd start worrying about bugs again."

"I'll say!" agreed Gabriel.

"In the city, the poorest classes stuffed their mattresses with rags," I continued. The 1895 Montgomery Ward catalog sold ready-made mattresses stuffed with husks, palm leaves imported from Africa, wool, hair, cotton, three different grades of moss, and "sanitary sea moss"—a type of seaweed touted as having tonic properties of particular benefit to "delicate or nervous persons." They also sold bed ticking fabric designed especially for use with straw or with feathers.[37]

"Feathers were the best across classes, if you could get them—whether by buying them or by raising the fowls yourself. It was pretty common to have two mattresses stacked on top of each other; the bottom one would just be for bulk—" I held up my hand, palm flat. "And the top mattress would be filled with the more luxurious padding you'd actually be sleeping on." I laid my other hand over top of the first. "Think the princess and the pea. Someone in our class and income bracket would probably have feathers in the upper mattress and some cheaper filler stuffed into the lower mattress."

The thickness of the feather mattress would vary by an individual's access to feathers, from a very thick, luxurious full mattress down to little more than a pad. In recent years, the concept of a feather bed has gotten rather fuzzy, since someone using the term now is less likely to be referring to an entire mattress stuffed with feathers than to a sort of thick, fluffy comforter intended to be used as a pad over a mattress. These pads are termed feather beds as a sort of honorary title, even in cases where their stuffing never made the acquaintance of a bird. (They can variously be stuffed with synthetic materials meant to be reminiscent of feathers or with cotton—presumably, in the latter case, by someone more competent than myself, as I was to discover all too soon.)

"I could stuff the lower mattress with cotton, and the upper mattress with feathers. I'd want to stuff the upper mattress with feathers anyway, regardless of what we put in the other one."

Gabriel looked doubtful again. "Where would you get that many feathers?"

I shrugged. "I'd order them, like we do with so many other things."

Living in a very small town, we have exactly some of the same problems our Victorian forebears had in small Western towns: lack of local availability. Starting in 1872, this issue was easily solved by ordering through the wonderful Montgomery Ward & Co. catalog, and in just a few years, consumers would have even more choices when Sears & Roebuck joined the mail-order business and prompted a rivalry that would lead to increasingly lower prices—and increasingly varied selection—for customers around the country.[38] By the end of the nineteenth century, these two companies were selling and shipping everything from horseshoe nails to houses, silk shirtwaists to Winchester repeating rifles. We had reprints of these old catalogs and pored over them for hours, marveling at the selection of materials they represented: corsets for every body style; guns for any quarry; dozens of different stoves that would run off of anything from wood to coal to oil to gas; tents (the kind people take camping and the kind put up at fairs to sell refreshments); rugs in a dizzying array; telephones; sandglasses thousands of different pocket-watch possibilities; toilet paper; tea sets; fancy stationery; fish hooks; shelf brackets . . . We often dreamed we had a magic mailbox that could receive just a few of these items through a time warp for us. Lacking this, we made do with the closest current equivalent: ordering things by Internet. Given that they still went through the mail (just like in the old Montgomery Ward days), it wasn't really that big of a leap. The main difference is that the modern 'net is slightly less convenient than the old catalogs, since the price lists are now significantly less consolidated. (Amazon.com may sell books on home decor, but they won't ship an actual house. Score one for the Victorians.)

When he heard my idea of ordering enough feathers to stuff a mattress, my husband gave me a dubious expression. "That's going to take a lot of feathers. Won't that be expensive?"

I shrugged and smiled at him. "Cheaper than a new mattress."

He conceded this point.

"Besides," I pointed out. "This way I can make it fit the bed exactly. Like you said, we'd have a hard time doing that with a modern mattress."

"We *couldn't* do it with a modern mattress," Gabriel asserted, inspecting the wooden frame and the metal box spring. It was significantly larger than a modern single bed, but smaller than a queen-sized one. It was meant to have a mattress made just for it—just for us! Not for bedbugs.

"Okay." Gabriel finally assented to my idea. "Let's do it!"

That afternoon, I sent in an order to a fabric supplier for canvas ticking and an order for feathers to a supplier that usually sold their product to people re-stuffing jackets and pillows. I initially wanted to buy at least the cotton locally, but when a search of the local stores revealed that buying every single cotton ball in Port Townsend might (possibly) yield enough to stuff a large teddy bear, I put in an order for cotton to yet a third source. In the 1890s, all three of these purchases would have involved filling out a single Montgomery Ward order form—and paying a single shipping fee. Furthermore, I would have had my choice from twelve separate ticking fabrics all specifically made for beds; these included three varieties of bed ticking designed especially to be stuffed with straw and four different fabrics (including a fancy variety striped in red, white, and blue) designed specifically for feather filling. (The remaining tickings—presumably good for use with any stuffing material—included another ticking under the "Fancy" heading—this time in blue plaid, available as either a medium or a large plaid pattern depending on the consumer's style choice.) Remember, these are just the varieties of ticking made specifically for beds! Tent duck, wide duck, and awning duck all had their own categories in Montgomery Ward. In the modern market, I had to send in an order for generic "duck ticking" and hope it would serve my purpose.

I based the quantity of my feather order on the supplier's suggestion for how many feathers it takes to fill an average pillow, multiplied by an educated guess about how many pillows it would take to cover our new bed. The result was an order for fifty pounds of steamed duck feathers. I hoped this would be enough.

When it came to the cotton, I had no idea how much I would need to complete the project. My first thought was to use cotton wadding, but I could find no suppliers selling the loose fiber to consumers and the variant sold to quilters (pressed into sheets as batting) was prohibitively expensive. After investigating a number of sources, I realized that buying enough cotton batting to fill a mattress would quickly add up to more than double the cost of the feathers I had ordered; since the entire purpose of filling the lower mattress with cotton was to keep it cheaper than the upper mattress we would be sleeping on, this would clearly be a foolish choice. I decided cotton was cotton; if upholstery was sometimes stuffed with rags, why couldn't I stuff a mattress with plain little cotton balls? I found a supplier for these and, since I had no idea how many I needed anyway, calculated my order on financial considerations alone. I ordered enough cotton balls to equal a total order price roughly half that I had spent on feathers and hoped for the best.

I was going for a walk afterward and contemplating my purchases when some arithmetic clicked over its counters in the back of my brain. "Huh," I said to myself. "That's interesting."

I was near a coffee shop where an acquaintance worked, so I went in and found him behind the counter. When he had a spare minute without customers, I sat down across from him at the bar and grinned. "I just ordered ten thousand cotton balls!" I told him perkily and without preamble.

He blinked in surprise. "Um, hello to you, too." He took off his glasses and started wiping them on the corner of his shirt. "Exactly how much—" he held his hands in various configurations in front of himself, "—volume does ten thousand cotton balls represent?"

I grinned. "I have absolutely no idea whatsoever. That's what I get for ordering by price point. After realizing how many I ordered, I have an image in my head now of coming home one day soon and finding my entire house covered in cotton balls."

One of the other baristas who had overheard the conversation chimed in. "Maybe they'll deliver them by helicopter!" she joked. "Wouldn't that be cool?" She spun around, hands uplifted, imagining a storm of cotton falling out of the sky. "It's snowing!" She caught something imaginary and squinted at the invisible item. "No, wait—it's cottoning!" She danced around again.

I laughed. "Or, for all I know, when it actually arrives, it might wind up being just a small box of them. I only hope it's enough for the project I'm planning."

The ticking was the first of the various orders to arrive. It appeared on our porch a few days later: a long bolt of fabric wrapped around a cardboard tube nearly as tall as I was. I heaved it inside, cut pieces to the dimensions I wanted for our bed, and started sewing two identical mattresses.

I do all my sewing by hand, and this project was no exception. Admittedly, this was a case where an average woman from our target period of around 1889 would probably consider *me* old-fashioned. In 1868 (twenty years before our house was built), Canadian diarist Lucy Ronalds Harris casually wrote in her journal that her husband had bought her a small sewing machine that she planned to change for a larger one.[39]

In 1853, the first Singer sewing machines sold for one hundred American dollars each. They weren't the only machines available, but thanks to enthusiastic sales tactics, by 1855 Singer was already "the world's largest sewing company." A Singer sewing machine won first place in the Paris World's Fair in 1855, and the next year salesman Edward Clark originated a purchase-by-installment plan that allowed even the lower classes to buy sewing machines. In 1863, around 20,000 sewing machines were sold annually by the Singer Company alone; and by 1870 this figure had jumped to 170,000! By 1880, Singer's worldwide sales exceeded 500,000 machines, and in 1889 (the year our beloved house was completed) the company produced their first electric sewing machine.[40]

Given how ubiquitous these devices were by our favorite period, I sometimes wonder myself why I cling so stubbornly to my needle and thread. The simple matter is: they suit me. I enjoy the calm, meditative control of a project lovingly finished. I'm not the first lady to be charmed in this way by the conservative side of women's work and doubtless I won't be the last. Nineteenth-century diarist Maude Franklin kept detailed records of all her daily activities from 1888 until 1899 and illustrated her journal with her own drawings and paintings of herself and her friends. She did own a sewing machine—it appears in a single drawing and one watercolor—but she depicts herself sewing by hand, as well, and recounts a story of a friend's young relative begging to be taught how to thread a needle.[41] Various modern women have confided to me (always in curiously hushed tones as if confessing something embarrassing or shameful) that they also prefer sewing by hand to using a machine. We're all unique, and the way we enjoy accomplishing things varies from individual to individual—no matter when we are living.

My grandmother's old sewing machine (a Brunswick model) was left to me after she died, and it lives in my guest room. The National Sewing Machine Company began manufacturing the Brunswick and the Damascus—another high-end model—for Montgomery Ward in 1889 (that magic year again!). Although it would be tempting to imagine my grandma's sewing machine coming off its assembly line as the last board was nailed onto our house, the design graphic on its box of attachments is far more consistent with the 1920s. The machine itself didn't change much in the intervening years, though, and Grandma's/mine is virtually a twin to the models I see when I linger over the old catalogs. Perhaps someday I'll learn how to use it. The attachments would certainly make pin tucks a less laborious part of my dress-making projects and, wherever my grandmother is now, she would doubtless prefer that I use her machine. Grandma never did approve of sewing by hand. (As I've said, every person is different, no matter when we're living.)

For tasks like the mattresses, though, the machine wouldn't help. If I had tried sewing through the multiple layers of thick ticking fabric with it, my only results would have been a broken machine and years of otherworldly scolding (my grandmother chiding me from beyond the grave). In any case, the project was nowhere near as complicated or time-consuming as dressmaking. It only took me a single day to complete the first mattress. Given that some of my dressmaking epics had stretched out for over a year, any project finished in but a single day had an air of fantastic speed! (Admittedly, I still had to fill and seal the tick once the stuffing materials arrived.) I was working on a seam for the second mattress when a gentle thump on the porch alerted me that another delivery had appeared.

Image courtesy Estar Hyo Gyung Choi, Mary Studio.

I looked outside and saw a petite little box, slightly smaller than the average microwave oven. I read the label and laughed. "So that's what ten thousand cotton balls looks like!" I chuckled, putting my hands on my hips. "Well, we'll see how this works!"

I used a kitchen knife to slice open the shipping tape on the box and pulled out dozens of dainty little plastic bags filled with cotton balls—the sort of packages one might expect to find on certain women's makeup shelves next to the toenail polish. Sitting surrounded by them on my kitchen floor, I reflected that if personal pedicures had been the motivation for my order, I would now have a lifetime supply of spacing fluff.

As mattress filling, however, the pile seemed a bit scanty. I laughed at its inadequacy, shook my head, and determined to do the best job possible with the materials I had. Then I scooped the heaps of little bags back into their box, carried them into the parlor, and set to work filling the first mattress tick. Pulling open bag after bag of the cotton balls and pouring them into the tick felt slightly like bailing out a boat in reverse. The balls expanded slightly once they were released from the compression enforced by their packaging; notwithstanding this, the most charitable assessment of how well they filled the mattress by the time I finished was that it was—at best—one-third of the way full.

Sewing projects invariably generate snips and snarls of fibers, and over the last three years I had gotten into the habit of saving these for use as pillow stuffing, pen-wipe material, and all the myriad employments scraps can be put toward. Seeing the inadequacy of the cotton balls, I jogged upstairs and fetched my overflowing scrap box and a half-finished pillow I had been filling with snippets of thread. I spent about an hour picking out the larger pieces from the scrap box that could still make useful patches, then poured all the smaller scraps into the mattress tick along with the cotton and all those thread snippets. Remembering I had a small portion of cotton quilt batting remaining from a recent project, I threw that into the tick as well and shook it up to fluff it.

The result still seemed rather flat. If a soft, welcoming mattress were likened to a puffy, huggable sheep, then this tick would more closely resemble an irate (and possibly malnourished) lamb after a particularly aggressive shearing. I gave it a lopsided grin and laughed good-humoredly at how entertaining this project was becoming. Then I put on my cycling clothes and set off to put a formerly discarded plan into action: I bought the city of Port Townsend out of its supply of cotton balls.

First I went to the local drugstore, which has been continuously in business so long that I've found their dusty leather-bound house account ledgers filed away in the county archives. (I've even read the charge accounts, written in flowing script with a steel-nibbed pen, for items purchased by the very family who lived in our house in the 1890s—but more on them later.) After buying their entire supply of cotton (and receiving a rather shocked look from the clerk at the register), I rode to the Safeway grocery store that came into town during the Great Depression of the 1930s, when circumstances were so straitened people were willing to change the shopping habits of lifetimes—leaving behind small local businesses and traveling outside what was then the city limit—to stretch their household budget just a little further. I bought out all their cotton as well and, like a little boll weevil, moved on to the last available source in my area: the QFC grocery store whose company had been founded in Bellevue, Washington, in 1955 and established a presence in Port Townsend in 1997.[42] After denuding this last supply, my bike's panniers were relatively full and the clerks of the several stores undoubtedly had some rather interesting speculations over their lunch tables.

I returned home and repeated the reverse-bailing procedure of emptying all my little plastic bags of cotton into the large canvas bag that was my mattress tick. This accomplished, I stepped back from my work and rubbed my chin, evaluating. The floppy, limp object oozing over my parlor floor was hardly the mattress of my dreams, but I judged that it would probably do acceptable service as an under-tick as long as the mattress on top of it was comfortable. I therefore pinned all my hopes on the fifty pounds of feathers, which had yet to arrive. I wondered—by no means for the first time—what that particular delivery would look like.

When the feathers arrived a few days later, I chewed my lower lip, worrying. The box they were in was certainly bigger than the shipping container for the cotton balls—it was taller than my waist—but it still didn't seem quite big enough to stuff the second large tick I had just finished sewing. I failed to take into account a significant difference in packing techniques between the two suppliers.

I should have gotten a clue about what to expect when I tried to bring the box inside and my arm muscles performed a jerky double take. Knowing it was full of feathers, I expected it to be light. Grabbing the box around its wide spaced edges, I casually tried to lift it—and it barely moved. After a brief flash of surprise I reminded myself, *Oh, yeah: fifty pounds of feathers!* I took a firmer grip and tried again. The fact that it was a particularly large box with smooth sides and no handholds to grip didn't help matters, but I managed to haul the package into the kitchen.

Inside the box I found two packages, each one consisting of a tightly compressed brick of feathers crammed into a fabric bag, which was in its turn encased in plastic. I carried the first of these into the parlor where the canvas tick I had sewn (and lined with a more tightly-woven broadcloth after a suggestion from my mother-in-law) was waiting. The parlor (which should be the cleanest room in a Victorian home) might not be the most appropriate venue for the notoriously messy task of filling a feather tick, but it was the largest room available to me and I reasoned that cleaning feathers off of the parlor floor would be easier than cleaning mud off of the mattress tick if I attempted to perform the operation outside in the rain. Of all the rooms in our house, the parlor had the most available floor space to maneuver bulky items. Our bedroom is located right above the parlor and is in many ways that room's plainer twin. However, most of the space there was taken up by the newly acquired antique bed and the futon that still served as our sleeping platform until I could get the new mattresses finished. Our parlor doubles as my sewing room, so in that sense it was an appropriate workspace.

I put the double-bagged sack into the tick, plastic and all, before I even tried to open it. Once it was thoroughly encased in canvas, I reached in and sliced open the plastic bag with a sharp knife. Even with most of the feathers still encased in the interior fabric bag, loose bunches of them already floated about in lazy circles.

Keeping both bags inside the tick, I disgorged the heavily filled fiber bag from its plastic *matroyshka* and gave the thin, clear wrap a vigorous shake before carefully removing it from the tick. Even with all these precautions, I laughed merrily to see a few feathers dancing free through the air of the room this early in the procedure.

When I used my knife on the fabric bag, a minor explosion occurred. With a sound like a soft sigh, the sack became a miniature Vesuvius and disgorged billowing clouds of velvet softness into the mattress. I blew away some down that had flown up into my face and, laughing, held the tick tightly closed until the eruption settled. When the feathers escaped from their compressed captivity, I was happy to see that they were filling the mattress rather nicely. I scraped the last stubborn quills from the inside of the fiber bag, then removed it from the tick. A cloud of feathers fled for liberty behind it. After brief reflection, I added this fiber bag to the other assorted stuffing in the cotton tick, then repeated the whole process to add the contents of the second bag of feathers to the first inside what would be the upper mattress.

The feathers filled and expanded the mattress into a cloud worthy of a slumbering goddess. The only thing keeping me from leaping onto it before I'd even sewn it shut was a vision of myself afterward chasing thousands of errant feathers throughout the house after my weight forced them from the open space that had allowed them into the bag. I quickly sewed this shut with the same thick, linen thread I had used to sew the seams. (Besides my natural propensity for hand-sewing and a conviction that my grandmother's machine couldn't have handled the canvas ticking fabric, the particular thread I was using on this project was another good reason to do it by hand. I was using waxed bookbinding thread, a single strand of which was several times thicker than dental floss. I couldn't have passed it through the eye of the needle of my grandmother's old sewing machine, but I could use it when sewing by hand, and it would definitely make the finished mattress seams strong!)

When Gabriel came home, I had both mattresses laid out on our magnificent antique bed. I pulled him eagerly upstairs, shouted, "Behold!" and plunged into the downy depths of the feather mattress. It was like falling into heaven, like swimming in a cloud. Languidly, I rolled over and smiled up at my husband.

He returned my happy expression, but then a curious look came into his eyes. "Didn't you make two mattresses?"

I turned sheepish. "Hmm? Umm, oh. Hmm . . ." Embarrassed, I rolled over and off the feathery cloud. "The other one didn't turn out so well," I confessed, standing. Grabbing a corner of the glorious downy corner of heaven, I peeled up the first mattress to reveal the misshapen lumpy mass underneath. I pushed and prodded the blob like a child picking at an unsavory (and particularly large) pile of raw liver covered in Brussels sprouts. "No matter what I do," I explained, first pushing at the lump, then picking up the mattress and shaking it, "the quilt batting I put in there won't lay flat." I tried grabbing it through the ticking fabric and ironing it with my hands to little avail. "And the cotton balls—" I shook the mattress again, "mostly want to stick together."

Gabriel helped me shake the abortive attempt at a cotton mattress until we were able to lay it out (relatively) flat. "I think—" Gabriel suggested, "that you would need a lot more cotton to get this to actually work right. The principle is good, but I think the mattress is supposed to actually be *stuffed* and not have the filling rolling around inside of it."

"I know, I know," I conceded. "If I'd had a better source for cotton that would have worked." I gave the under-mattress a last swipe. "As it was, though, that much cotton would have cost way more than the feathers. And," I added with a huge grin, pulling the feather tick back over its unsatisfactory sister, "I would much rather just have more of this." I snuggled into the cloud, sighing with absolute contentment. "Aaahhh!"

Gabriel chuckled and did a belly flop onto the space beside me.

After years of sleeping on our cozy little feather heaven every night, there are only two objections I can possibly imagine someone raising to it—someone not myself, certainly, but some hypothetical Fussy Flossy.

First, it does molt in a rather entertaining fashion. Presumably the various feather-ticking fabrics designed for the specific purpose of making feather mattresses and sold through the Montgomery Ward catalog in the nineteenth century had a tighter weave than the canvas I was able to procure from a modern supplier. Our feather mattress molts despite the fact that I backed the canvas with broadcloth before I sewed it. This is not a crippling obstacle, but it does sometimes look as though a bird had taken a test flight around our bedroom. (It never looks as though a bird lived there though; I've lived in households with pet birds and the space under their cages collected more feathers in a single afternoon than our whole bedroom does in an entire week.) Our summer sheets have a higher thread count than the flannel ones we use in winter, so when I do the seasonal changeover, I layer the winter sheets on top of the summer ones to minimize feather loss through the looser weave of the flannel. When I sewed the feather tick, I created one seam that would be easier to rip open than the others in case we might ever want to add fresh feathers in the future, but the feather seepage is so slow that after an entire year there was still no noticeable difference in the size of our marvelous cloud.

The other theoretical objection could only really be made by a particularly critical pessimist. As soon as one lies down on the mattress, the fluffed feathers immediately contour to one's body and remain in that shape. If one rolls around in the night, all the subsequent spaces covered by the sleeper will also be perfectly formed to one's body. Personally, I find this to be an absolute vision of heaven for slumber. Fussy Flossy, however, might point out that after an entire night of this behavior, a series of compressed clefts and mounds will be left behind and the mattress tick will want fluffing in the morning. What does this mean? How does one accomplish this esoteric practice that has Fussy screaming about the burdens of antiquity and frantically dialing for the most heavily formaldehyde-drenched polyurethane rectangle marketed to consumers?

The Chair of Ultimate Comfort!

For a single person, fluffing a mattress involves lifting up one side of the mattress, giving it a vigorous shake, then walking around to the other side of the bed and repeating the process. The entire maneuver takes less than fifteen seconds. (For a pair of people, it's even easier since they can shake both sides at once.) That's it! That's all it takes to reboot the software of this simple device and spend another night of dreams embraced in heaven.

6

Maligned Plumbing, a Beautiful Toilette Set, and a Surprise Visit from a Daughter of Arachne

"We now come to an all-important point—that of the water supply. The value of this necessary article has also been lately more and more recognized in connection with the question of health and life; and most houses are well supplied with every convenience connected with water."
—*The Book of Household Management*, 1893[43]

Plenty of structures built in 1888–89 had indoor plumbing from the start. Nearly forty years earlier, in 1853, Boston already had more than 27,000 plumbing fixtures, including 2,500 water closets.[44] Historian Maureen Ogle states that "during the mid-nineteenth century, plumbing technology spread from occasional use in the homes of the very rich to the homes of those of middling circumstances living in both city and country."[45] The 1880s were actually a sort of golden age for sanitary plumbing. Indoor plumbing and flush toilets had been extremely popular in the mid-nineteenth century, then experienced a temporary downturn in trendiness in the 1870s due to worries about sewer gases. After U-shaped traps were worked out to keep such gases where they belonged, indoor plumbing came back in the '80s with an absolute vengeance, and various US cities put regulations in place to enforce safety and hygiene of household plumbing.[46]

Our particular house, being on the very farthest western edge of US civilization, did not initially have indoor plumbing in 1888. The architect's intention was not to create a long-term home for himself but simply to throw up four walls and a roof and then sell it as quickly as possible, make as wide a profit as possible, then move on. He cut corners when he could and plumbing was one of

these corners. In the far west at the dawn of the last decade of the nineteenth century, attitudes were right at the tipping point about which social classes deserved
indoor plumbing. Public opinion was about to switch very quickly from viewing
it as an upper-class luxury to considering it an every-class necessity.

Our house's first plumbing was installed sometime between eighteen and
twenty-two years after the house was built. The downstairs bathroom was created by walling off an old porch just off the kitchen, and the construction
style of the slight amount of work that accomplished this is consistent with
the first decade of the twentieth century; it's plainer than the Eastlake style of
the rest of the house. We can guess rough dates from the style of the window
(a different shape from the others in the house) and the unornamented cast
iron, claw-footed bathtub that were installed at the same time. Records of city
laws pinpoint even more exact years. Port Townsend's first sanitary sewer lines
were established in 1906, and by 1910 City Ordinance #753 had banned privy
outhouses and mandated that anyone who could access public sewer lines was
required by law to connect to them.[47] Four years might seem like a short time
for such a sweeping change in every household within a community, but it's not
really such a short time for a change people are eager to support.

I generally don't feel too guilty about making use of this slightly post-
construction addition, given how common indoor plumbing was in other parts
of the world by the 1880s and '90s. Besides, the United Nations has declared
"the right to safe and clean drinking water and sanitation . . . a human right that
is essential for the full enjoyment of life and all human rights"[48]—and who am
I to argue with the UN?

When we moved into our house and found the toilets filled with solid
blocks of ice and icicles dangling from faucets, we metaphorically bit our fingernails, fearing the pipes had burst inside the walls of our new/old home.
We breathed a huge sigh of relief when we melted things a bit and were able
to establish there hadn't been any interior damage and that the plumbing still
functioned. However, when the thaw came to the outside world, things got
even more lively.

The soil of the Pacific Northwest is very well adapted to the typical weather
of the Pacific Northwest. It acts like a slow and inexorable sponge to the perpetual drizzle that gives Washington its nickname of the Evergreen State. It's
far less effective at soaking up sudden deluges—in fact, it flatly refuses to do
anything of the sort.

All the extra runoff from the storm left inadequate room for our own system to drain properly. (The problem was exacerbated by another factor we didn't

know of at the time, but which I will revisit soon.) Our domestic wastewater, instead of draining to the public sewer, pooled at the lowest possible point in our house: the downstairs bathroom drain.

An abnormal amount of time spent watching one's own feet while in motion can lead one to walk into walls, large animals, and other inconvenient obstacles. I try to keep my eyes focused at a reasonable level to avoid such collisions, but not watching one's step can have its downside as well. My first view of the flooded bathroom floor came about half a second after I had stridden right into the pool of icy gray water—runoff from the sinks and shower. (At least it wasn't sewage.)

"Oh, for goodness sakes!"

I'm proud of the fact that I managed not to curse when I saw my predicament. On the other hand, I am rather embarrassed to admit that my first thought was to back out of the mess again and let Gabriel find it so that he would clean it up. My better nature fought with my selfish side for a while, and at last I sighed, patted myself on the back, and grabbed the mop.

The first two plumbers we called were from separate companies and we called them at different times (we called the second because the first had been so disastrous), and yet they managed to be remarkably similar to each other. They were both older than Methuselah and looked like they hadn't combed or washed their hair since antediluvian times. Each was coated from above his waist to the soles of his boots in a viscous brown substance that I really, sincerely hoped was mud. They tracked it into nearly every room of the house, including several rooms without plumbing such as the parlor, leaving behind thick ovals of the *stuff* on the floor and even across Gogi's antique parlor carpet. (There is obviously no plumbing in the parlor. A sink in the parlor would be close to the oddest thing I can imagine in a house. The alleged plumbers' entire motivation for barging into the parlor seems to have been to gawk at things and ask what they cost.) After this march of mire, they each separately declared the problem was that the house was too old and we should tear it down (the whole house!) and build a new one. Then they handed us substantial bills, presumably for the cost of the sludge.

Discouraged but far from beaten, we evaluated the situation. We knew the storm and all its attendant runoff was a main contributing factor, so we crossed our fingers that the situation would get better once the weather improved. We asked our various neighbors if they were having similar problems; when they responded in the negative, we realized there must be something blocking our pipes somewhere, regardless of what the cretins from the Black Lagoon had told us.

I started a daily routine of pouring entire boxes of baking soda and gallons of vinegar down our pipes. It would bubble and burble its way down and, when I could no longer hear it, I would follow this chemical procedure with multiple gallons of boiling water. I reasoned that enough of this was bound to eventually have an effect over time, regardless of what the blockage was. Even a dead rat couldn't stand up to this treatment indefinitely. Gabriel had little faith in the baking soda/vinegar/boiling water technique of pipe clearage, so his contribution to the effort was several gallons of an intensely alkaline chemical purchased from the hardware store.

Meanwhile, I kept cleaning up the water when it created pools in the downstairs bathroom. After the storm water receded, the problem shrank from an outright flood to a small pool, which was still less than ideal but at least better than it had been. The drain from which the water crept up was the lowest one in the house, and since the water always appeared after our morning showers, it didn't place much burden on our cerebral functions to reason that we must be creating more wastewater than the drain could handle, for whatever reason. In addition to attempting to clear it then, the other thing we could clearly do was to reduce our water usage.

I have always adored the beauty of Victorian bowl and pitcher washing sets. The first ones I ever saw were in the bedrooms of the Flavel House Museum in Astoria, Oregon. The elegant porcelain pitchers to hold wash water paired with their matching basins to lather soap and rinse sponges in seemed like the ultimate way to combine beauty with utility. As an adult woman, I still didn't have an antique bowl and pitcher set, although I had managed to jerry-rig a functional equivalent during our short sojourn in Washington, DC. The city water in Gaithersburg (where we were staying while Gabriel worked at the Library of Congress) had been so contaminated and heavily chlorinated that daily showers made my sensitive skin break out in an angry rash that itched like hives and burned like fire. In desperation, I had pressed a large ceramic mixing bowl into service as a wash basin and started filtering or boiling as much chlorine as possible out of the water before I bathed with it.

In Port Townsend, the water was blessedly cleaner than what we'd dealt with in Gaithersburg. It smelled and tasted like water instead of like sewage laced with bleach. However, in the interest of conserving this precious resource and accomplishing damage control on the backup problem, I decided it would be prudent to revisit the bowl and pitcher scenario. I paired the same large mixing bowl with a jug and moved them both up to our bedroom. (I still wanted a real set, but these served the purpose for the time being.)

Every morning while Gabriel took his shower, I would fill up the bowl with water from the pitcher, lather up my washcloth with French soap I kept nearby, and thoroughly bathe myself from forehead to toes using two quarts of water instead of fifty gallons. (Incidentally, that fifty gallon figure is for a *short* shower. The Washington Suburban Sanitary Commission cites the average fifteen-minute shower as using 150 gallons of water! Even supposedly water-saving showerheads use two to four gallons per minute.[49]) The result was that the pool of wastewater downstairs (not to mention our water bill) was substantially reduced—and I reasoned that every little bit helps.

Even with the reduction in water consumption, I did get rather tired of mopping the downstairs bathroom every single morning. I also fretted about what all this extra moisture would do to the flooring. I passed a few worried weeks—and then we had a stroke of luck. A little angel visited us in the form of a clean and friendly young plumber in his twenties who knocked on our kitchen door one afternoon.

We hadn't called him. He just appeared unbidden, like a benevolent spirit in a fairy story, and he was as dissimilar from the previous plumbers as the plucky hero of such a tale is from the gruesome troll under the bridge. I could see his van across the street and it had an advertisement painted along its side. Given my recent experiences with other ostensible members of his profession, if not for the van I might not have guessed the calling of this friendly young man at all.

"Hi!" he greeted me, smiling. "I'm sorry to bother you but I was doing some work for the city and when I was down in the sewer I noticed that the pipes from your house to the main line out under the street are clogged really thick with roots. That can really slow down your drains, and I wondered if you'd like me to snake them out for you. It'll only take a few minutes."

Hallelujah! If I weren't a married woman, I would have kissed him!

I started to tell him the story of our problem and asked him to come in so I could show him the place where the water pooled every morning.

"Are you sure you want me to come in?" he asked, looking with concern at his shoes. They were substantially cleaner than those of the primordial ogres who had preceded him and I nodded vigorous encouragement. He wiped his feet very carefully and conscientiously on the mat outside the door and gingerly followed me to the bathroom through the kitchen.

When I had finished explaining the situation and had shown him the drain that was backing up every morning, he nodded. "Probably the roots," he said confidently. "Would you like me to take care of it for you?"

"Yes, please!" I was so excited I nearly shouted the words. "Thank you, thank you, thank you!"

He smiled at my enthusiasm, then paused to look at the structure of the building before going back outside again. "This is a beautiful house," he said approvingly. "I always love to see people taking care of these old ones."

This was a refreshing change in attitude from the costly but ineffectual men who had visited before and immediately raised the young man even higher in my estimation than he already was.

He went out to his van and through my kitchen window I watched him don a sturdy set of coveralls over his clothes. He disappeared briefly around the back of the house, carrying a stout plumber's snake. With a woman's natural curiosity, I listened at the kitchen sink and heard interesting grinding and chopping sounds conducted upward by the metal and amplified by the ceramic basin.

After about five minutes, the fresh-faced plumber appeared again and asked if he could use our garden hose. I would have gladly let him take the hose away with him in exchange for a functional drain, so I readily assented. He pulled it around back of the house and I heard it run a few minutes and then turn off.

The young workman went back to his van, put away the snake, and carefully removed his coveralls. Then casually, in a motion that was plainly second-nature, he stamped his boots against the street to knock off anything that might be clinging to them before coming back into my front yard. His hands were perfectly clean and a little damp; he had clearly used the garden hose to wash them and also to rinse off a thick piece of root that he brought up to the porch to show me.

"I don't think that drain's been snaked in years!" he commented cheerfully. "Did you guys just move here?"

I nodded and made some desultory comments about the absentee landlords who had been our home's previous owners. "But we love the house," I concluded.

He looked up at it approvingly. "It's a beautiful one," he said with admiration. After he spent a moment appreciating the house, he held up the woody root. It was slightly thicker than a pencil. "Here's an example of what your drainage pipe was full of," he explained. "It was nearly filled solid! I had a hard time even getting the snake through portions of it."

You could have fooled me! I thought. He had done the job quickly and efficiently and in far less time than either of old ogres had spent lecturing me that I needed to tear my whole house down.

"In a neighborhood with this many trees and plantings," the wonderful young plumber continued, looking up and down the street, "the pipes can get a little like clogged arteries from all the roots. You might want to think about having them snaked out every six months or so, just as general maintenance to keep things under control."

He said this as matter-of-factly as a dentist would advise regular cleaning visits. I wondered how the old trolls had missed something that a person less than half their ages seemed to consider totally basic. Then I privately told myself just to be grateful for this serendipitous visitation by a person of competence. I thanked the young plumber profusely and asked how much I owed him.

The young man's bill for actually accomplishing something was far less than what we'd been charged for the privilege of having our house insulted and watching mud tracked all over it. (I really hope it was mud.) He smiled brightly as I wished him a good day and gave the house an admiring pat as he left, like a good horseman patting a thoroughbred. As he drove away, I laughed at the witty advertisement on the side of his van. It involved the best pun imaginable for a plumber: "Don't sleep with that drip!"

After he had gone, I ran upstairs and carefully stored his business card in an old Hershey's chocolates tin in my desk for future reference. I've called him every six months or so ever since—every time we notice the old sluggishness returning. Far from the ogres' horrendous exhortations to tear down our beautiful house, once we found a plumber who actually knew his business, there's never been a problem he couldn't handle. It's not easy to find someone who understands the way old things work, but when we do, they are gold among the lead.

Even after our plumbing was draining properly again, I kept up my habit of a thorough washing and scrubbing with a jug of water and a large bowl every morning, interspersed with a long soak in our claw-foot bathtub once or twice a week. With a bit of care and diligence, it's easy to stay just as clean this way as by letting 150 gallons of water run down the drain every morning. The bowl-and-pitcher method of bathing is kinder on both our local aquifer and our water bill. It's also much gentler on my skin and—most importantly—better for household felicity, since my husband and I never fight over the bathroom in the morning.

The method was working fine, but I had one qualm with its execution: the mixing bowl and water jug looked rather silly in our bedroom. I started setting money aside to buy a nice antique wash set and began my hunt for the coveted ideal set that would suit me best.

I had wanted a porcelain washbowl and pitcher from such an early age that, looking back on my childhood, I can't remember a time when I *didn't* dream of owning one. I never fantasized about owning a car. The subject was so far from my mind that when we did a survey project in fourth grade and a classmate asked me what sort of car I wanted when I grew up, I got in trouble for being the only student in the class who couldn't name a brand of automobile I desired. However, I fantasized endlessly about porcelain washbowls and pitchers.

As a little girl in the 1980s, my exposure to such bowls and pitchers bore a resemblance to a contemporary boy's experience of a Lamborghini Countach; I had seen them in pictures and in movies and that was the limit of my exposure. The closest I came to owning one myself was when I was twelve years old and saw a minute set in a store's toy aisle. The bowl had about the same diameter as a quarter and the pitcher could have held one teaspoonful of water. I was a little too old to play with dolls, but I bought them anyway. They inspired me to ask my teacher if I could earn extra credit by making a model of a nineteenth-century mansion, and she told me I could. The little bowl and pitcher took prominent place in the window of the little cardboard house I made. In another window I put a tiny faux oil lamp I manufactured out of a hazelnut shell and little bits of clear plastic glued together in the rough shape of a glass chimney with yellow and red beads inside to represent the flame.

Not all bowls and pitchers are created equal, of course, any more than all automobiles are. Just as some of my old classmates might have sniggered behind their backs at certain cars and chased after others for blocks, longing to get a better look at them, so too it was with bowls and pitchers and me. When I was an adult, I admired them in antiques stores, seeking the perfect one. I saw certain toilette sets painted such a ghastly mishmash of clashing colors I wondered what their designers had been thinking; others nearly made me want to cry for the sheer beauty of them. I dreamed of the day I would have my own set, but it had to be just the right one.

Because washbowls and their corresponding pitchers started as matched pairs, they make a particularly good example of something archivists call "survival bias." Survival bias is the tendency of artifacts to survive—or be destroyed—out of proportion to their original numbers. It works against fragile or common items and in favor of sturdy or unusual ones. Survival bias is the reason sturdy meat grinders and cherished wedding dresses appear in antiques stores in larger numbers than fragile champagne flutes or boring work clothes. At any given time, there are far more work clothes than wedding dresses in the world, but the latter get saved while the former are generally used until nothing is left of them. This is also why extremely small shoes survive into antiquity in greater numbers than normal sizes do. People who don't understand survival bias assume that the prevalence of size 3 or smaller shoes in antiques collections mean that everyone in the past had tiny feet. In fact the opposite is the case: these very small shoes survived because they weren't wearable by most people.

Over the course of the twentieth century, survival bias worked solidly in favor of the bowls of wash sets and solidly against their corresponding pitchers. This was just an obvious result of the physical nature of the two pieces. A toilette set's washbowl is shallow (which gives it an extremely low center of gravity) and it typically has very thick sides. Knocking one over would be like trying to upset a tire already lying on its broad axis, tread-side out. Occasionally they do get dropped, which can break them if they land on a hard enough surface like stone or brickwork. Most of them are too thick to smash on a carpeted floor. In a washbowl versus wooden floor contest, the winner will likely depend on the hardness of the wood, the length of the fall, and the thickness of the bowl's edges. Hunting for the perfect set, I saw many relatively cheap bowls, but it took me a while to save up for a matched pitcher and bowl set.

After dreaming about such a set since childhood, when I finally was able to buy one at a local antiques store, my heart swelled with joy. I cradled it in my arms as I walked home, taking particular care not to misstep or do anything to endanger my long-coveted treasure. I stopped at Aldrich's (the corner grocery that dates to 1895) just long enough to buy one of each of the four flavors of Swiss chocolates they were selling by their counter: milk chocolate, dark chocolate, mint, and stracciatella. They were made by Lindt, a company that originated in 1845, so this treat struck me as being particularly appropriate. I slipped them into my pocket then lifted up my wash set again with exquisite care and carried it home. It had been very dusty in the antique store and the pitcher had a dead moth in it, so I washed and polished it before bringing it upstairs and setting it on my dresser. I fixed myself a nice cup of tea and a big bowlful of strawberries and whipped cream, laid my chocolates alongside the strawberries, and set up a chair in front of my beautiful new wash set so that I could gaze lovingly at my prize while I enjoyed my treat.

It seemed that, slowly but surely, I was finally turning my childhood dreams into reality.

The pitcher of the wash set proved to hold one of the wonderful subtle lessons that can only be learned by using an authentic antique instead of a reproduction. At the top of the handle are two little curls in the china pottery. I barely noticed them at first, and even if I had, my only thought would have been that they were a pretty bit of ornamentation. However, after I had been using my wash set a few days, I noticed that the pitcher's weight was designed for perfect balance. I realized that when I carried it upstairs full of water, my thumb automatically braced itself against the larger of the two curls on the handle to steady it. When I poured out my morning toilette, my fingers naturally wrapped around the curls of their own accord. The design was so simple and so perfect that I didn't even have to think about it.

When Gabriel gave me an antique milk jug that Christmas, I noticed that it, too, had a bracing-curl for the hand holding it. I started paying close attention to vessels of various sorts from the nineteenth century and noticed this practical detail to be a common theme. It even appears on some teapots. On wash pitchers, it is absolutely de rigueur—probably because they are so heavy when they are full that proper balance and bracing is especially important. The sweet little curl is an instant clue as to the age of a wash pitcher. The pitchers made for use in the nineteenth century have this important and useful detail; pitchers made for later "Victorian revival" fashions such as those of the 1960s almost always leave off the curl because the artists who designed them were ignorant of their function. Some did try to put some sort of nub there, but since they didn't know it actually had a purpose, they never put it in quite the right place. The difference becomes obvious when lifting the pitcher into a pouring position: on an authentic nineteenth-century example, the thumb just naturally braces itself in position, whereas on a reproduction it fumbles about, seeking purchase.

These little curls—so subtle and yet such a great source of insight—are the sort of thing a person only notices when they deal with an item every day. The "Victorian Revival" artists missed them because they saw only the rough outlines of the object's form and totally divorced it from its function. Part of why Gabriel and I admire the Victorians so much is because they did such an incredible job of seamlessly marrying form *and* function. As William Morris said, "Have nothing in your houses that you do not know to be useful or believe to be beautiful"[50]—but preferably both.

I've only ever had one problem with my wonderful wash set. Honestly, it was more amusing than challenging—even at the time, let alone in retrospect. The incident involved a most unwelcome visit by one of Arachne's descendants.

One pleasant, misty summer morning, I was still feeling a bit sleepy as I went about my morning tasks after my ablutions. I slowly made the bed and then wandered downstairs to put the kettle on for my tea. Still yawning, I returned upstairs to finish the routine. I emptied the soapy water from my washbowl and carried it back into the bedroom, where a glance out the large bay window put me in a soft, romantic frame of mind as I saw a fog bank sweeping in from Puget Sound and ushering in a gentle rain. I dreamily watched this dove-gray veil drawing itself over my beloved Victorian town as I wiped my washbowl dry and set it carefully upon the marble of my washbasin.

The pitcher holds twice as much water as the corresponding bowl, so it only wants filling every other day. I had started with a full pitcher on this particular morning and there was still a considerable amount of water in it even after my ablutions. I closed my fingers around the pitcher's handle and hefted it up to its customary place in the bowl to be ready for the next morning. Glancing inside, I was abruptly startled out of my dreams.

"Gracious!"

An enormous black spider, nearly as big as the palm of my hand, had fallen into the open-mouthed pitcher. She was desperately treading the thin meniscus of water tension, trying to stay afloat. Later, when I described the arachnid to my friend Meredith (who is a research biologist), I learned that I had encountered a species known as a European giant house spider. At the time though, all I knew was that *this was one huge spider*!

For a brief, horrified flash of a microsecond, I wondered if the arachnid had been there when I had poured my morning wash water from the pitcher, but I quickly realized that if this were the case, she would have long since drowned. The frantic motions keeping her atop the water were of a panicked nature that could certainly not be maintained for long.

If it had been a cockroach in my wash pitcher, I'm sure Gabriel would have heard my shrieks distinctly at his job in a different county. When he came home, he would have found me clinging to the ceiling in a hysterical condition. Getting me down again would have involved using a crowbar to pry my fingers out of deep grooves carved in the plaster by my fingernails.

Spiders, however, don't concern me overmuch—even one that happens to be the size of a young rat. I had been startled by the bulk of her, though! In any case, the predicament she was in was far more terrifying than my own.

The steeply sloping sides of the pitcher's wet interior trapped the arachnid completely, and she was totally at my mercy. I took the pitcher downstairs and emptied its entire contents, spider and all, into the garden.

"Don't come back inside!" I hissed over the porch railing and went back into the house, slamming the kitchen door behind me.

In the multiple years I've been using my bowl and pitcher for washing, that one formidable spider was the only example of an unwelcome visitor I've come across thus far. I'm sure she won't be the last, just as I'm absolutely positive she wasn't the first arachnid to startle someone at their morning toilette. I do not by any means find this worrisome, as the presence of a single innocuous invertebrate once every four years is by no means a threat. I think I could even handle a cockroach with that sort of infrequency—although admittedly the ceiling plaster might suffer.

7

A Detail as Fine as a Hair

"The hair should be carefully combed, and shampooed from root to point with the shampoo wash; it should then be rinsed with tepid water, until the water running off is quite clear... The hair can be dried partially with a Turkish towel, by twisting the towel round it and wringing."
—Mons A. Mallemont, 1899[51]

I first came across the idea of using castile soap to wash my hair while reading an 1889 copy of *Good Housekeeping* before bed one night during our first winter in our home. It was just past the solstice and thickly overcast, so the sun had disappeared long hours before and neither stars nor moon could take its place through the dense clouds. When I had been moving about the ground floor of the house earlier in the evening, my breath condensed around me in white clouds against the dark shadows of the night. I had retreated to the bedroom early and lit the kerosene heater before burying myself under many layers of thick blankets and curling close around my hot water bottle. Outside, the night was coated with a thick darkness like chilled velvet, but within the snug little room, the heater and my reading lamp complemented each other to brighten and warm the room. I could feel the lamp's radiant warmth against my face as it illuminated the words on the pages in my hands. "Once a fortnight is often enough to wash well-brushed hair . . . Frequent washing keeps the hair too dry for vigorous growth. Use tepid water and old castile soap."[52]

Outside of shampoo commercials, opinions (past and present) on how often one should wash one's hair vary wildly between individuals. Writing in 1888, Maude Berkeley mentioned in her diary that she kept dust out of her hair by covering it with a bandana while she moved furniture "to avoid the penalty of shampooing twice in a week," which implies that she considered once a week normal.[53] In the twenty-first century, advocates of the "No 'Poo" trend such as

Picture from an advertisement in *The Youth's Companion*, December 29, 1892.

blogger Lucy Aitken Read don't shampoo their hair at all.[54] It really shouldn't be a surprise that such a range of self-treatments exist. Every person is a unique individual, not only in the biology of their scalp's oil glands but also in the amount of dirt to which they expose themselves on a regular basis.

Since frequency of hair washing is such a private matter, I didn't particularly intend to reduce mine to once every two weeks as the *Good Housekeeping* article suggested. However, washing it with castile soap was an intriguing idea and I decided to give it a try.

As is the case with most grocery stores, my local supermarket stocks a rainbow array of brands of modern shampoo that battle for space at eye-level along an entire aisle. It took me a few minutes to locate the castile soap on the lowest shelf of the bath section only a few inches above the floor. When I read the label, I was immensely pleased with my find. The bars of soap came five to a package, each wrapped in white paper with the no-nonsense description, KIRK'S CASTILE: HEALTHY, BEAUTIFUL SKIN SINCE 1839. A soap company that had started business only one year after Queen Victoria was crowned? Now that was the product for me! I have an unusual relationship to branding: I don't give a fig for the endorsements of modern celebrities, and quite frankly most of the advertisements in twenty-first-century women's magazines mystify more than entice me. However, a date of origin before 1900 on a product's label is a major way to catch my attention.

Most soaps are based in animal fat in the form of sodium tallowate. (Note the root *tallow*: it's usually derived from beef fat.) Castile soap, however, has a vegetable oil base. Originally made from olive oil in the Castile region of Spain, now the appellation can apply to any vegetable-based soap. Kirk's uses coconut oil.[55]

As with many other things in my life, there was a lot of trial-and-error involved since I didn't really know what I was doing when I started. The idea seemed so simple: just wash my hair with a bar of soap. What could possibly be complicated about that? At first I tried wetting down my hair and then rubbing the bar of soap against my head. The hard bar scraped uncomfortably against my scalp and the friction pulled my hair—not good. Next I tried lathering the soap in my hands and applying it to my wet hair. This was a little more agreeable since I no longer felt like I was scraping a brick over my head, but the soapsuds slid off of my wet hair so quickly that seemed like they couldn't possibly have had time to do any cleaning. When my hair dried, I saw that they hadn't.

I finally hit upon the solution when I remembered some advice I'd tried years earlier when researching and experimenting with hot oil treatments for hair. A book I'd read on the subject had pointed out that since oil and water don't mix, after a hot oil treatment, shampoo should be applied to hair before it gets wet. (Applying oil, then water, then shampoo results in a frustrating mess that refuses to emulsify.)

I reasoned that the natural oils on my scalp and hair might be creating a similar scenario on a milder scale. I tried lathering the bar of soap with my

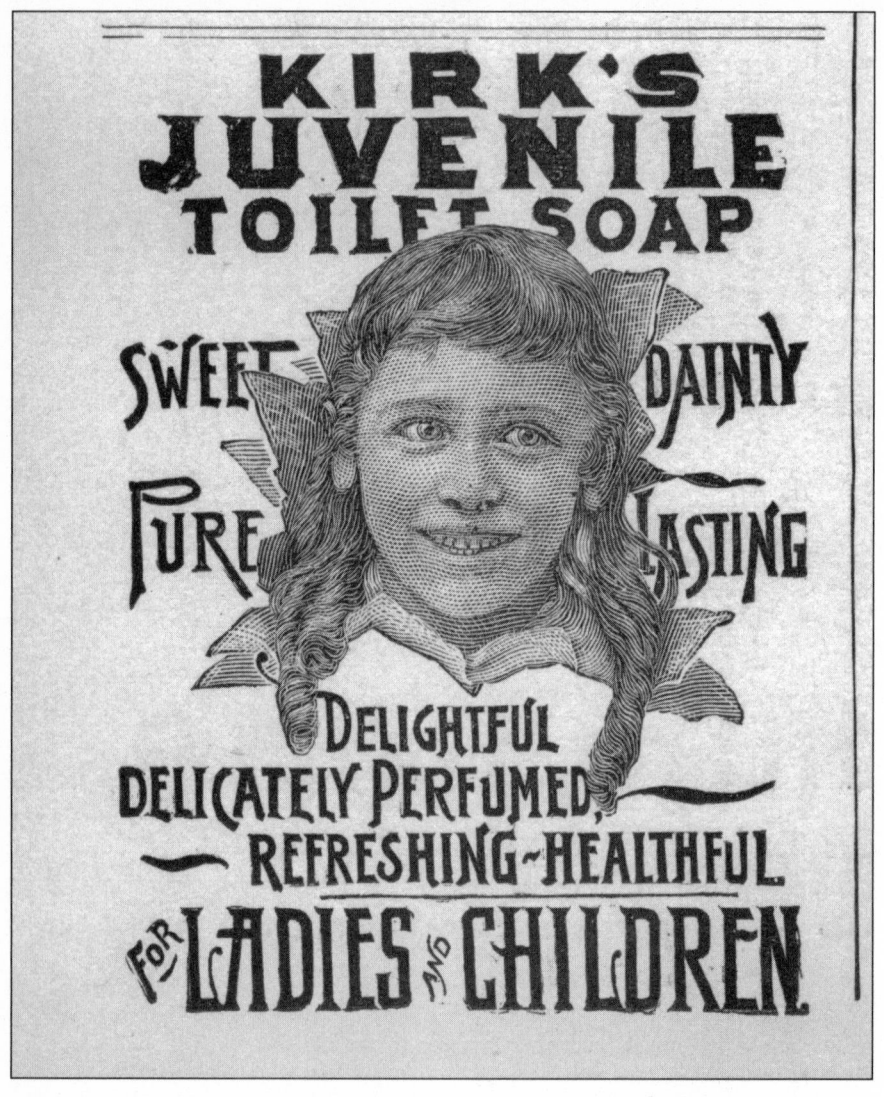

Kirk's soap advertisement, circa 1890s.

hands, then rubbing the suds over my scalp and petting them into my hair while it was still dry. I spent a few minutes massaging it in, then added some cool water. Bingo! The soap layered over my head and hair turned into a snowy crown of bubbles. I spent a few minutes running my hands through it and delighting in the sensation before rinsing it out. When I ran my fingers through my damp hair afterward, it was so clean it squeaked!

The castile soap didn't make my hair slippery in the way modern shampoo did, and I found this to be a great advantage when arranging my hair in Victorian updos. My previous attempts at achieving the swooping curls of hairstyles I had seen in nineteenth-century photographs had mostly resulted in unwieldy masses of limp hair sliding into my face. However, as soon as I made the switch to shampooing with castile soap, I found that my hair stayed where I put it and did what I wanted without a struggle. I hadn't been expecting this outcome, but (like the curls on the wash pitcher) it is a good example of exactly why my husband and I find immersion to be such a useful method of studying history. The tiniest details in life are often the most revealing ones.

PORT TOWNSEND.

Port Townsend, 1870. Illustration from *Harper's Magazine*, September, 1870.

8

The Brackens

"The upper story of Port Townsend is charmingly located, wide bright
waters on one side, flowing evergreen woods on the other. The streets
are well laid out and well tended, and the houses, with their luxuriant
gardens about them, have an air of taste and refinement seldom found in
towns on the edge of a wild forest. The people seem to have come here
to make true homes . . ."

—John Muir, 1889[56]

One of the first things Gabriel and I did together when we moved to Port
Townsend was to start researching the history of our house and the people
who had lived here in the nineteenth century. The tale is an intriguing one—
and, moreover, one that is wonderfully representative of the settlement of the
area. In a way, the story of our house and the people who have passed through
it is the story of Port Townsend. First, though, let's take a very brief detour
out east.

In the 1850s, Boston was completely flooded with Irish refugees from the
recent potato famine. What work existed (and there was precious little of it)
might be completely barred to people of Irish heritage on grounds of prejudice:
the classic signs saying No Irish Need Apply were well-known. Immigrants
who did manage to find work were lucky to earn starvation wages for their
long hours of labor and would often go home to crowded slums. Amid this
background, imagine a young man—American-born but the son of Irish immigrants and therefore bearing the stigma attached to his race—coming to the
age of manhood and looking for his first employment. Is it any wonder that
Thomas Bracken left Boston and came west—even though it meant leaving his
parents and everything familiar to scrabble a living out of an unknown wilderness? The unknown land of the territories (not yet states) tempted with siren
calls of opportunities, even if they were uncertain ones.

Young Mr. Bracken came to Washington Territory in 1853[57]—there's no record as to how, but the greatest likelihood is that he took the overland route across the continent. This was long before the Panama Canal was dug, so getting to the Northwest from Boston by sea would have involved sailing all the way around the southern tip of South America and back north again. It is highly doubtful Bracken had the money to accomplish this as a passenger, and signing on to a ship's crew for the purpose of free passage was an experience so unpleasant that most men preferred the overland route. He settled in a very small community of dubious promise but great stubbornness. This first place he took up residence was not Port Townsend, but a mainland community on the west side of Puget Sound that was called Alki—the Chinook Jargon word for "by and by."* The overwhelming features of Alki were tidal mudflats and an incessant gray drizzle that would eventually be known around the world. By that point, though, the term *Alki* would be forgotten by all but locals. The place would be known internationally by the name of the Duwamish chief who allied his tribe with the white settlers: Seattle.

Something often forgotten in modern discussions—but which is absolutely vital to remember if one would understand the political situation in the nineteenth century—is that each tribe of American Indians constituted its own sovereign nation (and incidentally, still does). In her book *Indians in the Making*,[58] Dr. Alexandra Harmon (Professor of American Indian Studies at the University of Washington) discusses how the concept of "Native American" as a generic, blanket term to describe anyone whose ancestors inhabited North America prior to 1492 is an artificial construct—and a fairly new one, at that. The indigenous peoples of this country were a diverse array of nations with cultures as distinct, and relationships to each other every bit as complicated, as those seen in the countries of Europe.**

---

*Various sources attribute the name to white settlers asserting that "by and by" their community would amount to something. My cynical ninth-grade history teacher used to tell students that the natives had given the place its name with the idea that "by and by" the whites would give up and leave.

**A few words might be in order here regarding the hot-button topic of terminology. Partly because the concept of an overarching culture of Native Americans is such an artificial construct, and partly due to linguistic issues, in the twenty-first century many modern tribes are going back to using the term *Indian* or *American Indian*. As Dennis W. Zotigh, a member of the Kiowa, Santee Dakota, and Ohkay Owingeh tribes, points out in his blog, "[T]echnically a native American, [is] a label that literally describes anyone who was born in and remains a citizen of a country in North, South, or Central America."[59] (By this definition, technically *I'm* a native American because I was born in Washington state, even though all my ancestors crossed an ocean to get here.) A 1995 census survey found that "49.76 percent of American Indians preferred that term, compared to 37.35 percent preferring *Native American* and much smaller numbers preferring other terms."[60] Because the largest portion of individuals in the survey chose *Indian* as their preferred term and also because the Klallam and the Clallam tribes—the groups with the closest historical ties to Port Townsend—officially prefer that term as well, I use it to respect their wishes.

Now, back to 1850s Alki, where young Thomas Bracken (the American-born son of Irish immigrants) had just arrived. It was a gray beach with a precarious trading post and a bleak outlook. The future of the settlement was uncertain; the futures of the individuals living there even more so.

The tribes of the Puget Sound region had been people of trade since time immemorial. Any economy of trade between nations (be it the medieval Silk Road or modern NAFTA) inevitably involves complicated and ever-changing relationships between the peoples involved. Some were trading partners. Some were allies. Some were enemies.

The settlers were every bit as diverse as the natives. Some were American-born, others were from countries all across the globe and didn't even necessarily speak English. They also had their own friendships and enmities, as well as prejudices, both positive and negative. The one thing all these various individuals of both groups had in common was that they were all human, with all the intrinsic passions and foibles of our species.

When young Thomas Bracken arrived at Alki among this complex cultural stew in the early 1850s, he soon found himself involved in an intricate set of alliances. Chief Leschi of the Nisqually had declared war on the white settlers, who were allied with Chief Seattle's Duwamish tribe and also with Chief Patkanim's Snoqualmies.[61] When news of Leschi's hostile intentions spread, a group of settlers was asked to find Leschi and escort him to Olympia to meet with Acting Governor Charles Mason. This group was led by Captain Charles Eaton and called themselves "Eaton's Rangers." Thomas Bracken became one of their scouts.

The ensuing conflict is known to historians as the Indian War of 1855–56, or the Puget Sound War. The details were too complicated to recount fully here. For the purposes of this narrative, suffice it to say that it was a series of guerrilla assaults and that partisans on all sides of the conflict performed actions that would now be classified as war crimes.[62]

Beyond the fact that Bracken scouted for Eaton's Rangers (which was mentioned in his obituary), no record survives to report the details of Bracken's participation in the conflict. Men in his position seldom kept diaries; they were more concerned with immediate issues of remaining alive. There is no way to know how he felt about the whole scenario. We do know that as soon as the conflict was over, Bracken left the Alki community for good and settled in what is now Port Townsend.

He partnered with an Indian woman from the local Klallam tribe who went by the name of Mary, and their first child (Charles) was born in 1860.[63] Over the course of the next nine years, they had three more children: Henry came along in 1865, Mathilda (called Tillie by her family and Mattie by the clerk who kept the records in the local drugstore) in 1867, then Edward in 1869.[64] In 1871, when their oldest son was eleven years old and the local community was gentrifying, Thomas and Mary seem to have decided it might be a good idea to get married. The official wedding was performed by Catholic priest Father Prefontaine on October 23, 1871, presumably with the four Bracken children in attendance.[65] Thomas and Mary would go on to have two more sons: Daniel was born in 1872 and Thomas Jr. (the baby of the family) arrived in May of 1884.[66]

When Gabriel and I tell visitors to our home about the Brackens, they often express great surprise at several elements of the family's history. First, they are astonished that a man who fought in the Indian Wars would go on to marry a native woman, then they are equally surprised that the ostensibly Catholic couple would wait until they had four children to get married. Yet the situation would have seemed quite normal to a couple in Thomas and Mary's position in the 1850s and '60s, no matter how it might shock the narrow-minded sensibilities of modern people.

On the frontier in the early days of settlement, partnerships between white men and Indian women were actually fairly common, for the simple reason that there weren't anywhere near enough white women to go around. Frontiersmen aren't exactly known for celibacy. Missionaries were often required to marry and go to their assignments in pairs specifically to avoid their marrying the natives. As for Thomas having fought in the Indian War, his enemies in that conflict had been Chief Leschi's Nisqually tribe; Mary was a Klallam. To even understand (let alone honor) the history of mid-nineteenth-century America, it is important to remember the very real distinctions between the sovereign nations involved. Thomas Bracken would certainly have understood that the two tribes were entirely different entities.

Children born out of legal wedlock were also more common on the frontier than many modern people realize. This was especially true when their mothers came from cultures with different views of marriage than those recognized by the US government. Historical matters of legitimacy were often as much or more about legalities of inheritance than about morality.

The Brackens homesteaded a farm on a piece of land still marked on Port Townsend zoning maps as "The Bracken Addition." The location is a beautiful one, with morning views of the shimmering waters of a peaceful lagoon like something out of a dream from a fairytale. To this day, it is still one of the best areas to pick wild thimbleberries.

When the economic boom hit Port Townsend and property values soared in the 1880s, Thomas Sr. platted his farmland (had it mapped out into parcels on legal records).[67] With everyone expecting hordes of new people to rush into town, this made good economic sense. Thomas Sr. could sell the land he had worked so hard for—now freshly zoned for residences, thanks to the platting. He could set up a comfortable life for his wife and six children and retire from the backbreaking labor of farm work. He must have reflected on how fulfilling it would be to meet all the new people moving into the city he had helped pioneer.

Then the bust hit.

With the economy in free fall, Thomas Sr. could no longer pay the taxes on his farm—the farm he had homesteaded with his own hands. Because of the platting, for tax purposes, the government no longer saw that farm as agricultural land. Rather, they considered it to be twenty-one blocks of city real estate, and they demanded full taxes on it as such.[68] But it was still just a farm, just a bit of earth to grow food with hard work and toil. Thomas couldn't possibly pay what the government felt he owed. Many other Port Townsend residents were in the same position.

In a futile attempt to force them to pay taxes they couldn't in any way afford, the local newspaper ran lists of citizens' delinquent tax records. On September 1, 1895, Thomas Sr.'s tax delinquencies took up half a column in the Sunday newspaper.[69]

In the early 1890s, the Bracken brothers (all except little Tom Jr.) were young men and Tillie was a young woman, but their father's tax troubles were making it difficult for them to earn a living. Ed and Dan were both teamsters, men who drove teams of horses. In 1895, Dan performed this service for the Port Townsend fire department, and duly submitted his request for pay. The fire chief signed off, certifying he had done the work, and the finance committee recommended the sum be paid, but the payment was rejected by the city council.[70]

The Bracken siblings might have hoped that some distance from the farm might help them escape the taint of their father's tax debts and earn a living for themselves despite the economic depression. They may have felt that closer proximity to the city center would help them find work; or they might simply have wanted to experience independence as adults. Most likely it was a combination of all of these that made Charles, Edward, Dan, and Tillie move to Uptown Port Townsend in the 1890s. They brought little Tom Jr. with them; we know this because at the local drugstore the charges for Tom Jr.'s schoolbooks went on Charles's house account, not their father's.[71]

Thomas Bracken, Jr., 1898, from a school photo. Image printed with permission of Jefferson County Historical Society.

They rented a beautiful new Eastlake-style house on Taylor Street—building had just finished on it in 1889.[72] There was a bright, sunny bay window in the parlor where Tillie could sit with her sewing, framed by elegant plaster molding. Upstairs, the master bedroom for Charles (as the oldest) was a plainer twin to the parlor, with the same bay window but no fancy plasterwork. Dan might have chosen the bedroom overlooking the Queen Anne mansion behind their house; Ed and Tom Jr. might have shared the room with a view of ships passing on Puget Sound. Downstairs, there was an isolated bedroom on the main floor—perfect to give Tillie some privacy from her rowdy brothers and also to keep her close to the warmth of the kitchen.

Daniel Bracken, from his football team photo, 1895.
Image printed with permission of Jefferson County
Historical Society.

In short, it was our house!

I hardly ever go into my massage studio without at least some thought to it
being Tillie's room. Sadly, there are no photos of her at the archive, but I picture
her as a kind woman with a round face like her little brother Tom Jr.'s and a warm,
motherly nature. Her purchases recorded in the charge accounts at the local drugstore have a nurturing connection. She bought lots of hydrogen peroxide and
wood alcohol, probably to patch up Ed after his baseball games or to tend to Dan,
who was known as the "smashing fullback" on the local football team.

She doubtless also brought them out when little Tom Jr. got cuts and
scrapes. Her charge account also reflects a woman who cared about ladylike
things, no matter how meager her circumstances might be. She bought rosewa-
ter, glycerin, bitter almond oil, and spermaceti: all ingredients for making fine
soaps and skin creams.[73]

When I first saw these purchases written with a fine steel-nibbed pen in a heavy leather ledger, they gave me distinct pause. I had recently made myself some skin cream out of virtually the same ingredients, based on a recipe I had seen in a nineteenth-century massage text. (I had substituted shea butter for the spermaceti, since stores no longer sell oil from whales.) When I saw Tillie's account in the archive, I set my hands in my lap, leaned away from the accounts book, and smiled at the words upon the page.

The pharmacy in Port Townsend has moved a few blocks down the street, but I was very familiar with the space where Tillie would have shopped. I pictured her making her purchases there, then walking up the steep path to Uptown. The stairs would have been wooden then, not the concrete steps that replaced them in the early twentieth century, but the difference was only a slight one. I pictured her coming home—to my house—and mixing the same lotion I had made myself.

I thought through all this, then a frown creased my brow. I wondered if it was presumptuous of me to be comparing myself to a woman from whom I was separated by so many years and experiences. Then I remembered how dearly the friends I have made in other countries always relish sharing our common interests, no matter how specific details might vary. I thought back on going shopping or sharing sweets with companions in France and Japan and sharing these very same experiences in America with friends from all around the world. I smiled again, reflecting that some things can be shared across cultural boundaries—even ones of time.

9

Ghost Stories

Nineteenth-century illustration of a young woman reading ghost stories, circa 1890s.

"They filled her mind with the superstitions which are still respected
as truths in the wild north—especially the superstition called the
Second Sight.
"'God bless me!' cried the captain, 'you don't mean to say she believes in
such stuff as that? In these enlightened times, too?'
Mrs. Crayford looked at her partner with a satirical smile.
'In these enlightened times, Captain Helding, we only believe
in dancing tables, and in messages sent from the other world by
spirits who can't spell!'"

—*The Frozen Deep,* 1874[74]

There are interesting associations between the Victorian era and ghost stories. Many of these come from the Victorians themselves, of course, who dearly loved a ghoulish tale. From Dickens's notorious Christmas Carolers to the more sinister specters found in James's *The Turn of the Screw*, there was a tremendous popularity of tales of the dead—and the not quite so dead as they should be. In modern reflections on Victoriana, there is also the painfully obvious fact that the Victorians are, sadly, virtually all gone now.*

The concept of a ghostly visitation by someone out of the past has a certain appeal. However, it is interesting to notice how many more Victorian ghosts inhabit people's imaginations than phantoms from other generations.

Go to a typical American elementary school a day or so before Hallowe'en and ask a classroom of schoolchildren to draw a ghost's house. If our culture simply associated ghosts with any general group of people who have passed on, one would expect a broad range of dwellings to be represented in the children's drawing, representing a span across human history: caves, huts, castles, etc. Yet it's rare for our culture to conjure these as their first impulse picture of a ghost's abode. With the possible exception of classrooms in certain New England communities, I expect that even an eighteenth-century home would be the exception rather than the rule in the drawings produced by our theoretical class of children—with most of the boys and girls happily sketching away at nearly identical images of decayed Victorian mansions while one or two immigrant children wondered why their classmates' drawings had such a striking uniformity. Their puzzlement would be entirely legitimate. After all, why isn't an American's first thought when they hear the word *ghost* an eighteenth- or a seventeenth-century specter? If it's simply a matter of accessibility and familiarity, why don't we think of twentieth-century ghosts? It's not as though no one died in the past hundred years.

There is an immense amount of cultural baggage tied up with the idea of a haunted house, and nearly all of the images first appearing when the phrase is invoked are Victorian in nature. Simply utter the words *haunted house* and the average American mind instantly conjures up a silhouette of a Queen Anne mansion with crumbling gables and a small graveyard to the side, the whole

---

* I say "virtually" because, incredible as it is, as of this writing, there are a handful of people born in the nineteenth century who are still alive—although admittedly they are extremely advanced in years. A *USA Today* article published on September 5, 2014, lists six people still alive who were born before the turn of the twentieth century. They are, by order of birth: Misao Okawa (Japanese, born March 5, 1898), Gertrude Weaver (American, born July 4, 1898), Jeralean Talley (American, born May 23, 1899), Susannah Mushatt Jones (American, born July 6, 1899), Bernice Madigan (American, born July 24, 1899), and Emma Morano-Martinuzzi (Italian, born November 29, 1899).[75]

scene backlit by a huge harvest moon. Few would associate the term with a 1950s rambler or a tract house quite so quickly, no matter how many grisly murders had been committed there. So intertwined has Victorian imagery become with the idea of ghosts that one of the common questions I am asked about my tidy nineteenth-century home in its pleasant and well-mannered neighborhood is whether it might be haunted.

How did such lovely examples of architecture as Victorian houses become associated with dead people who can't make up their minds about an afterlife? Culturally speaking, much of the ectoplasmic trail can be followed back to the economic depression of the 1930s. At that time, Victorian buildings were seen as white elephants: embarrassing remembrances of a more affluent time. No one could afford their upkeep any longer and they were thus left to rot and become infested by unpleasant creatures making frightening sounds in the dark. As disenfranchised people wandered the country looking for work and scraping for food, they hated these empty reminders of an ancestral prosperity and dignity now lost, with their broken windows that leered like the disapproving eyes of the dead. The *New Yorker* cartoonist Charles Addams illustrated the spirit of that discomfort in his Addams Family drawings, macabre caricatures of ghoulish creatures living amid decayed Victorian settings. In doing so, he cemented these images in the American subconscious for decades to come. It can be quite interesting to see how modern purveyors of the macabre take advantage of this permeating connection lingering in our minds.

During our first October in Port Townsend, Gabriel and I were out for a walk on the particularly grim sort of autumn day to which the Pacific Northwest is subjected. In northern latitudes, the equinox of fall can seem like a mortal wound to all natural illumination: each passing day bleeds progressively more and more daylight hours from the world and shrouds of rainclouds conspire with this dying of the light to cast the world into sepulchral tones of tombstone gray. As we took our constitutional against this backdrop, with mud pulling at our feet like an eager grave and rain soaking our clothes like groundwater filtering through a coffin lid, my husband spontaneously suggested the cheering activity of visiting a cemetery.

To be fair, it was archival interest rather than sheer morbidity that prompted the detour. We thought that more data about the Brackens might be inscribed on their grave markers. I personally might have chosen a sunnier day for trudging through a quagmire of mud that held dead bodies, but it was hard to argue with my husband's very logical citation of the fact that we were very close to the graveyard already.

We spent about an hour examining gravestones. Gabriel was more efficient at it than I was, since he had no qualms whatsoever about where he trod. I was so concertedly trying not to step directly on any of the graves in the crowded cemetery that my husband laughed at my superstitious nature. We didn't manage to locate the resting places of our house's former family, although we did see the graves of many others whose lives we had read about in the archive.

The substance pelting us was closer to sleet than rain. Gabriel nearly ruined his shoes in the mud, and I was drenched through my cape, shirtwaist, skirts, and all my undergarments including my corset, so we decided to complete our examination on another day.

While walking home, we saw a large sign advertising a temporary attraction: HAUNTED COURTHOUSE. We later investigated and learned more or less what I had suspected based on the sign: as an autumnal holiday stunt, the historic nineteenth-century county courthouse would be draped with Hallowe'en decorations, and actors dressed as ghouls would charge admission to individuals seeking thrills. Someone had created a rather absurd story about a lost group of carnival performers to accompany the attraction. The tale of them encountering evil in the town's empty buildings was easily dismissed from my mind. However, the season, and too many other ghost stories read at late hours in the dark, had far creepier effects on my nervous disposition.

Gabriel was gone the next night visiting his mother, and the early sunset of an October night spattered blood over everything it touched before dying in the west. I was alone in a house filled with shadows and silence, and I was thoroughly spooked.

The cold deepened as the scant warmth given by the angled sun departed. We were saving money for house repairs (and our historical research) by exercising draconian frugality in some aspects of our life, and heat was one of these. We kept our home just warm enough to avoid moisture damage to our books and antique clothing; our own comfort did not come into consideration. The temperature inside the house barely differed from that of the outer world, which had been a comfortable enough situation when summer warmed the Earth. Now, though, we were deep in the season when frost stalks the night and rips the green life out of tender plants.

I pulled my wool cape around myself in my frigid dining room and huddled close to my oil lamp, straining for the palpable warmth it cast into the gloom along with its light. If I moved back from this radiance just a few feet, I could see my breath against the darkness, yet two nights previously that merry glow of the wick's fire had focused my attention and made my heart smile.

Now it was the darkness that drew all my senses. My eyes searched a shifting blackness beyond the oil's glow for a presence the upright hairs at the back of my neck knew was there. My ears strained and stretched to hear scurrying footsteps that didn't exist. Close by the lamplight, I looked into the inky air and imagined vaguely human, shifting shapes outside my vision. A terror of unseen menace urged me, begged me, to throw the switch on the electric lights and banish these terrors from the night, but I would not give in to this superstition. *People lived their entire lives without electric light for thousands of years*, I told myself. *I will not be afraid of the dark.* It was more of a command than a conviction.

I finished my dinner and attempted to sew, but the dim light swallowed up my dark stitches on dark fabric. I managed a few seams before putting the project away and climbing upstairs to fetch a book and retreat to the cold and empty bed. I am right-handed so I held my little fingerlamp on that side, although being in my dominant hand did not stop its shaking. The lamplight cast long shadows on the steep steps, curving in strange ways as a dim glow hit corners and attenuated itself in stretching for the high ceiling. The stair's railing is positioned to be on the right side when ascending, and since my right hand held the lamp, I gripped nothing but my own terror as I climbed the steps. It seemed like specters were reaching to douse my feeble light. Suddenly, a weak spot in a stair, a place where cheap twentieth-century carpeting deceptively covered the broken edge of a nineteenth-century wooden step, rejected my foot. I slipped. I was falling, and the handrail was on the wrong side of me. If I dropped my fingerlamp to grab it, the glass could shatter in a blaze of oil. In the brief instant as I fell downwards, I felt the acute terror of something far more tangible and far more immediate than ghosts: *Fire!* If the oil spilled and ignited, could I put it out before it consumed the house? Could I get out myself, or would I fall prey to that most primal of terrors?

In the flash of the short distance to the carpet, scenes from a dozen movies where a massive inferno was started by a falling oil lamp flashed through my head. Then I hit the stairs. The lamp went out. I think my heart went out with the light.

I looked into the darkness. No light. No light meant no fire. I took a full, relieved breath. I still wasn't entirely convinced the house was safe, though. *Where's the oil? Is the oil spilling?*

I had twisted onto my side when I fell, so although I was lying on the stairs now, I was unhurt. As the lamp had gone out, I had heard the glass-on-metal clink of the fragile chimney falling from the burner, but there had been no shattering sound, so presumably nothing was broken. To maintain this situation I would have to locate the pieces of the lamp—both the delicate chimney and the oil-filled base, the latter of which might be pouring flammable liquid all over the dark stairs at that very moment—before I attempted to stand. Otherwise, I could easily step on one or the other, which would do neither my foot nor the lamp any good.

Gently, I probed the dark where I thought the lamp had fallen. My fingertips touched the thick glass of the base, and I was relieved to feel by its position on the pitch-black step that it had fallen and landed in an upright position.* I cautiously felt the carpet around the base of the lamp and was hugely relieved to find it dry. No oil had spilled. I took another deep breath, although my anxiety wasn't entirely chased away yet. I rubbed my hands repeatedly over the dry carpet, reassuring myself.

Clink! My fingernail hit the lamp's glass chimney, and I carefully fitted it back onto the burner by touch. I felt the carpet again, just to be sure, then lifted myself from my diagonal position and cautiously felt my way down the stairs.

The adrenaline fire-fear had chased away some of my anxieties about specters. I concentrated on making my way through a room that now lacked even the dim light of my lamp. Trying to remember the exact positions of the furniture and incidental articles, I realized the room was not as completely black as I might have expected: a dim illumination the color of old spiderwebs hung in the air, visible now that my lamp was no longer overpowering it with firelight. It was the light of a full October moon, half-drowned by the decaying leaves on the trees outside.

Maneuvering by memory and moonlight, I made my way around the larger furniture, although I did stumble over a footstool and cursed softly, vowing to never again violate the old mantra, "A place for everything and everything in its place."

My barked shin might be paying the price for my negligence in this rule concerning the hassock, but at least I had followed the advice with my storage of the matches. I felt their box where I had placed it earlier, high on the corner of a top shelf. Concentrating on motions my hands had learned even without my eyes to guide them, I struck a light and relit the lamp. This time I held it in my left hand so that my right would be free to grip the handrail. My second ascent of the stairs was without incident, but what I saw when I reached the top nearly made me scream.

---

* Much later, upon reflection, I realized that the bottom-heavy shape of a fingerlamp's base predisposes it to land this way if it is dropped. I very much doubt I am the first person in history to experience such a mishap. I would not, however, wish to repeat it as an intentional experiment.

Something was moving in the spare room.

I told myself nothing *could* be moving in the spare room. I was the only human in the house and we hadn't owned a pet since my dear old Pretty Kitty had passed on to the next of her nine lives. But something was in there: something alive. What I saw—first with just the corners of my vision, then with the full focus of my gaze as I turned to face the sight—were not the small scurryings of an insect or even a mouse, but the large motions of a form as big as a human. And whatever was making those movements was glowing bright as silver.

I clutched the oil lamp, my heart thudding. *Turn on the light, turn on the light!* something infantile and terror-stricken begged within me. I grabbed the fear and gripped it in a choke hold.

No! I insisted to myself. *I'm the only one in the house.*

But it's—

It can't be a ghost. I refuted my own thoughts.

At least run in the bedroom and shut the door!

No.

Hide! Barricade yourself in bed!

No. I have to find out what this is.

Whatever this was, it was not imaginary. It was not like the fearful delusions of my own imagination that had made sinister shapes out of the shadows downstairs. This was real, I could tell that much. And I had to find out what it was.

The shimmering, human-sized shape grew brighter, reached out to me, dimmed, grew brighter. Heart thumping, I stepped toward it.

Frightened as I was, I had not forgotten my sore-shinned lesson from the footstool downstairs. I carefully held the lamp out and scanned the floor, locating the piles of antique artifacts we stored in the spare room and gingerly stepping around them. The silver-bright thing was still in the room. It was not running from me like a ghost in a story; it was facing me down. I walked toward it—

—And found a mirror. I glanced quickly outside at the huge moon in the sky and, with a sudden gasp of cold-sweat relief, understood what I had been seeing. Here on the upper floor of the house, fewer tree branches blocked the light of the enormous full moon, and its light was reflected and intensified by a full-length mirror we had placed in the spare room. The few tree branches that did reach this high swayed in the wind outside, shadowing and moving the light at random intervals, and the whole eerie play of illumination was made stranger still by the movements of my own lamp. The angles in the situation were such that the mirror didn't show the classic cratered-orb shape of the moon—the source of so much of this otherworldly light—but the glass caught and reflected its illumination, warped and reflected by an infinite array of harmless objects. The whole effect was magnified and compounded by the natural biology of my sight being blurred by the light level in the room: it was too dark for the cone cells of my eyes to pick up explicit details, and my rod cells were detecting blurry images of light and darkness. I sighed in relief and went into the bedroom.

The mystery was solved, but I will confess that some still-uneasy part of me wished that our bedroom door had a lock. Looking about my dark room, I shivered. Superstition might still be holding me in its sway, but I told myself it was the cold making me shake. In the nineteenth century, the chimney running up our house's center had presumably helped to keep the upstairs warm. Now, though, with the kitchen stove gone and the old brick chimney blocked up, nonfunctional, the bedroom was exceedingly frigid.

I lit the Perfection heater and undressed as quickly as possible before diving underneath the thick strata of blankets on the bed. The hot water bottle I had buried there earlier radiated a warmth that contrasted starkly with the sepulchral cold of the room. I cuddled it to me like a long-departed lover. Orange firelight played on the ceiling as I waited for the room to warm to a point that permitted my hands and arms to release their desperate embrace of the rubber bottle. Until the bedroom reached a temperature sufficient to make my breath invisible, I had no desire to expose my arms to hold my reading material.

The design painted by fire upon my ceiling was like a Rorschach test: its interpretation depended on the viewer's frame of mind, and mine was unsettled. First the pattern of interlaced circles was an orange flower upon an October grave; next it was a biohazard symbol.

When the room was finally warm enough to read, I found myself too unnerved to concentrate on the pages of my antique magazine. I put it away, then stepped out of bed. I stood close enough to the heater to be bathed in a last wave of warmth as I loosened my corset a few inches and retied the bow at the small of my back. Then I turned the key controlling the heater's wick and snuffed the flame. I raced to bed, blowing out the lamp as a last, quick action before pulling the covers over my head. I told myself I was simply conserving heat, but the Perfection heater is a remarkably well-engineered device and it had raised the temperature of the room considerably. In truth, I was sweating.

The room spun around me with the same vertigo I remembered from childhood retreats under the covers when I had been small and afraid of ghosts.

As the air under the thick blankets grew stale and humid from my breath, I confessed to myself that I truly was engaging in a most childish cowardice. The weird sensations of spinning were probably due to the lack of oxygen under the thick blankets.

Chiding myself for superstitious illogic, I raised my head from its burial under the quilts and breathed in the air of the wider room, perfumed with the ghost of the recently extinguished heater's kerosene. It was not the first occasion on which I speculated as to the likelihood that the Brackens had owned a Perfection heater, but it was the first time I wondered if their spirits could smell the scent of my own.

Then something dawned on me.

If there was a Victorian ghost in my house, it would probably be one of the Brackens. What unearthly reason could they have for haunting here, of all places? The house had been a rental property in the 1890s. Surely if they were going to haunt somewhere, they would choose a place with more sentimental connections.

The Bracken brothers had moved from Port Townsend and lived out their lives in other cities, or altogether different states. The master bedroom Gabriel and I shared had most likely belonged to Charles, the eldest brother. He had gone to Montana, married, raised a family, and died in the shadow of the Rockies. Surely Butte to Port Townsend was a long way to come simply to give me an uneasy evening. Thinking of the drugstore charge account I had seen listing Charles paying for little Tom Jr.'s school books, I could hardly imagine he would be the sort of man to make an interstate, multidimensional trip for the sole purpose of unsettling a woman he had never met.

I couldn't remember the last time I had visited a former residence that I had rented myself. In my case, these had all been dorm rooms, and walking across campus had seemed like too much trouble to simply knock on a stranger's door. Even now I can't think of any earthly motivation I could have ever had for doing so. I doubt that such eccentric activity would have been welcomed, and the most I can imagine resulting from it would have been an awkward moment of staring at the new occupant before parting ways.

Even if Charles did come back to visit his old bedroom for some enigmatic ghostly motive, a man who would buy his kid brother books and make sure he finished school seemed far more likely to protect me from malignant poltergeists than to be one himself. A very similar line of reasoning held true for Tillie, whose (likely) old bedroom was now my massage studio, and who had filled her charge account at the drugstore with first-aid supplies and soap-making ingredients. She was the Bracken sibling who had spent the most time in Port Townsend; if any of them were lingering here in spirit, it should by rights be her. Tillie had raised her children (and lost one) in a house just a block away. If she were haunting anywhere, surely it would be there. Why hang out in a place she had lived a few years, when her home of decades was just down the street? I certainly don't barge into my neighbors' houses in the middle of the night and then loiter for no apparent reason. Assuming she did haunt her old house down the street, and stretching incredulity still further to suppose she would take time out of however ghosts spend their hours to come calling on me, everything I'd learned about her through my research implied that the most threatening thing she would ever do would be to pointedly jiggle the soap dish and lock the door if I tried to leave home without washing behind my ears.

Realizing how benign the ghosts of this home would be (even on the weird chance they chose to linger here), I felt a tremendous reassurance. I snuggled deep into my down pillow and drifted to peaceful sleep.

Humans have had a rather extended fascination with ghosts, the afterlife, and mortality in general. A little over a year after I scared myself silly over the moonlight in my mirror, I encountered an interesting Victorian death tradition while sorting through photographs in an antiques shop.

I had fairly specific parameters for my search that afternoon: I was seeking photos from the 1880s and '90s of women whose full dresses were visible in the portraits. The first antiques store I had visited yielded one such photo from their stock, but at the second shop I was met only with a pained look and an annoyed expression. At the last store, though, the owner told me I was in luck. He blessed me with a huge grin and pulled huge plastic crate after huge plastic crate from their places under the counter. Each one was filled with photographs; they were so full that none of their lids would settle. The pictures weren't organized, but they *were* numerous.

"The interesting thing about the city," I mused to the shop owner after an hour or so spent sorting through the huge stock of black and white pictures, "is how much it's been a microcosm of the history of the country." I paused in digging through the pile of silvered paper and held my hands out as if encompassing an invisible map. "Everything that happened in the country at large, or in the whole world—" I drew an even broader compass in the air, "—happened here, but more so." I pulled my hands together and clasped them tightly. "It's like the events that shaped the rest of the world were magnified here, then froze in time and are preserved."

The shop owner nodded, lifting up and musing over a few of the photographs I had discarded. "That's why we've got such great Victorian architecture here." He set the pictures aside. "Are you finding what you're looking for?"

"A few. The problem, of course, is that people weren't taking quite as many pictures yet in the period I like."

Photography was certainly popular in the 1880s and '90s, but still a bit expensive. The price of portraits or of pursuing the art as a private hobby was dropping rapidly, but was not quite conducive yet to the same bulk quantities of pictures that would document the twentieth century.* Photos were becoming common, but weren't entirely ubiquitous yet.

"Oh!" I held up a portrait of a small baby, startled by a detail on the card holding the picture. "That black wreath—"

The shopkeeper looked more closely. "You're thinking of memento mori?"

I nodded slowly.

The store owner squinted at the baby. "Yeah, I don't think this one is—he looks pretty lively. But if you do come across any death portraits, let me know." He wrinkled one corner of his mouth, thinking over what he had just said. "That sounds so morbid." He shook his head, rubbing his eyes with the backs of his wrists.

"No, it's okay. I know what you meant."

Photographs were, in fact, so expensive in the nineteenth century that some families could not afford to have them taken in life. In certain cases, people would scrape together enough money for a portrait of a recently deceased family member because it would be the only photo they would have of their loved one. Fortunately, however, pictures of the living do outnumber pictures of the dead. As a consequence, death portraits, or memento mori, are valuable and particularly sought by certain collectors. However, browsers who do not collect pictures of dead bodies can be disturbed by coming upon them suddenly. Both attitudes—attraction and repulsion—are good motivations for storekeepers to keep these particular items separate from the rest of their stock.

---

* Of course, neither the nineteenth- nor twentieth-century photographers would approach the expansive boom in photographing all the minutiae of daily life that is coming to characterize the digital age. I used to feel flattered when people asked to take my picture, but it seems less complimentary when they move on to just as eagerly photograph coffee, rocks, or other pointless subjects for which they won't care a fig in ten minutes' time.

I found two memento mori as I sorted through the bins. One was from a considerably later period than one usually finds such pictures, which probably explains why the body itself was not visible. The photo showed a small group of sad-faced men in 1930s work clothes, using straps to lower a simple firwood coffin into a grave. The other photo was older, and the coffin was open. The man inside was gaunt, as though he had died of a wasting illness or possibly a dehydrating one such as cholera. Social training told me I should shiver as I looked at it, but somehow I didn't. I felt solemn, but in a respectful way rather than a particularly sad one. This was a page in a human existence, neither more nor less than the others that spilled over the counter.

I cast my eyes over the huge pile of silvered faces. *In a way*, I thought, *they're all death portraits.* Even the happiest ones and the shots of people fullest of life. They're all gone now. At that thought I did shudder, and I was a bit sad. "It's hard to think about how every single one of these—" I gestured at the photos overflowing the storage bin and counter and spilling onto the floor, "is a life. Each one of these people lived and had a whole story around them."

The shopkeeper nodded solemnly. "Yeah, each one is a story," he agreed. Then a set of pictures we had sorted earlier caught his eye and he smirked, picking up a particular one to lighten our dark mood. "Some more so than others."

I looked at the woman with perfect hair and garish lipstick whom we had seen in half a dozen 1930s portraits, each with a different (but always seedy-looking) man. "Definitely." I shook my head. "Whatever hers was, though, I'm not the one to tell it." I held up my small collection of Victorian women in long dresses. "I'll take these."

As I wandered home with my photos—a voyeur's purchased peepholes into other lives—I thought about the various stories I had read or been told about spirits in the town.

There is a beautiful Queen Anne–style house down the street from mine with a tidy yard and well-maintained climbing toys out back. The children always seem to be smiling over some energetic game of ball, and their parents are a helpful pair who gave us their medical tape one holiday morning when the shops were all closed and Gabriel managed to break his little toe. The home seemed like an idyll from the front of a Christmas postcard; I was completely shocked when I met one of its former residents and she told me how uncomfortable she had been when she lived there.

"It's haunted," she told me, absolute conviction filling the wide brown eyes behind her glasses. "That whole house just has a weird vibe. I grew up there, and there was this one landing—" She cut herself off, shuddering. "My mom called in a psychic who did a reading on the place, and then did an exorcism."

"Really?" I asked, intrigued but trying very hard to hide my skepticism.

The storyteller nodded. "She didn't tell me about it until years later. The psychic came in and said right away, 'Oh, this spirit that's here *does not* like men!'" She emphasized "does not" with particular force. She went on to tell a tale of a Chinese woman who had been held captive in the house by a white man, buried her baby in the backyard, and was still haunting the place until the psychic performed her exorcism.

I refrained from asking how much the psychic had charged for this service.

"And, you know what?" the storyteller went on, shuddering, "When I used to dig around in the backyard—I didn't know any of this!" she added hastily. "I used to find bits of Chinese glass and once I found a piece of Chinese pottery!"

I thought about all the conversations I'd had with other town residents living in nineteenth-century homes, and about the major recurring question that inevitably popped up among those with a fondness for either history or gardens: "Have you found any glass yet?" I always felt somehow deficient for not having found any glass myself. (I had, however, turned up the rusty hardware from an old hitching post.) When Port Townsend was the Pacific Northwest customs port for the United States, it was a common landing point for trans-Pacific vessels. There are so many bits of cheap china pottery and old bottles under the ground in the area and its environs that a resourceful pair of gypsies supplement their fortune-telling business by selling glass bottles to tourists.*

It seemed impolitic to mention any of this, though. The young woman telling the story had always been kind to me and there was nothing to be gained by dismissing her story without examining it. I was, however, very curious to check the historical record. I thanked her for the story and shifted the date of my next archive visit.

The late nineteenth century is a time just close enough to touch us, if barely. Records survive from that era in fairly large numbers, and even if they don't always tell a researcher every minute detail, they can convey quite a bit of information. I had already spent a considerable amount of time scouring the census and city directory records related to my own house and some of the immediately neighboring addresses. I knew that careful reading of the records told everything from the occupations of every inhabitant to a good guess as to

---

* This might sound like a rhetorical metaphor, but I am actually describing two dear and friendly women who live in a brightly painted wooden gypsy wagon. Near their advertisement for Tarot readings sits a quaintly chalked sign reading, Hand-Dug Glass. Priced as Marked.

whom had answered the door for the census taker. (The inhabitants' names were usually recorded by the census taker not in priority of age or importance to the household, but simply by virtue of the order in which they came to the door or were listed off to the government official. I always smiled when I saw a servant get top-billing over the head of the household.)

I hadn't told the young woman of my plan to search the records, because (although I had tried to be polite) I considered her story implausible in the extreme. When I looked up the census account, I anticipated finding little to distinguish that neat and tidy home from any of the others on the block. I guessed it to be the home of a hardworking middle-class family, maybe with a boarder, and I fully expected the actual facts of the address's history to make the ghost story seem absurd.

When I found the census line listing the address of the beautiful Queen Anne home and its inhabitants, I saw that I had been correct about the record not substantiating the exorcist's story: There was no mention at all of a Chinese woman—or any woman, abused or otherwise—living there in the nineteenth century. Eerily, though, the census didn't exactly disprove the involvement of ghosts with the location—at least, it didn't do so in quite the way I had expected. What the census did do was make the small hairs on the back of my neck stand on end.

The city's undertaker had lived there.

Every community needs someone to care for the dead, of course, and it stands to reason that person would have to live somewhere. I simply hadn't expected to turn up a mortician's name while sleuthing out the truth behind a ghost story. A more credulous personality might spin out tales of unsettled ghosts following home the man who had prepared their bodies for burial, but I tried to stop my imagination from weaving such cobweb stories.

When I related this whole interesting tale of rumor and research to my neighbor who lives kitty-corner from the old undertaker's house, she laughed along with me at the improbable beginning. When I reached the conclusion, however, she paused and looked up from her gardening, a thoughtful expression on her face. "Huh," she said quietly. "That explains it. I'd always wondered about that." She shifted on her haunches in the turned soil and gazed up at her own house pensively.

I gave her a curious look.

She wiped her forehead with the back of her wrist and used her garden spade to gesture toward the top of her home. "When I redid my attic," she explained, small particles of soil falling from her spade and returning to the earth, "we tore out the old walls to put in new insulation, and underneath we found that the inside panels of the walls had been made out of old shipping crates for coffins."

My eyes went wide and another neighbor who was with us shuddered visibly. "You're kidding!"

The gardening neighbor stood up from her flowers and brushed the soil off her jeans, folding her arms in front of herself as she looked up toward her attic. "The boards were all marked," she explained. "That's how we knew where they had come from."

I speculated, "When they built the house, or at least did that part of it, they must have gotten the boards from the undertaker." I gestured across the quiet intersection to the house where the man with the solemn occupation had lived.

"I suppose it makes sense," said the third neighbor. "You'd use what you had handy."

"Well, they were sure good, strong boards!" asserted the woman whose attic had been paneled in them.

I laughed in a wry, dark sort of way. "I guess they'd have to be! I suppose it would have been wasteful to throw them away."

We looked at each other with half-restrained guilty smiles, sharing a shamefaced amusement at the practicality of building a home for the living out of boards that had once shipped vessels for the dead. It seemed macabre to end on that note, and I tried to think of something to liven up the mortuary conversation.

I remembered a particular herb in my front yard that had been especially profuse that season, and as a way of changing the topic from the dark ruminations that had occupied us, I asked my neighbors if they would like some salad burnet. Neither of them were familiar with the plant, so I jogged home and returned with two handfuls of feather-soft leaves, so green they seemed like the very color of springtime rebirth.

"Burnet doesn't get cooked," I explained, stroking the silk-soft fronds. "It's a green for salads—it tastes a bit like cucumbers." I smiled and held out a handful to each neighbor. "If we don't eat it the deer will just come in and wipe it out, so we might as well enjoy it while we can."

I wandered home, feeling a quiet pride in having produced an upbeat ending to the conversation. I looked at the bunch of feathery leaves growing by my door, speckled with their tiny, red-flecked flowers, and reflected that a new piece of knowledge was a good way to distract people's minds from morbid topics such as coffins and undertakers. It wasn't until much later that I would look up salad burnet in my book of herbal references and learn that the plant's scientific name of *Sanguisorba minor* is Latin for "I soak up blood."[76] Perhaps morbidity is never quite so distant as modern people would like to believe.

When people present me with ghost stories, I enter much the same frame of mind I would have if the same person told me that they had awoken to find a live zebra in their kitchen. I don't totally discount the possibility there might be some truth involved in the matter; I can think of a few (highly theoretical) scenarios that might conceivably get a zebra into a kitchen. However, I do get very curious about the details.

The sentimental portion of me would like to believe that specters exist. The pragmatic element of my nature is inclined to think that if spirits really can pass from one world to another, then they surely must have better things to occupy themselves with than the petty mischief generally attributed to poltergeists. Finally, the analytical section of my brain finds that the rational explanation behind a ghost story is often the most intriguing part of the tale.

One of my favorite haunting tales involves an Edwardian family in a Victorian house. I like it because it has all the hallmarks of a classic ghost story—and a perfectly scientific explanation. The case was described in a medical journal in 1921—not a psychological journal as one might expect when alleged ghosts are involved, but a journal of ophthalmology. The incident was incredibly well documented; to protect the family's privacy, they were identified only by their initials: Mrs. H. and her husband G.

In October 1912, the H. family were driven out of their townhouse by a fire and forced to find new lodgings at short notice. After much difficulty owing to the lateness of the season, they at last found a home for rent: " . . . a large, rambling, high-studded house, built around 1870, and much out of repair. It had not been occupied by the owners for the past ten years."

Shortly after the family moved in, the house's furnace broke down and new parts had to be made for it in a different city. "It was a very old furnace, built thirty years or more ago, with a combination of hot air and steam, with a boiler suspended over the fire." Little did the family suspect what a horrifying role that furnace was to play in their destinies, or how near it would bring them all to death.

When they had only been in the house a couple weeks, Mrs. H. started experiencing severe headaches and feelings of fatigue. Lying down and resting only made her headaches worse, and even taking iron pills three times a day didn't help her feelings of weakness. Meanwhile, her husband G. started to feel the overwhelming sensation of being watched at night. "The children grew pale and listless and lost their appetites." They abandoned their playroom at the top of the stairs, despite all their toys being there, and begged to be allowed to stay in their bedroom.

The state of things grew so bad that Mrs. H. took the children away from the house for the holidays. While they were gone, G. was repeatedly awakened by loud bells and other noises in the night. Yet when he investigated the sounds, he found them to be without cause or explanation.

The children benefitted from their time away from the house, but when Mrs. H. returned with them, they were sicker than ever. ". . . [T]he gloom of the house began to cast a shadow over us once more," Mrs. H. later wrote. Her headaches resumed and she "frequently felt as if a string had been tied tightly around [her] left arm." At night, she and her husband heard phantom footsteps where no one could be, along with impossible crashing noises and slamming of doors.

One morning, Mrs. H. saw "a strange woman, dark haired and dressed in black" coming toward her. When Mrs. H. walked toward her, the apparition vanished and Mrs. H. found herself facing her own reflection in a mirror. She later reported, "I laughed at myself, and wondered how the lights and mirrors could have played me such a trick." But it was a trick that was repeated three times.

One morning, her four-year-old son B. entered her room and asked why she had called him. When she said that she hadn't, the child was shocked. He insisted that someone had called him and made a pounding noise. Nothing his mother said could persuade him otherwise.

The children lost their appetites again and didn't want to leave their beds. While playing with a toy on the floor, the little four-year-old B. would lapse into an apparently trance-like state and "would lie, stretched out, limp and listless upon the floor, a toy in front of him clasped in his hand, his eyes glued upon it yet apparently neither seeing nor thinking about it."

Mrs. H.'s plants died, and the whole family continued to grow sicker. One night, G. woke up to a vivid sensation of strangulation and, looking over at his wife, found her in a heavy stupor as though drugged. Even their servants were affected: They too were ill and saw and heard impossible things.

The servants charged with caring for the children claimed the house was haunted. They reported that the four-year-old had run screaming down the hall begging them, "Don't let that fat man touch me." But there was no man.

The children's nurse reported sensations of being followed and of having her bedclothes ripped off of her at night by invisible hands. Once, when she woke up, she saw a man and woman sitting on the front of her bed and they quickly vanished. Another servant felt her bed being shaken by an unseen presence. They had all heard mysterious loud noises after dark and reported sensations of *something* creeping over them at night while they lay literally paralyzed—not by fear, but by something likewise invisible and even more sinister.

G. and Mrs. H. tracked down former occupants of the house and found that they had all had similar experiences. The last residents had seen figures in purple and white creeping around their beds at night.

The ghastly mystery was solved when G.'s brother recalled an article he had read several years before. He speculated that all of the sensations and visions experienced within the house were the result of something unseen yet horribly real: carbon monoxide poisoning.

A man of science was brought in to evaluate the situation. He found that, as the brother had suspected, the house's faulty furnace was pouring deadly gas into the rooms. He told G. and Mrs. H. not to let their children sleep in the house another night, warning that if they did they might find "one of them would never wake again."

The family's physician was summoned and confirmed that they were all suffering symptoms of prolonged carbon monoxide poisoning. He ordered them to flee the house and prescribed iron supplements to help them regain their strength. In time, they gradually recovered. Little B.'s eyes remained affected for years afterward though—which explains how the case found its way into a journal of ophthalmology.[77]

Some alleged ghost stories involve neither spirits nor anything sinister, but simple cases of mistaken identity. After several years in Port Townsend, most people of the small town knew me, but once in a while new residents move here with interesting results. In our fourth year of residence here, I was given occasion to wonder how many superstitious people there might be in the general population.

A new couple had moved to the general neighborhood, accompanied by their two dogs. Exactly where this foursome had taken up residence I had no interest in knowing, but it must have been within a short walking distance of my home because they started (ahem) pausing by my yard on a regular basis. I can forgive the dogs for pausing; all biological creatures are subject to natural functions. However, I was irritated by the owners' complete nonchalance as they watched the action being performed on someone else's property—and their total lack of any scoop or bag. I even witnessed them changing their path and crossing the street to single out my yard in particular for their functions. It was a distinction I really didn't appreciate.

Some people like dogs and others don't, but I have never yet met a person who relishes finding the discarded digestions of someone else's animal directly in the middle of their walkway. I'm sure even the most avid dog-lover will understand my irritation after three weeks of this daily performance. When they came back and stopped in front of my house and the overture began again, I contemplated an appropriate way to bring it to a close.

My first impulse—which was to rush out the door, start screaming, and possibly throw something—seemed a bit heavy-handed and possibly wanting in dignity. I decided an escalating approach was more sensible. First I would stand very visibly in my window, making it very clear to the owners that they were being watched. Any halfway decent person would slink away, ashamed of themselves.

If they persisted in behaving badly in front of a witness, I decided I would tap on the glass, point at the defecating dogs, and shake my finger a very stern, "No!" If even this proved insufficient, I would open my front door and take one step outside, glaring at them. (The dogs might take this as enough of a hint, even if the humans didn't.) I saved screaming and throwing things as a last resort.

As it turned out, the very first step in this chain proved far more effective than I had imagined it would be.

I saw the overture commencing: the owners pulled the dogs across the street and pointed at my front walkway. At their masters' command, one dog squatted and the other lifted its leg.

I was wearing my pure white summer dress so I knew I was visible, but to make extra certain I would be seen, I waited until one of the owners happened to glance upward. Then I stepped into the alcove of my bay view window, right up against the glass, glaring downward with the strongest expression of disapproval I could manage.

Just as I had hoped, the man's eye was caught by my movement and he saw me. I expected him to look embarrassed and make an awkward retreat. His actual behavior, though, proved far more amusing. It was almost worth my irritation at the dogs' digested matter.

The man's eyes grew wide as saucers, and all the blood completely drained from his face. I saw his mouth shape a word. It took a moment for my mind to interpret it, by which time he had already grabbed the arm of his female companion and had started running, dragging both her and the dogs with him.

They were halfway down the block by the time I deciphered the word I had seen his mouth form. When I had, I looked down at my 1870s-style dress (copied from an antique in our collection) and then at the 1888 bay window framing me. Then I laughed out loud.

The word the man had spoken as all color drained from his face just before he started running had been "Ghost!"

I chuckled as I drew the curtain on the retreating forms. These things happen to me from time to time. I once got a free lunch from a pair of amused actors by telling them about being mistaken for a specter when I first moved into my home. On another occasion, I thought a tourist was going to start screaming when I slipped past her on the steps separating the Uptown and Downtown districts of Port Townsend. When she saw me, she gasped in a great lungful of air and stumbled backward—uphill—over her own feet.

Ghosts hadn't really entered into my plan for shooing away the unwanted visitation, but the encounter was effective: they never came back.

10

Writing

"Letter-writing as it was in its golden age is almost a lost art. Telegram
and postal card, telephone and 'letter-sheet,' are fast pushing it into
the background, and while it certainly is as pleasant to hear from one's
friend as ever, one must be content with the brief lines which the rush
and hurry of our days permit."

—Anna Sawyer, 1889[78]

I seldom paid attention to liquid inks in the days before I had a pen compatible with them. (As a child, I had tried scavenging feathers from underneath the cages of my mother's pet parrots and dipping the quills into the contents of ballpoint pens I had eviscerated, but these experiments proved unsatisfactory.) Without a pen that could use them, the inks had no utility for me so they fell beneath the radar of my consciousness. I knew that liquid inks are manufactured in a variety of colors in much the same way that I (as a non-driver) was aware that gasoline comes in different grades; it was a somewhat mundane bit of knowledge with no significance to me personally.

The nuances between the different shades of these valuable liquids took on new meaning for me when Gabriel gave me my first dip pen. As I unwrapped the thin wand of mother-of-pearl one Christmas, my husband explained that it differed from a fountain pen in not having a reservoir to pump and hold liquid ink. Fountain pens get their name from their artesian quality—their ink flows like the water from a fountain. A dip pen can also be called a straight pen or a steel-nibbed pen. (Admittedly, this latter nomenclature can be confusing, because fountain pens may also have steel nibs, and some high-end nibs for straight pens are made out of gold to give them greater flexibility in writing.)

The one thing a dip/straight/steel-nibbed pen is not is a quill pen. Quills come from feathers and straight pens are more advanced technology. In an

interesting way, the shift from quills to steel nibs can be seen as representative of the movement from artisan production to mass manufacture. Carving a
bird's feather into a usable pen is actually a more complicated skill than a casual
observer might realize. When Gabriel studied library and information science
at the University of Washington, one of his professors was a former computer
programmer who gave up the dot-com world to study the technologies involved
in medieval manuscripts. He spent years learning the proper way to prepare
quills, first shaving off the barbs from the shafts, then perfectly baking the quills
in sand to harden them before carefully carving a painstakingly sculpted writing
utensil.

One weekend, I coerced Gabriel into helping me replicate the process his
professor had described and the results were embarrassingly dilettante. The
quills we produced could be used to write something a castaway might throw
out to sea in a bottle, but they were far from optimal. Lest we forget our failure,
for days after our pen-making exercise our kitchen was haunted by the unpleasant reek of low tide. The odor was a foul reminder of my error in thinking that
it was acceptable to bake our goose quills in beach sand instead of the clean
sand we should have used. Just because a technology is old does not mean that
it is easy to produce—on the contrary, sometimes the older a technology is, the
more art it requires.

Turning bird feathers into pens is an acquired skill, but for many centuries
writers of European languages had little choice. Western alphabets were ill-
suited to the brushes favored in various Asian countries (besides, these were
probably no easier to produce than quill pens). Stylus-type writing tools made
out of reed, wood, or other materials were still older technologies with their
own issues. A type of metal stylus was used by engineers and draftsmen, but
ordinary people found the stiffness of these instruments inconvenient. In 1890,
the author of *Birmingham Inventors and Inventions* wrote to a researcher compiling a history of the pen:

> It has often occurred to me that some of the very early references to
> metallic pens may perhaps be the draughtsman's 'ruling pen,' and not an
> instrument made after the fashion of a quill pen with a slit in it. That it is
> possible to write with such an instrument this paragraph will show, but I
> must admit that it is not equal to one of Perry's J's.[79]

Until around 1830, making metal nibs for pens was an artisanal skill even more
specific than trimming feather quills: nibs from precious metals such as gold

or silver were made by jewelers, while steel nibs were made by cutlers (the men who forged and ground knife blades). Then mass production entered the picture—and writing became much more advanced.

During the Industrial Revolution of the eighteenth and nineteenth centuries, rapid expansion of technologies in a variety of areas contributed significantly to each other. Advances in book and paper production led to greater literacy—and a greater need for pens. Moreover, in the early 1800s, the expectation of where things should come from was changing. Hand-produced goods were seen as antiquated and inferior; machine-made products were state-of-the-art and desirable.*

In the early 1800s, demand for metal-nibbed pens rose swiftly, and a number of cutlers found that it was increasingly more profitable to manufacture pen-nibs than knives. The question of which specific individual deserves credit for being the first to mass-produce metal nibs is debatable; pen historian Henry Bore divides the credit between three men around 1830: John Mitchell, Joseph Gillot, and Josiah Mason.[80]

When Gabriel gave me my straight pen, he accompanied it with a short educational lecture about the history of the pen. Experiments with using it became a succession of experiential lessons about the nature of ink. The classic black inks come in varying qualities and prices, and I found that very cheap ink tends to dry into clumps on the pen or fade on the page. The highest grades of ink are those that not only flow the most smoothly for writing, but also last with a dark permanence. Besides basic black, there exists a choice of colors so varied as to put any rainbow to shame and convince even the most resplendent peacock he should resign himself to a bachelor's existence. Experience taught me to be cautious of lovely marbled and metallic inks that mimic precious ores or lustrous tropical beetles; the suspended metallic particles that give them their sheen tend to clot when exposed to air and foul the nibs of pens, making it difficult to write neatly with them.

When I saw that the J. Herbin Company made inks, I was intrigued because I had long been a devotee of their high-quality sealing wax. Being me, of course I couldn't be content with simply testing the product but felt obliged to research the story of the company—and it proved a fascinating one. The

---

*By the late nineteenth century, a backlash movement had sprung up against this attitude, with philosophers such as John Ruskin and William Morris touting the value of handmade goods. Then the early twentieth century saw a resurgence in the "better living through technology" attitude and there were mixed reactions in the immediate aftermath of each world war. The 1950s space era idolized technology. The hippies of the 1960s despised it. Around and around . . .

tale goes all the way back to the seventeenth century. The original Monsieur Herbin was a French sailor who collected ingredients and formulas on visits to India. Settling down on his return to his homeland, he founded his sealing wax company in 1670 and began selling inks in his Parisian shop on the Rue des Fosses Saint-Germain at the turn of the century in 1700. Over the years, the company's prestigious list of customers has included Louis XIV and Victor Hugo. The author of *Les Misérables* and *The Hunchback of Notre Dame* had his own private ink formula, and the recipe for it is still archived in the company's Paris headquarters.[81] Herbin's inks are made with all-natural dyes, which give them a very neutral pH (an important quality in archival terms, since acidic elements can eat through documents).

The natural ingredients of a particular line of inks give them a very special quality indeed. In the nineteenth century, ink manufacturers started making ink from hydrosols, the aromatic waters distilled from flowers during perfume making. Herbin uses hydrosols from a Provençal town in southern France famous for its perfume to produce inks smelling of roses (red), violets (blue), lavender, oranges, and other delicious fragrances.

Scented inks! The discovery brought an array of childhood memories of old markers I had cherished. In the early years of my elementary school education, my teachers and all the luckier children in the classrooms possessed a particular brand of colored marker that we all unilaterally agreed were astronomically better than any other felt-tipped pens on the market. This superiority was due not to greater availability of shading (the standard set only contained nine colors) or any particular persistency of ink (although they seemed more vibrant than the pens of other brands). These markers—these wonderful pens—were prized because they smelled of fruits and candies. Many years later when I was in college, a classmate and I waxed nostalgic for those dear old scented markers, and we imagined what adult, less-sugared versions would be like. We fantasized about red ink that smelled of rose petals or lavender scented with the eponymous herb. We joked about making our fortune by manufacturing such clever products. Little did we dream that companies manufacturing liquid ink had anticipated our idea by more than a century. Finding the scented inks produced by J. Herbin took me back to childhood delights and adult daydreams, then pushed them both up a notch.

Victorian stationery paper could also be scented by adding perfumed sachets to the boxes in which it was stored. By the 1890s, scented letters were so common that advice columnists writing on correspondence discussed fragrance as a matter of course. Unsurprisingly, their specific suggestions on the subject

Writing tools, left to right: Back: Scented inks (30 mL bottles), black unscented ink (100 mL bottle), antique inkwell (circa 1890s), flannel scraps (for wiping pens), antique rocker blotter. Front: antique mother-of-pearl fountain pen (circa 1900), antique mother-of-pearl straight pen, antique sterling silver straight pen, blotter pad.

were influenced by their own opinions, although as a general rule they advised their readers to save perfume for personal (never business) letters and to err on the side of subtlety. Writing for *The Woman's Book* in 1894, Constance Cary Harrison boldly declared that "[s]trong, vivid odors intended for the masses, so frankly vulgarize everything they touch, it seems hardly worthwhile to urge that the sachets containing them be thrown into the fire."[82] *Good Housekeeping*'s Anna Sawyer was more indulgent and saw no objection to delicately scented personal correspondence. However, even she drew the line at patchouli, which she found "vulgar in the extreme."[83]

In exaggerated cases, the offense could go beyond olfactory aversion. A work of short fiction originally published in 1867 gives a fantastic account of a lady who was driven so wild with jealousy after seeing her husband meet a young blonde woman that she poisoned him with laudanum. When a scented letter arrives from the blonde, the murderess's "jealousy and anger rushed to life again . . . Did she *dare* to call him *her* dear Lionel! Ay, there it was, written on pink paper with perfumed ink." Only after reading the scented letter does the self-made widow learn that the pretty blonde was her husband's favorite sister. Oops![84]

I am inclined to think that strongly scented letters affect some people in the way that text alerts on modern devices affect others. There is a natural human curiosity about other people's messages—and an equally natural desire for the addressees to be possessive of private missives. The challenging thing about scents and audible signals is that they both force a teasing fragment of a private item into the public domain. The Victorian advice guide *Hill's Manual of Social and Business Forms* includes the commandment, "Never read letters which you may find addressed to others."[85] When the mailman delivers envelopes with other people's names on them or when electronic devices are dormant, decency generally overcomes curiosity. However, when the missives attract the attention of our other senses through scent or sound, restraint becomes just a little bit more difficult. Luckily, outside the fictitious world of Gothic romance, people are less likely to go around poisoning each other over such things.

Considering etiquette's emphasis on maintaining subtlety of scent in letters, it shouldn't be surprising that the J. Herbin company has actually named their line of scented inks *Les Subtiles*—"The Subtles." I absolutely adore the fragrance of roses, and when I found an ink that smelled of them, I stepped up my writing of personal letters just to increase my exposure to that beloved perfume. I was intrigued to find that the fragrance, which was so heady in the ink bottle, disappeared very quickly after words were set to paper—in other words, the ink is fragrant when wet and nearly scentless when dry. With their line of *Les Subtiles*, Herbin seems to have struck the perfect compromise between scented and unscented: the writer smells the fragrance but the reader does not. They also produce inks that aren't scented at all for formal correspondence as well as for people who simply don't care for fragrance.

As Goldilocks said about Baby Bear's possessions, Herbin's ink was "just right": it flowed smoothly without clumping and left bold marks upon the page once dry. I was to especially appreciate this latter quality when I acquired an antique fountain pen.

Fountain pens may seem old-fashioned to most Americans, but this is more of a commentary on Americans than on fountain pens. In Europe and in Japan, they are still common and readily available. Department stores sell them in a broad range of prices and qualities, from cheap examples in the school supply section to beautiful, artisan-quality specimens under glass in their own department. Worldwide, fountain pen sales are on the rise: Parker, which has manufactured fountain pens since 1888, says that the years since 2006 have demonstrated a "resurgence" in fountain pen popularity; and Amazon reported in 2012 that online fountain pen sales were double what they had been in 2011 and four times what they had been in 2010.[86]

Even in America, fountain pens still have their adherents. Antique and vintage fountain pens have particularly devoted followers. Pen historian Jonathan Steinberg cites the inherent superiority of the older pens as the reason for their devout followings. He points out that, owing to differences in flexible and rigid nibs, antique pens write in a completely different way from newer models. The nibs of the earliest fountain pens (like the nibs of straight pens before them) replicated the flexibility of feather quills; they curved and flexed very slightly as the words were formed on a page. Rigid nibs (which didn't flex to shape words and were rather scratchy to use) existed, but they were specialized implements used primarily for writing through multiple layers of carbon paper—this earned them the nickname "manifold" nibs. Flexible nibs were preferred as being far more comfortable to write with.[87]

The same pliancy that made flexible nibs comfortable to write with also made them slightly more delicate than their rigid counterparts. This wasn't a huge problem as long as writers were careful. However, in the 1920s, companies started introducing the idea of lifetime warranties—which meant that people were no longer responsible for their own breakages. It became prudent business practice to make nibs as indestructible as possible, no matter that some of the comfort in writing was sacrificed.[88]

Fountain pens aren't actually that old of an idea in the grand timeline of human history. They first became a mass-market item in my favorite period—the 1880s. Various small-scale inventors had been experimenting with primitive fountain pens since the eighteenth century (Thomas Jefferson made one for himself), but they all faced the same frustrating problem: the ink tended to form a vacuum inside the tube of the pen. Various methods were attempted to overcome this obstacle, and in 1882, Lewis Waterman developed a channel feed for fountain pen nibs that let air in at the same time it let ink out. In 1884, he started commercial production of this new technology and a number of other companies followed suit.[89]

When I set out to buy an antique fountain pen with part of my first book advance, Gabriel helped me find just the right one. This took some searching, because for such a major watermark celebration, I was determined that it had to be perfect. We visited every fountain pen seller in Seattle (sadly, not a large number these days), then we started looking into dealers online. Gabriel managed to track down a seller in British Columbia who refurbished antique pens and had a few my husband thought might be right for me. I chose a beautiful model with a gilt cap and mother-of-pearl inlay, from right around 1900. (Prior to the turn of the twentieth century most fountain pens had very plain black exteriors, and I wanted something a little showy.)

My particular pen is a style with a reservoir the writer fills with ink from an eyedropper. When I first acquired it, I had some official letters to write; colored ink would have been inappropriate, so I went to the only shop in Port Townsend that sells liquid ink and bought a bottle of black off their shelf. (The ink was from a company that shall remain nameless, but let the record show that it wasn't my beloved Herbin.) Buying ink from a store with a low turnover rate of products was a mistake I will never be repeating, but at least it taught me a lesson. If asked to name materials with expiration dates, a person might list milk, meat, poultry, and other edibles. Ink probably wouldn't come up high on most people's lists. However, if it spends enough time sitting on a shelf, even a decent ink will start to dry out and the pigments suspended in the liquid will clump together. For several frustrating weeks, every ten to thirty minutes of my writing would be halted by the necessity to wash yet another clog out of my beautiful new fountain pen. Some people would wrongfully lay the blame on the antique pen, but I knew it had been fully serviced by the collector who sold it to me. (Buying a fountain pen is like buying any piece of technology: It helps to make the purchase from a reputable buyer who knows how to repair the product before they pass it on. Think of it as buying a used laptop from a reputable dealer with guaranteed tech support instead of pulling one from the back of a Goodwill store and expecting quality results.)

I have a general inclination to "make do," and for a while I dealt with a maddening ritual imposed by the clump-prone ink: Write for ten minutes, see that words have stopped appearing, shake pen, try to write again with no results, take pen to bathroom, wash out pen, wash out bathroom sink (now stained black), refill pen, still have no luck writing, shake pen again, reflect that my desk is starting to resemble a Dalmatian, apply pen to paper, curse giant blot that has emerged on page, rewrite page (if a formal letter), repeat entire process in ten to thirty minutes. Finally I decided the time this was costing me in terms of inefficiency was more valuable than the negligible sum I had spent on the world's most infuriating bottle of ink. I sent away for fresh black ink from my favorite company.

As long as I was ordering from J. Herbin, I ordered some blotting paper from them as well. Blotting paper is to regular paper what a diaper is to a handkerchief: it is extremely thick and absorbent, which makes it perfect for testing a newly filled pen or as a space to hold a clogged pen over when shaking it. (When the clog is shaken free of the nib, it will—hopefully—fall onto the blotting paper.)

Having blotting paper also made it possible for me to use an item Gabriel had given me for Christmas: a rocker-blotter. This tool is often simply referred to as a blotter, but since that term can also refer to a pad that holds a stack of blotting paper in place horizontally, I'll use the full name to avoid confusion. It is a pad about the size of a deck of cards, with a curved bottom and a handle on the top. A piece of blotting paper is fitted over the curved bottom, and the tool is pressed over freshly inked words in a rocking motion. Its purpose is to soak up extra ink so that it won't smear when a page is turned over or folded.

Once the new ink arrived (straight from the factory), writing became a lot more pleasurable. Clogs and blots decreased dramatically—although they didn't disappear completely yet, because, as with so many worthwhile things in life, the lessons involved were arrayed upward on a steep learning curve. I started to look on my eyedropper pen a bit like a Persian cat: It was fussy, yet I was confident it would become a worthy companion once we became accustomed to each other. Also like a Persian cat, it had specific needs I did not fully understand at first.

My writing desk is what the British would call a bureau: the lower portion consists of three broad drawers like a dresser, and these support a slanted top that folds down to provide support for the writing materials. Behind this movable slanted portion are seven little drawers, only two-and-a-half inches deep: three each are stacked vertically on the left and right and a broader but equally shallow drawer is situated between these.

At the time I was still learning how to tend the needs of a fountain pen, my desk was situated next to one of the hottest windows in our house. We had placed it there in the winter when the house was cold and the sun came through the glass panes at low angles; the warm spot seemed like a good place for a writing desk at the time.

Starting with desks that had perpetually exasperated my elementary school teachers and all the way through my stewardship of this family heirloom as an adult, I considered myself congenitally incapable of keeping a tidy desk. I'm far from alone in this. Between 2001 and 2005, a team of UCLA archaeologists and anthropologists examined the houses of a number of different families, counting artifact totals in each room. Most of the home office spaces included in the study were so cluttered that the researchers gave up on counting paper items—"abundant stacks of papers, mail and magazines, which we deemed impossible to tally with accuracy." Even ignoring these documents (and also ignoring hidden objects shoved behind other items), the researchers documented as many as 2,337 plainly visible non-paper objects in a home office space—and they didn't even look in the drawers or file cabinets.[90]

All the little drawers in my desk were perpetually stuffed with detritus. Not wanting a valuable (and potentially leaky) pen to get mixed up with the mess, it seemed logical to leave my fountain pen resting at the open space at the front of the desk when I wasn't actively writing. I found a little ceramic flower (intended to be a chopstick holder) to use as a pen-rest and laid my fountain pen horizontally across it on full display—in the bright, pretty sunshine. In retrospect, as far as sensible actions are concerned, this was about on par with leaving a laptop computer on the dashboard of a sealed car at the height of summer.

I overlooked one of the most basic properties of water: it expands when heated. Since liquid ink is primarily water with tinting materials added, it should surprise no one that I had quite a few more messes to deal with before I finally considered the chemistry of the situation. (I doubt the hot window did any good to the antique gutta-percha of the pen's body, either.) Feeling chagrined at my oversight, I cleaned out the broad drawer at the center of my desk's top so that I could give my poor pen some shelter from the sun. While I lined the drawer with cotton flannel (to soak up any further leaks), I reflected that this particular space was probably intended for pens all along. So many things in people's daily lives are designed expressly for their purpose; the trick lies in discerning that purpose.

Storing the pen in a shaded portion of the desk ameliorated my problems, but they weren't completely eliminated yet. That took moving the desk to a cooler portion of the house; of course, this also made it a much more pleasant space for *me* to work in the summer. Once this was accomplished, clogs and blots dwindled to being only occasional, minor annoyances, about on par with an abnormally slow program running on a usually fast computer.

Trial, error, and a bit of research would inform me about the proper procedure for operating a fountain pen. Different varieties of inks should never be mixed together; even if they are each fine examples of ink on their own, they tend to get fussy when mixed. The pen should always be capped when not in use, even for short periods of time such as stopping to talk to someone or daydream out the window (otherwise the ink can start to dry and clog the nib). Also, if the pen is left unused for a few days, a slight bit of attention (in the form of gentle shaking and/or a warm water rinse) might be necessary to reboot it and get the ink flowing again—or at least, this is the case with my particular eyedropper fountain pen. I don't presume to speak of pens everywhere.

I ultimately came to understand that my fountain pen and I have more than a little in common: We both appreciate good ink; we don't like taking in material that doesn't agree with us; we dislike excessive heat; and we both become neurotic if we're not allowed to write every day.

There was still one more application to acquire for successful running of the fountain pen program, and that was proper paper. In the nineteenth century, it was naturally assumed that all writing was done with liquid ink or with pencils, and paper was manufactured accordingly. A paper company whose product splayed out ink as quickly as water seeps through toilet paper would not have remained in business very long. Unfortunately for aficionados of Victorian pens, expectations have changed, and the types of paper most compatible with electronic equipment are actually the least compatible with liquid ink.

When I was a junior at the University of Washington, a minor incident occurred that left a lasting impression on my memory. At the beginning of a particular class, the professor handed out the notes for the day, just as she always did. Right away, we all noticed something out of the ordinary about the paper on which these particular notes were printed. It was thick, with a slightly cloth-like texture. I looked around and saw the other students fingering it, hefting it, squinting at it quizzically. One girl held it up and rubbed it against her cheek, a slight smile on her face.

"This paper—" someone asked.

"Is it—" another student began at the same time.

We all looked at each other and the paper, then someone tried again. "What's going on with it?"

"Hmm?" asked our white-haired professor distractedly. She turned from the board at the front of the room where she'd been writing the day's itinerary. Looking around the class, she noticed the ways in which we were all engaged in a total sensory experience of our assignment. "Oh, I'm sorry. I ran out of computer paper. I had some old typewriter paper at the back of my office, so I used that instead." She smiled at the girl who had been rubbing her cheek on the novel item. Distinctive as it was to the students, our professor saw nothing extraordinary in it. "It used to be that the higher-quality papers had a higher rag content so the ink wouldn't smear," she explained.

"Why did they ever stop?" asked the dreamy-eyed student with the sensitive cheeks.

"Well,"—our professor looked over at the streamlined new Apple at the front of the classroom—"anything connected with computers or printers has to be kept as dust-free as possible." She gestured up at the whiteboard. "That's why all the classrooms are switching over to these from chalkboards." She wiped her hands to clean them of clinging dry-ink particles from the marker she had just used, then looked out over the pieces of paper we were holding. "Technically, I probably shouldn't have run that paper through my printer. Doing that too much is liable to clog the printer with lint. I was in a tight spot, though." She looked back up at the board. "Can we move on to the lesson now?"

We all set our papers down, slightly embarrassed—and yet a little reluctant to let them go.

When I started using liquid ink, I discovered the corollary to the problem described by my professor. Running too much high-rag content paper through a computer printer might jam it, but writing with liquid ink on most printer paper leads to a rather unsightly mess. Instead of drying neatly in place, the ink seeps through the paper and leaves spots all over the back of it. In the worst cases, the ink also bleeds out across the front of the paper and turns even neatly written words into odd approximations of Rorschach tests.

Since printer paper has become the default sold in most office supply stores, paper that is actually intended for use with proper ink instead of toner can be a bit difficult to locate. Looking for ink-compatible paper one day, I made a trip to Seattle and visited the huge bookstore attached to my old alma mater. I spent half an hour frowning at and feeling the pages of nearly every notebook and journal in the school supply section when it finally occurred to me to cross over to the art supplies. I found some broad, blank-paged artists' journals. I checked the labels to make sure they were acid-free (and therefore wouldn't self-destruct as they aged), then asked the clerk behind the counter how well they would handle fountain-pen ink.

"I know it's not reasonable to expect you to have intimate knowledge of every single product in your store—" I apologized.

"No, that's a great question!" she assured me. She smiled, inspecting the blank-paged books. "I understand exactly what you mean. Let me ask my boss!"

She disappeared into a back room and returned after only a brief absence. "They can take a light wash, so they should be fine for liquid ink." She smiled brightly at me, and I thanked her.

When I brought the journals home and interfaced them with my fountain pen, I found the technical support to have been sound: they were compatible.

Gabriel pointed out to me that, from an archivist's perspective, it's particularly important to use good-quality paper for correspondence. A lot of what historians know about people from the past comes from what can be gleaned from the writings they leave behind. Not everyone keeps a diary, and even when they do, they or their executors don't always allow it to become public. Therefore, letters constitute valuable windows into people's thoughts. As such, they merit preservation, and a letter on good-quality paper has a better chance at long-term preservation than a letter on paper that will become fragile over time. In 1895, Thomas Hill wrote:

> You little dream how much that letter may influence your future. How much it may give of hope and happiness to the one receiving it. How much it may be examined, thought of, laughed over, and commented on; and when you suppose it has long since been destroyed, it may be brought forth, placed in type, and published broadcast to millions of readers.[91]

About the same time I acquired an antique fountain pen, I made a resolution to conduct as much of my personal correspondence as possible by actual letter. I knew that in the realm of business, trying to enforce handwritten correspondence upon my poor, hardworking editor would doubtless simply drive her to finding less-eccentric writers to publish, and quite frankly I wouldn't blame her. There was no reason not to use it for personal correspondence, though, and a number of my friends proved wonderfully amenable to the idea. The quickest to catch on was my old buddy Tom, which never really surprised me because he's been my most faithful correspondent over the years.

I met Tom when I joined the University of Washington's archery club back in college. He was the club president—his hobby while he multiple-majored in what seemed to me like every branch of science known to man. Graduation inevitably leads to a bit of a diaspora of school chums, but Tom and I managed to stay in touch, and he always responded cheerfully to any missive I sent him, whether it was simply an inquiry into how he was doing or a request for a pile of case studies regarding mechanical testing to establish the force necessary to fracture human ribs. When I started sending him physical letters in lieu of the emails I'd been writing him for years, he took it completely in stride. When he responded by email to tell me he was enjoying the letters and that I should keep them coming, I considered the multi-media approach of the whole scenario to be a charming way for two old friends to communicate. When I receive one of his electronic messages and I pull out my pen and ink to respond, the heart-warming subtext of the exchange seems to be, "I respect your choices and I'm glad you respect mine, and I'm so happy we're friends." Such statements risk sounding a bit sappy when stated outright, but the details of how we communicate can sometimes express them as well as words.

I was incredibly pleased when some of my lady-friends started responding to my letters with their own and missives started popping up in the post with increasing frequency. There is an intimacy to physical letters that cold pixels cannot match. They turn the mailbox from a hated messenger of junk and bills to a carrier dove that can deliver a friend's smile.

They can also deliver things that are far less pleasant. In 2013, I received a thick manila envelope stuffed with a rambling and ungrammatical piece of lengthy hate mail. The letter repeated "kill" a number of times and ordered both me and my husband to leave town, as well as stating that we had no right to be here. It is unfortunate that a society that ostensibly prides itself on diversity contains so many people who don't accept it.

Physical mail is an interesting example of a way in which the late nineteenth and very early twentieth centuries were actually significantly more advanced than the twenty-first. From the time that free mail delivery was authorized in US cities in 1863, "carriers were expected to make deliveries 'as frequently as the public convenience . . . shall require,' Monday through Saturday."[92] Big cities had several deliveries per day; by 1905, Baltimore and Philadelphia each had seven deliveries per day, most of New York City had nine, and Brooklyn had five. When Thomas E. Hill wrote advice on answering letters in 1891, he included sample letters as forms to follow for various situations. It is revealing that a number of his examples and their corresponding responses are marked with the exact same date, implying that they were received just a few hours after they were sent and answered by the next mail a short time afterward.[93] (I know plenty of people who can't manage this with email.)

Rapid delivery of mail was so taken for granted in big cities that residents of small towns seem to have been resentful that they did not enjoy the same perquisite—they had to be content with only getting their mail once a day. In an article in a Port Townsend newspaper in 1889, a journalist demanded two daily mails for the city in extremely strong terms. He declared that the unacceptable situation of only one delivery per day here had come about because "In an insane desire to reduce tariff and pile up a surplus in the United States treasury, the government has in recent years allowed the postal department to degenerate to the inefficient service of a beggarly nation." Washington wasn't even quite a state yet when the article went to press, yet its writer felt that the idea of a letter sometimes taking as many as three days to get from Port Townsend down to Portland, Oregon (209 miles away), was a sign of "how wretched our service has become."[94] One hundred and twenty-six years later, I'm very happy if the post office delivers a letter the same distance in so *little* a time! And of course if the mail proved insufficient in the nineteenth century, there was always the telegraph.

I'm often amused by the fact that the only way to make a twenty-first-century message travel as quickly as a nineteenth-century one is to send it by email.

No matter how slow the post office gets, though, physical objects do have advantages over their electronic equivalents. One interesting example of this is their ability to preserve and transmit incidental information. When Gabriel was in library school, one of his professors told a particularly interesting story about the sort of information that gets completely lost when something is digitized. The tale, as he told it, ran thus:

An archivist was monitoring the collection of a major institution when a researcher came in requesting a number of documents. The archivist found them in storage, noticed that they were letters from various places, and brought them out to the researcher without noticing anything extraordinary. The archivist returned to his desk, but soon he noticed the researcher behaving very strangely. The man would pick up a letter, check the date, hold it to his face and inhale deeply, then sort it into one of two piles he was stacking without reading it. When the piles had grown fairly high and the man still hadn't read a single letter, the archivist's curiosity finally got the better of him.

"What on Earth are you doing?" he asked.

The researcher looked up and smiled. He explained that he was an epidemiologist researching the history of a particular outbreak. At the time of the disease he was studying, letters out of quarantined areas would be disinfected with vinegar before being passed along in the post. The scent was still discernible many years later, and he was smelling for it to determine which letters merited further investigation. People would often specifically avoid mentioning outbreaks in their words; the text of the letter might be something as innocuous as "You'll be happy to know that our business is thriving!" In the context of an outbreak, however, those words can have very different implications. Digitizing the letters would have stripped them of this context and thus a significant portion of their meaning.

All people live surrounded by details they don't necessarily consider or even notice. Yet sometimes those seemingly trivial points provide the greatest insight into a situation.

Illustration of fruit from Mrs. Beeton's Book.

11

The Book of Household Management

"The world-wide renown of 'Household Management' is not at all surprising, even to those who are but slightly acquainted with its merits; but the present editors, who have carefully examined it line by line, page by page . . . cannot but express their unqualified admiration of the marvellous skill, care and labour bestowed on the work by Mrs. Beeton, and the thoroughness apparent in every detail."
—Preface to the 1893 edition of Mrs. Beeton's
The Book of Household Management[95]

Over the years, Gabriel and I have been ramping up the Victorian aspects of our home by a series of dares to each other. "What if we added this nineteenth-century element?" "What if we added that one?" In one of these lighthearted challenges, Gabriel bought me an 1893 copy of *The Book of Household Management* for our eleventh wedding anniversary. Later, in what was not exactly a countermove but was nonetheless related, I pressed for selling the electric refrigerator that came with our house, thus forcing us to use our period icebox.

Isabella Beeton's *The Book of Household Management* is known familiarly among historians as "Mrs. Beeton's Book." The volume's full title is of rather astounding length: *The Book of Household Management: Comprising Information for the Mistress, Housekeeper, Cook, Kitchen-Maid, Butler, Footman, Coachman, Valet, Parlour-Maid, Housemaid, Lady's-Maid, General Servant, Laundry-Maid, Nurse and Nursemaid, Monthly, Wet and Sick-nurse, Governess. Also Sanitary, Medical and Legal Memoranda. With a History of the Origin, Properties and Uses of all Things Connected with Home Life and Comfort.* It is not difficult to understand why this gets abbreviated.

Illustration of parrot pie from Mrs. Beeton's Book.

This pivotal work was an invaluable resource for women of the Victorian era. Covering every element of running a household, from the average wages of various servants to the proper way to cook a bible-length collection of recipes, Mrs. Beeton's was the ultimate go-to guide for busy Victorian women. Today it provides a plethora of fascinating insights into nineteenth-century life. Flipping through the pages, I could definitely see that the volume was intended for an audience who already had a firm grasp on the business of cookery. In Victorian parlance, it was the sort of book that made a good servant but a poor mistress. There are thousands of recipes in Mrs. Beeton's book and a person could hardly expect them all to be perfect. When I saw the recipes for Australian cooking, I couldn't resist bringing the book down to my Aussie friend Pippa's teashop. She agreed with me that the recipes for parrot pie (calling for "1 dozen paraqueets"[96]) and roast wallaby were best left untried.

As long as I used my good judgment, though, I found many of the recipes to be quite excellent. One of my particular favorites is Beeton's vanilla custard sauce[97]:

Vanilla Custard Sauce (To Serve with Puddings)

Ingredients.—1/2 pint of milk, 2 eggs, 2 oz. of sugar, 10 drops of essence of vanilla.

Mode.—Beat the eggs, sweeten the milk; stir these ingredients well together, and flavour them with the essence of vanilla, regulating the proportions of this latter ingredient by the strength of the essence, the size of the eggs, &c. Put the mixture into a small jug, place this jug in a saucepan of boiling water, and stir the sauce one way until it thickens; but do not allow it to boil, or it will instantly curdle. Serve in a boat or tureen separately, with plum, bread, or any kind of dry pudding. Essence of bitter almonds or lemon-rind may be substituted for the vanilla, when they are more in accordance with the flavor of the pudding with which the sauce is intended to be served.

Time.—To be stirred in the jug from 8 to 10 minutes.
Average cost, 4*d*.
Sufficient for 4 or 5 persons.
Seasonable at any time.

When Gabriel gave me a copy of Mrs. Beeton's Book I decided that a more nineteenth-century diet might be both interesting and educational. Reading the volume and doing other research into the matter, I was pleased to learn this would not involve much sacrifice. As *Good Housekeeping* said in 1889, "In these days of quick transportation there is a sort of millennium of all [food] products the year round."[98]

The first experiment in packing tropical oranges, plantains, bananas, and coconuts in ice and shipping them from Cuba to New England happened all the way back in 1816. Like many first experiments, it was unfortunately not very successful. Too little ice had been used, and most of the fruit arrived too rotten for sale.[99] However, by the 1880s, tropical fruit was relatively familiar to any Victorian household in a locality served by the refrigerated railroad cars of either of the two huge Chicago meat-packing companies, Armour and Swift. Bananas and other fruits that arrived in New Orleans via ships from South America would be loaded onto railroad cars to Chicago and from there dispersed to locales all over the United States.[100]

The specially designed refrigerated railroad cars (known colloquially as "reefers") that transported this tropical cornucopia trace their origins back to the 1840s.[101] Originally developed to transport milk and butter for sale to broader markets than their producers could reach locally, refrigerated railroad cars were "re-iced" at many of the same stations where the engines hauling them were refueled with coal and water. Ice was stored at the railroad depots next to these other vital supplies.[102] These cars were improved throughout the nineteenth century, and ice-cooling remained the standard in American railroad cars through the 1960s. Mechanically powered refrigerator cars (as opposed to ice-cooled ones) weren't invented until the 1950s and didn't replace their traditional ice-cooled counterparts in the United States until the 1970s. (The Whippany Railroad Museum in New Jersey still displays one of the old ice-cooling refrigerated railroad cars decommissioned in 1972.)[103]

Since tropical fruit was available in the nineteenth century, I didn't eliminate it from my diet altogether. I did, however, shift my attitude to thinking of it as more of a treat. Researching the history of food transportation made me contemplate more thoroughly just how far these delicacies were traveling to reach me—and made me appreciate them all the more.

The biggest shift to a more "Beeton approved" diet involved concentrating more on seasonal foods. Mrs. Beeton's charts of what is in season when were a great help in this. Grocery stores' produce aisles are stocked with such a diverse combination of items that at times it can be easy to forget what is truly at its peak of freshness versus what has been picked unripe and transported long distances. Mrs. Beeton's charts on when things are available and when they are "best and cheapest" helped sort out some of the confusion. Produce tastes better when it is in season—which is a big part of the impetus behind the modern trend in seasonal foods, although I do find it amusing that some people consider this a new idea.

People's relationships with their cooking spaces are as old as the cave-sheltered campfires of *Homo erectus*. (Evolutionary scientist Richard Wrangham theorizes that cooking actually allowed our anthropoid ancestors to evolve into modern humans in the first place, since cooking food relieves part of the burden of the digestive tract's labor and frees up more calories for developing bigger brains.)[104]

In the nineteenth century, the kitchen was the warm heart of the home, and at the same time the bastion of its queen. The very first line of Mrs. Beeton's Book reads, "As with the commander of an army, or the leader of an enterprise, so it is with the mistress of a house."[105] A woman's home was her domain to tend and control, and the kitchen was a particular guardroom of responsibility, both symbolically and in actual fact. "It must be remembered that . . . much of the family 'weal or woe,' as far as regards bodily health, depends upon the nature of the preparations concocted within its walls."[106] After all, proper nutrition influences not only our physical health but our emotional well-being, too. (Hungry people are seldom happy people.)

In the mid-twentieth century, designers and architects (most of them male) decided that comfortable kitchens were obsolete, so the room devoted to meal preparation shrank into cramped quarters. Unsurprisingly, since people still needed to eat, shrinking the kitchens made them more awkward, but no less important to daily life. In a study of modern, middle-class American families in the twenty-first century, a group of UCLA researchers likens a kitchen in a family home to a command center and documents it as "perhaps the most important space in daily family life: a site of frequent congregation, information exchange, collaboration, negotiation, and child socialization . . . a crucial hub of logistical organization and everyday operations . . ." In more than ninety percent of homes in the 2001 to 2005 study, "the small kitchens of [the 1940s through 1970] rank among the top three spaces used by family members. Indeed, the kitchen often ranks first."[107] Regardless of fads among architects, the kitchen is still the hub around which life turns in many households—and it is likely to remain so.

Gabriel brought home a metal-lined wooden icebox fairly soon after we moved to Port Townsend, but it took us a couple of years to actually commit to using this Victorian cooling cupboard for its intended purpose. There was never any question that we would store our food in it eventually; Gabriel bought it for use, not just to look pretty in the kitchen.

The size and layout of iceboxes varied widely between manufacturers. Our particular example is fifty-four inches tall (its top is a handbreadth below my shoulder), thirty-three inches wide, and twenty inches deep. Its exterior is oak; combined with the metal lining this makes it (as my grandmother would have said) "heavy as sin." Getting it maneuvered into the kitchen when Gabriel brought it home was rather a Herculean task, but luckily once it was in place there was little reason to move it further.

It has four doors, each with a latch that Gabriel had to replace. The top right-hand door opens directly into the ice compartment; the lower food compartment is the coldest (non-ice holding) portion of the appliance and has two doors; and the warmest section of the appliance is accessed by a door to the left of the ice compartment. At the bottom of the icebox there is a long, swinging hatch to allow access to the drip tray that collects meltwater from the ice. The original drip tray is long gone—doubtless fallen prey to a World War II metal drive. Gabriel made a replacement by ordering a large pan from a baking supply company and gluing wheels to the bottom. The original tube that had drained the ice compartment had also been removed long ago, so Gabriel replaced it with a bicycle tube. (Everyone's interactions with the world are influenced by what they're familiar with. Gabriel has worked with bikes since before we met, so bicycles infiltrate a wide variety of things in our life, sometimes in unorthodox ways.)

When we moved into our house, a 1980s-era electric refrigerator was one of the very few possessions the previous owners left behind besides their mountain of years-old trash in the backyard. Not expecting the electric fridge to be long for this world, we did extensive research into the history of food preservation and what would be involved in recommissioning our icebox.

Technically, the term *refrigerator* referred to iceboxes long before the electric type were invented. Any writers who want to try their pens at historical fiction should be aware that refrigerator was the preferred term for the ice-chilled cooling boxes in the nineteenth century.[108] To avoid confusion, though, in this narrative I'll use the term *icebox* to refer to our Victorian food chilling unit and *electric refrigerator* to refer to the modern type.

People have been using ice to chill their foods and beverages since the dawn of civilization. Ancient Mesopotamians sold ice in settlements along the Euphrates River four thousand years ago.[109] For thousands of years, ice was brought down from hills and mountains for use at warmer elevations; and in lowlands it was cut out of ponds and rivers during cold months and stored in specially constructed icehouses (usually underground) for use in the summer. The first really large trade in frozen water on a global scale began in the early nineteenth century, when an enterprising New Englander began shipping ice as ballast in ships bound for the West Indies. His first shipment of this cold commodity landed in Martinique on January 10, 1806, and pioneered an industry that would expand throughout the nineteenth century.

Some house-icebox systems in the nineteenth century were set up with a hole in the house that perfectly fit a hole with a grate over it in the icebox, so that in the winter people could just open the doors to the two holes and let the cold directly into where the food was. (They closed them in summer, of course.) Gabriel and I discussed this idea briefly, but decided chopping holes in the house might be something we would regret later.

By our favorite period of the 1880s and '90s, Americans had long ceased considering ice a luxury and had been considering it a necessity of life for decades.[110] It was delivered from door to door by men driving special wagons, in precisely the way that milk and other heavy commodities such as kerosene were delivered. In the summer of 1894, the *Port Townsend Leader* advertised that Edward's market was selling blocks of ice for one cent per pound and delivering them free of charge anywhere in the city.[111]

Because icemen were necessarily strong and came right into women's kitchens to deliver their product, bawdy jokes about icemen were fairly common. A popular one ran along the general lines of, "That baby doesn't look like anyone in your family—but he looks like the iceman!" Similar remarks were made about milkmen.

The infrastructure involved in the frozen water trade was enormous. The connections and interconnections that allowed a block of ice that had originally frozen in a New England lake to cool food half a world away was incredibly complicated; nearly as much so as the connections that now allow oil drilled in Alaska to power motorcars around the globe. But this infrastructure has entirely vanished. Artificially created ice made natural harvests on winter lakes obsolete in the early twentieth century. As private ownership of electric refrigerators became commonplace, icemen lost their employment and their service vanished from the American landscape.

Gabriel and I didn't necessarily require our ice to originate in a frozen lake, but we did need ice from somewhere to make our icebox function. Without an iceman to make regular deliveries, this was a challenge. If we were acting in a BBC series or a so-called "reality television" program, the production company orchestrating the scenario would doubtless hire someone to artificially fill the role of an iceman. Our lives being actual reality, however, we were on our own.

Iceboxes are designed to be refrigerated by hard ice—ice chilled to a significantly lower temperature than the soft ice sold in blocks at grocery stores. The companies producing hard ice in the twenty-first century are precious few and exceedingly far between. In Ohio, the Millersburg Ice Company sells hard ice chilled to 12 degrees Fahrenheit and delivers it to nearby Amish communities.[112] However, Ohio to Washington State is not a viable delivery range.

In most cases when my husband and I can't find a Victorian item locally, we can often track down some equivalent elsewhere. However, unlike fabric or feathers, ice was not a commodity we could order for shipment through the mail. Moreover, the very nature of the situation meant that we would need it quite regularly.

We asked all the local fish suppliers about hard ice and even telephoned the companies that supplied the fish companies and grocery stores, but only encountered dead ends. No one sold hard ice. Furthermore, no one would deliver ice of any sort—hard or soft—to a private residence. Brainstorming possible solutions, we even toyed with the idea of running the icebox on dry ice and got curious enough to try it once. As a cooling technique it worked admirably, but its cost made it impractical for regular use. Besides, it was certainly not authentic, so we simply chalked it up as an interesting experiment.

For three years, we kept searching for hard ice while we waited for our electric refrigerator to expire. We honestly hadn't expected the fridge to last six months (or a year at the very most), so its obstinate refusal to die seemed perversely frustrating.

When we had exhausted every possible line of inquiry regarding hard ice in the Port Townsend area, we finally adopted a "damn the torpedoes" approach to the matter. We decided to fill the icebox with soft ice from the grocery store and see how things went. A significant number of people who live on boats in coastal areas ("live aboards") keep their food fresh with soft ice in coolers, so it wasn't a terribly strange idea, even if it was technologically inferior to the way things were done in the nineteenth century. We knew that soft ice would melt significantly faster than the hard ice used by the Victorians. Since it was all that was available to us, though, we decided to make do with it.

Like someone who takes a series of deep breaths to brace themselves before jumping into an icy lake, we worked up to the switchover gradually. By the time we started using the icebox for food, we had already shifted to a far more Victorian diet. For a full year before we made the switch, there hadn't been much in our freezer beyond ice cube trays; and the truly perishable contents of the fridge were at a minimum. Gabriel had a bit of lunch meat, I had milk and butter, and we shared cheeses. Our various condiments and our vegetables probably didn't need refrigeration at all, strictly speaking, so we weren't terribly worried about them.

We filled the ice compartment with six ten-pound blocks of ice (the biggest we could buy) and hoped for the best. We moved the condiments and vegetables first, putting them in the upper left-hand section of the ice box since that was the warmest compartment. Eggs, butter, and cheese went in the medium-temperature section in the lower left-hand portion of the ice box. We reasoned that since cold sinks and heat rises, we should put the milk and meat below the ice, and at first that was exactly what we did. After we had been doing this a few weeks, though, Gabriel's grandmother mentioned in a letter that when her family used an icebox, they had put the meat directly on the ice itself. Gabriel immediately moved his meat up to the ice compartment and was quite happy with the result. I wanted to do the same with my milk and the cream I drink with my tea but I had one concern with this idea. Since most milk products are sold in waxed cardboard cartons now, I worried that the dampness of the ice would slowly compromise the integrity of the containers. The cartons were obviously waterproof on the inside, since that was where the milk was, but I didn't trust them to be quite as impermeable to liquid working its way in from the outside over the course of several days. Despite ice's notoriously slick nature, impurities often give it abrasive edges and I could easily imagine these rough spots wearing holes in the cartons, which all-around dampness would exacerbate. I had no desire to contemplate what a huge mess would be created by a half-gallon of milk seeping all over the inside of the ice compartment.

There is one local dairy that still sells their products in glass bottles; their milk comes from Jersey cows and is absolutely amazing. Unfortunately, it is also one of the more expensive brands on the market and is rarely in our budget. I usually only buy it on special occasions like my birthday or holidays. So I came up with a compromise: I bought the amazing milk once when we first started using the icebox—one half-gallon, one pint. Now, whenever I buy milk or cream in cartons, I pour it into the glass containers as soon as I get home.* When I was thus able to start putting my milk directly on the ice, I was charmed to see that this method actually kept it colder than the old electric fridge had.

When we sold our electric refrigerator, we talked about it being somewhat like Cortés's destruction of his ships upon reaching the New World: there was no turning back now. We were committed to our course of action.

---

* I scald the bottles between refills to prevent any bacteria buildup. Admittedly, scalding glass takes a bit of care. Once when it was too cold in the kitchen, the boiling water cracked the glass bottle and I had to buy a new one. I'll confess that I didn't really mind too much, since it gave me an excuse to buy the exceptional milk.

It proved remarkably easy, although we do go through a lot of ice. Along with the constant ticking of our mechanical clocks, occasional clunks were added to the sounds of our home when blocks of melting ice settled themselves into new positions. We usually put sixty pounds of ice in the compartment to fill it (we can cram in seventy if we really try), and since soft ice isn't very cold, it melts quickly and the box wants refilling about twice a week in the summer, once in the winter. This adds up, and in months when the budget is particularly tight, we'll eat up our perishables then go a week or two without ice. It's extremely easy to tell when this is going to happen; since we watch the ice supply shrinking, we can anticipate the situation clearly. It's not like electricity or many other modern commodities that come from a black hole, are tallied in a black hole, and suddenly demand payment in the form of an enigmatic bill.

We've only been caught in a situation where a perishable outlasted the ice a couple of times. It's always milk, so I simply do what people throughout history have been doing when they found themselves with too much milk to drink before it would go bad at room temperature: I made cheese out of it and salted it heavily. It's all part of the learning experience.

I honestly wouldn't be surprised if similarly ice-frugal behavior occurred in poorer households in the nineteenth and early twentieth centuries, even though ice was cheaper then as well as more effective (being colder, hard ice). This might seem ironic, but it's a case of supply and demand. In the late nineteenth century, ice was considered a necessity of life; people demanded that the product be good and prices be affordable. A huge public demand meant that suppliers could rely on bulk sales to keep prices down. Now, suppliers treat even soft block ice almost as a novelty, and it's priced accordingly.

There is no longer an iceman to deliver the cold commodity in Port Townsend, so Gabriel buys it on his way home from work at a large grocery store at the halfway point of his commute from work and transports it home in a cooler. We've developed a routine around refilling the ice compartment. When I see Gabriel drive up, I run out and we each take one side of the cooler holding our sixty pounds of ice. We carry it into the kitchen and Gabriel takes the milk, cream, and meats out of the ice compartment while I start cutting open the plastic bags that ice is sold in now. The remainder of the ice that is already in the ice box has, of course, always melted to an amorphous shape; Gabriel takes it out as well so that he can stack the new blocks neatly on top of each other. As he lifts each block, I pull off its bag and consolidate any shards or fragments of ice; then he refills the ice compartment with the amorphous lumps of ice and the foods that he had taken out earlier while I throw the bags away. It's a fun little task that brings us closer together since it requires so much coordination.

Even after we jettisoned our electric refrigerator, one item remained in our kitchen that sheer necessity made us tolerate: the electric stove. I often considered setting up my own version of the jars used in some offices and homes to discourage obscenities: Instead of imposing a fine for swearing, I would demand a contribution from everyone who asked why we don't have a wood-burning stove yet. If everyone who asked that question put five dollars in the jar, I'm sure we would have a wood-burning stove by now instead of an ongoing frustration with the electric stove that came with our house. We must have something to cook our food, though, and the item serves a function until we can replace it.

People see stoves every day and take them for granted, so they tend to forget what complex pieces of technology they are. Individuals who would never dream of buying a used car that had been sitting around rusting for thirty, forty, or fifty years somehow manage to overlook the inherent absurdity of asking why we simply can't use a stove that's been neglected more than twice that long. Restoring an antique stove from the ground up is a professional skill that takes years to master; it's an expertise we don't possess ourselves.

Almost as soon we moved to Port Townsend, we started a special savings fund specifically to buy an appropriate antique stove that had been refurbished by someone who (unlike us) knew what they were doing. Like everything in life, though, it's a project that will take time. Meanwhile I'll keep making faces at the electric anachronism in my kitchen and dreaming of how much more educational (and fun!) cooking will be when I have a stove to match my cookbooks.

Advertisement for meat grinder, 1893.

12

An Exotic Flavor

"Every family has its favorite list of pickles and sauces . . ."
—*Good Housekeeping*, 1893[113]

It's interesting to note that certain ancient customs like pickling are far more a part of ongoing, everyday life in some cultures than others.

Many twenty-first century Americans seem to view home food preservation more as an eccentric hobby than as a life skill, and for a while I had dismally little luck in finding an instructor. Any time I considered diving into the operation on my own without help, I could only imagine two possible outcomes: either an entire room full of spoiled food, or my own death by botulism. I experienced a stroke of good fortune when a friend (a sweet Korean lady whom I'd been helping to study English) asked if there was anything about Korean culture she could teach me.

"Would you show me how to make kimchi?" I asked excitedly. Food preservation from a culture where the tradition was still alive and current! My mind raced at the opportunity.

She looked surprised. "Sure—no problem!"

When the big day arrived, Estar came to my house with a whole carload full of Korean groceries in tow, a large, cheerful red bowl, and a blender. I made a mental note that I would have to acquire a sausage grinder if I were to repeat this exercise on my own—sausage grinders being the Victorian equivalent of blenders.*

Estar is a professional photographer, so she also brought her camera and tripod in the hopes of getting some shots that might be suitable to submit

___
* I had been meaning to buy one for a while, but I so seldom have occasion to purée my food that up until this point it had never occupied a high-enough priority to squeeze it into my perpetually small budget. I realized that I would now have a reason to push it higher up my list.

to collections of stock photography images. While she was engaged in doing something enigmatic and mysterious with the complicated digital camera apparatus, I looked on the large pile of Napa cabbage she had brought.

"Should I start chopping things?" I asked. It was a total stab in the dark as to what I should be doing. I had no idea what was involved in making kimchi, but when faced with large sections of cabbage, chopping it into smaller sections seemed like a reasonable idea. I felt that I should be doing something while she was setting up her camera, and attempting to "help" with a complicated electronic device about which I knew absolutely nothing could have only ended badly. Cameras are fragile and expensive. There was a limit to how badly I could mess up a cabbage.

"Yes, go ahead!" Estar nodded encouragingly. She gave me lots of kind smiles and compliments that I'm sure I didn't deserve as I turned the large pile of big cabbage sections into an even larger pile of small cabbage pieces. I am invariably amused by the physical mechanics involved with preparing food— the way that some foods shrink in size when chopped while others increase drastically. If I ever come to comprehend the physics of this, I think I'll apply for a job at a shipping factory.

After a while Estar nibbled one of the pieces of cabbage and instructed me to do the same. "Wait, wait!" she said suddenly while I lifted a chunk of a floppy yellow leaf to my lips. She ran over to her camera and tripod. "Okay, now!" she directed, poised for action.

I smiled and popped the cabbage into my mouth. It was less crisp than I had expected, and—what surprised me even more—already salty. Estar explained that she had soaked the cabbage sections in saltwater the night before, then run them through two rinses of freshwater. "It starts the—" She paused, searching for the English word she wanted. "Kimchi is a—" She stopped short again, looking to me for linguistic help. "—It's a kind of food that you need to do this," she said, her brow furrowed in concentration as she searched for a term that seemed to be on the tip of her tongue.

I tried to think of a term that might be applicable. *What would a food be required to do overnight?* "Ferment?" I guessed.

Estar's face lit up. "Yes, that's right! Kimchi is a ferment food!" She popped the lid off the little blender she had brought and showed me the contents: about a handful of cooked brown rice. She explained that the rice provided special bacteria to help the fermentation process.

I was surprised that no vinegar was going into the kimchi; I had assumed that anything pickled would have vinegar in it, but apparently that's not the case.

I was far more surprised by the next two ingredients that went into our recipe: a dried persimmon and three-fourths of a fresh green pear. Estar explained that these ingredients were for sweetness, and they went into the blender with the rice. Pondering the matter later, I started to put my friend's comment about sweetness together with her information about the rice providing some of the bacterial starter culture for the fermentation process. Considered in that light, the fruit seemed analogous to the pinch of sugar that gets added to yeast in bread-making to start the rising process.

After the rice and fruits had been run through the blender along with a few garlic cloves, Estar added a copious quantity of dried ginger, blended the mixture some more, and poured the resultant orange sauce over our mix of brined cabbage and fresh vegetables (daikon, Korean watercress, and onion). She had me fetch a spoon and measure out sea salt. I sprinkled what I thought was a rather liberal amount over the vegetables and looked nervously at Estar, afraid I might be over-salting the mixture. She giggled at my trepidation. "More, please!" she commanded with a smile.

Time after time, I plunged my tablespoon into the large bag of salt and poured white crystals over the salad-like mixture, growing more and more nervous as I did so. (The cabbage, after all, had already been pre-salted before we started.) Each time, Estar just laughed at my uncertainty and repeated her

Photo—and kimchi lesson!—courtesy Estar Hyo Gyung Choi, Mary Studio.

cheerful, "More, please!" After a while, she started joking by adopting the high-pitched tone she used to playfully mimic her young daughter. "More salt, please!"

After I had added what seemed to me to be enough salt to dehydrate a small whale, I started to understand why vinegar wasn't necessary. Salt is probably humanity's oldest food preservative. Around the year 2800 BC, salted fish was a major export involved in the economy of ancient Egypt, and salt historian Mark Kurlansky calls salt a "bacteria slayer."[114] Adding acid as well would have been overkill.

We added pungent chili powder, then mixed everything together with our hands. (We tasted it along the way and Estar snapped a number of additional pictures.) That was all there was to it. I was even more surprised to realize there hadn't been any cooking involved than I had been to learn that vinegar was unnecessary. Again, the quantity of salt (probably enough to model an entire limb from the biblical Lot's wife) provides the explanation. Salt breaks down protein in much the same way that heat does,[115] so we were essentially cooking our vegetables by a chemical process. We packed the salad-like kimchi into containers, and Estar explained that it would settle and take up less space as the salt forced water out of the various vegetables and created flavorful juice.

After Estar left, I ransacked my cabinets for jars to store all the kimchi. As I put away my trove, I reflected on how good it was for me to be reminded that history is not limited to America alone.

13

Our Daily Bread

"In our own times, and among civilised peoples, bread has become
an article of food of the first necessity; and properly so, for it constitutes
of itself a complete life-sustainer, the gluten, fibrin, fat, phosphates,
starch and sugar, which it contains, representing all the necessary
classes of food. There is too little fat and too little flesh-former
if used as a sole article of food . . . The finest, wholesomest, and
most savoury bread is made from wheaten flour."
—*The Book of Household Management*, p. 1081[116]

It is difficult to overemphasize the role played by bread in the Victorian household. It was an absolute staple, and a standard daily prayer beseeched God,
"Give us this day our daily bread." Bread was life, and sustenance, and pride, all
rolled into one vital source of nourishment. It might come from a local bakery
or be produced within an individual household, but it must be present. In *The
Book of Household Management*, Mrs. Beeton recommended a daily ration of
one pound of bread for every person in a household.[117] She cautioned that in
households where more than this is used, some wastage is likely to be occurring,
and the fact that Beeton felt this caveat to be necessary is a telling commentary
on what a large percentage of people's diet bread represented. A full pound of
bread is a considerable amount; it's equivalent to an entire loaf. In Britain at
the time Mrs. Beeton was writing, this wasn't just a rule of thumb but an actual
law. The Bread Act of 1822 had mandated that loaves sold in Britain weigh one
pound or a multiple thereof.

In the late nineteenth century, there was a bakery down the street from
our house; there is still one in virtually the same location. For any business to survive, people have to pay for its services, so clearly an appreciable
number of individuals in this neighborhood were buying their bread instead

Image courtesy Estar Hyo Gyung Choi, Mary Studio.

of making it, even as early as the 1890s. This makes sense, since the census records for the area show numbers of unattached men (and a few women) renting single rooms; people in such situations are less likely to have the time or inclination to bake for themselves. Even if they had wanted to bake their own bread, their situation might not have allowed it; many of these renters lodged in single rooms within family dwellings, and their access to the family kitchen was doubtless restricted. This is often still the case when families take in lodgers, but a Victorian woman was far more territorial about her kitchen than her modern counterpart. The kitchen was *her* domain as much as a manager's office was his. Even her own husband might not be welcome there. A February 1889 *Good Housekeeping* article about "A Man In the Kitchen" asserts:

> Most women heartily despise a "Betty," by which is usually meant a man who pokes his nose into the details of household affairs, dabbles in the work of the kitchen and irritates the housewife by assuming, regularly or occasionally, functions which she deems exclusive to herself. The dislike of women for this kind of man is well-grounded. The average man is unfortunately unable to make himself useful in household work, without making himself, also, more or less of a nuisance . . . The genuine "Betty" is a genuine meddler, whose zeal is without knowledge, whose helpfulness is without discretion and whose officiousness and conceit neutralize what might be useful in his makeup. Womankind is excusable for detesting him.[118]

So, no lodgers in the kitchen.

Yet American women with their own homes often saw breadmaking as a sacred duty, as well as a mark of economic prudence. Another 1889 *Good Housekeeping* article advised:

> The economical housewife has no need for [the baker's] services except in an emergency. One dollar's worth of flour will make twenty loaves of bread, while the same number from the bakery will cost one dollar and sixty cents. The saving is not alone in money. Home-made bread (it need never be anything but good) is more nutritious, more substantial, and "goes further" than the best baker's loaves. It is the cheapest of foods and, when good, will make an ordinary, perhaps scanty, meal satisfying and appetizing.[119]

Even in the best of households, though, the bread sometimes failed. Yeast is a finicky organism. As Mrs. Beeton said, "Extremes of cold and heat kill it, and a temperature that it does not like prevents it from growing actively . . ."[120] When a failure of fungal alchemy prevented the standard bread from rising—or if a busy schedule simply prevented the mistress of a house from setting her bread to rise in time for supper—there were a number of other options in the late Victorian kitchen. Baking-powder biscuits were a particularly popular choice of quick bread in the summer, since they didn't necessarily require firing up an entire wood oven—they could be cooked on a much smaller oil stove. Graham gems (which are similar to biscuits but made with coarser graham flour) were thought to be so easy that even a man could manage them![121] Muffins, popovers, buns, and various sorts of breakfast cakes were all perennially popular. In America, there were so many different recipes for corn bread and its cousins sometimes a person gets the impression that hardly any two localities made this classic in precisely the same way. (Mrs. Beeton's recipe for American bread is, in fact, a type of corn bread.)

And of course, if all else failed, there was always the local bakery to fall back on.

Nineteenth-century writings about bread-making range from texts that seem virtually religious in tone to stories that are outright comic. In 1889, writer Pauline Adelaide Hardy used bread-making as a metaphor for the formation of personality:

> I thought what a comfort it is to mould something to one's own liking, if it is only bread, and what strength is needed, not only of arm, but of purpose also, to make even the few attempts which we are daily making to mould our own characters to anything near a semblance of what we have wished it to be; for we continually show by our daily life what we are making and have made of ourselves.
>
> It makes no difference how much flour and water there is in bread, there is always some rising. With many this good quality has little effect unless carefully nurtured, while in another it makes its way through every obstacle. Perhaps the material was poor to begin with, or there was careless sifting by those who had control, that is, the correcting of the bad and encouraging of the good; but as everything in nature proceeds from the general to the special, so I fell to meditating on the similarity of character between bread and people . . .[122]

One of my favorite comic bread articles (which left me shaking with laughter the first few times I read it) is an 1890 *Good Housekeeping* piece. In "Buried Bread: How It First Rose and Then Fell, To Rise Again," a young woman admits that when she was married she "knew no more about cooking than this Persian kitten here in my lap." When she tries to bake bread, a number of callers continually interrupt her until she rushes to the kitchen and sees that her bread dough "had evidently made a frantic rush for the ceiling, but foiled in that scheme had revenged itself by running all over the edges of the tins, on to the table, from which it was fast traveling towards the floor." She is so disappointed with her disastrous bread dough that she buries it in the garden. Unfortunately, although the dough is defunct, the yeast within it isn't quite dead yet. When the outside temperature rises and the mass expands outward and upward from its burial plot, the failed baker's husband comes into the house quizzically remarking on a queer new fungus he has found in the yard![123]

Thankfully, none of my early experiments in bread-making were quite that disastrous—although admittedly over the years some of them have been pretty bad. A particular one that causes giggles every time I mention it to Gabriel is the incident of the rye-brick.

My first forays into bread-making involved focaccia bread when I was in high school, then again as a freshman in college. When I met Gabriel (and before learning that he really doesn't like focaccia bread), I tried making some for him. His response to this was to tell me that one of his favorite foods was rye bread—"without any white flour in it!"

I expressed some rather extreme doubts about the feasibility of this food product, because every rye bread recipe I had ever seen involved quite a substantial amount of wheat flour. (Rye is very heavy on its own.) If I had possessed a copy of Mrs. Beeton's Book back then I might have quoted a line from it: "Everybody knows that wheat flour yields the best bread. Rye-bread is viscous, hard, less easily soluble by the gastric juice and not so rich in nutritive power."[124]

Gabriel (who baked very little) assured me that all I would have to do would be to directly substitute rye flour for all of the wheat flour in any bread recipe, and the result would be delicious bread, "just the way I like it!"

I was nineteen at the time, and like any other besotted teenage girl, I was desperately eager to please the object of my affections. I didn't argue the point, but set to work producing the desired loaf.

The result was barely chewable when it emerged hot from the oven. By the time it cooled, it seemed significantly more resistant to fire, flood, or earthquakes than my dormitory's concrete walls. After a brief discussion, Gabriel and I both decided that this rye-brick was more appropriate food for crows than for humans. I carried the slab to the balcony of my eighth-floor dormitory apartment, expecting that a fall from that height would smash it to crumbs.

I peered over the edge to make sure no one was below me; I didn't want to drop the hardened mass onto someone's head and make a murderess of myself. After verifying that the concrete walkway below was clear, I dropped the rye-brick over the side of the balcony. Down, down, it plummeted—past the seventh floor, the sixth, the fifth . . . Nearly a hundred feet below, and traveling somewhere around eighty feet per second, the rye-brick finally hit the ground—and didn't break.

Despite an eight-story drop onto concrete, the rye-brick maintained its integrity. One of my roommates inspected the situation and expressed surprise that the stones of the walkway itself remained unscathed.

I didn't try making any wheat-free loaves for a while after that.

After the incident of the rye-brick I went back to making focaccia for a while, but I was still in college and my student budget deeply resented the strain I was putting upon it with all the olive oil I was buying. I knew there were breads baked all over the world without involving any oil or fat at all, but no matter how I tried, I could never make a loaf turn out entirely to my satisfaction. When I went home from school for a long weekend, I asked my grandmother to teach me how to bake bread. I pictured a Rockwellian idyll where she would impart some great wisdom of the ages. I imagined how in future years I would wax nostalgic over the day my grandmother taught me the secret of bread. Instead, she dug around for a few minutes in the bottom of an old desk and brought out a 1956 Betty Crocker cookbook. She handed the volume to me and promptly returned to her soap opera.

I regarded the book with slight surprise. "Don't you have any advice for me?" I asked bemusedly.

"There's a good recipe in there," she assured me, and this statement composed the entirety of her instruction. I went back to my experiments.

Through trial and error I was eventually able to produce loaves that suited me tolerably well, that Gabriel was willing to eat, and that (unlike the rye-brick) couldn't double as building materials or bludgeons. Bread-making became a casual activity for me over the years; a hobby to be taken or set aside as the fancy struck me. When we moved into our Victorian home, I decided it was time to get serious.

Since I had been baking bread for years already when I stepped up to the role of baker-in-ordinary for our house, the manufacture of this staple didn't pose much of a problem. The rye-brick incident was over a decade in the past and by now I could bake a good loaf fairly easily. The problem was that I was producing too many of them. Homemade bread lacks the artificial preservatives that give store-bought American bread a disconcertingly long shelf-life, so to keep fresh bread in the cupboard I had to bake a new loaf every other day or so. The work itself was not an issue—I very much enjoy baking and am happy to do it as often as necessary! The problem was that we couldn't always finish one loaf before it went stale and wanted replacement. I tried baking smaller loaves, but they were inconvenient for the sandwiches Gabriel prefers. (Also, they went stale even faster than the full-sized bread.) I kept up my fresh bread production, but the old ends of stale loaves started to accumulate.

At first this wasn't a hardship. I simply took down my trusty copy of Mrs. Beeton's Book and looked for recipes based around stale bread. Numerous people had shared my problem in Mrs. Beeton's day and her book has a large number of suggestions. (My personal favorites are Welsh rarebit and bread pudding.) No matter how well-prepared or how deliciously disguised though, eating stale bread at every meal does lose its appeal after a while.

I couldn't blame Gabriel for not wanting stale bread on his sandwiches. Yet one morning as I took a fresh loaf out of the oven and set it in the middle of piles of dried crusts, I let out a deep sigh. The loaf was beautifully brown and smelled delicious right at that moment, yet it seemed doomed to be only partially eaten before being added to the pile of rusks. Then an idea occurred to me.

"Hey—" I said to Gabriel as he entered the kitchen. "You're visiting your mom tonight, aren't you?"

"Yeah." Gabriel nodded.

"Do you think she'd like some of this bread?" I asked. "The fresh stuff, I mean, not the pile o' rusks."

Gabriel looked surprised, then pleased. "Probably. It would save her from buying any from the bakery by her house."

I cut off two slices for Gabriel's lunch sandwich, then wrapped the rest of the loaf in waxed paper for his mom. Looking at the pile of crusts on my counter, I knew that I would still be eating Welsh rarebit for both lunch and dinner that day, but at least this would give me a chance to make a dent in the stale bread supply before I augmented it again.

A couple days later, Gabriel reported on his mom's reaction to the bread. "She loved it!" he told me proudly. "She said it's better than what she can buy at the bakery and asked if she could have some on a regular basis."

Eureka! I grinned at my husband. "As much as she likes!"

Now I supply Gabriel's mom with bread as well as making it for us, which lets me bake a fresh loaf every two days or so without things getting out of hand.

Getting dressed in front of our antique armoire. Image courtesy Estar Hyo Gyung Choi, Mary Studio.

Fixing my hair. Image courtesy Estar Hyo Gyung Choi, Mary Studio.

Antique bowl and pitcher.

My chatelaine. The tools, from left to right, are: book-shaped pincushion, aide-memoire embossed with stylized orchids, walnut-shaped thimble holder, book-shaped vesta, embroidery scissors, and sheath.

Tiny gears inside Gabriel's watch. Image courtesy Estar Hyo Gyung Choi, Mary Studio.

Opening the parlor door. The morning light is shining through the flash glass in the outer door. Image courtesy Estar Hyo Gyung Choi, Mary Studio.

Lighting the Perfection kerosene heater. Image courtesy Estar Hyo Gyung Choi, Mary Studio.

Gabriel sitting by the Perfection heater and reading to me from an antique cycling magazine while I sew. Image courtesy Estar Hyo Gyung Choi, Mary Studio.

Filling my fountain pen with an eye dropper. Image courtesy Estar Hyo Gyung Choi, Mary Studio.

Thimbleberries. Image courtesy Estar Hyo Gyung Choi, Mary Studio.

Berry picking. Image courtesy Estar Hyo Gyung Choi,
Mary Studio.

Close up of the vasculum in the picture on the left.

Photo of two children, circa 1890s. The boy has a small, painted vasculum.

Collecting fossils with my vasculum.

Gabriel and his Wheel, by Frances Gace. Image courtesy Fracis Gace.

Modeling Perugini's *In the Orangerie*. Image courtesy Elizabeth Ogle.

Modeling Manet's *Nan*. Image courtesy Francis Gace.

Gabriel after crossing Deception Pass.

My trusty steed of steel! Image courtesy Tanya Pilant.

14

Chestnut Shrapnel, "Pure Evil," and A Few Sweet Delights

"Now, any woman who has struggled with old-time cookery books and careless recipes will heartily sympathize with these poor novices. Most of us, however capable . . . have known what it is to spoil materials, and retire from the kitchen with an aching head and back."
—Catherine Owen, 1889[125]

One of my most amusing cooking incidents involved that beloved classic of Christmas carols: roast chestnuts.

Humanity's connection to the chestnut tree is very, very old. In Genesis 30:37, Jacob takes rods from chestnut trees and places them by the place where his father-in-law Laban's livestock come to drink.* In Victorian literature, Charles Dickens's Scrooge peers in at the Cratchit family and sees them roasting a shovelful of chestnuts on their fire after dinner. In 1881, a periodical edited by Dickens reported, "One of the most welcome signs of winter is the appearance, at stray nooks and corners of the streets, of the roast chestnut vendor . . . The roast chestnut has a peculiar charm of its own, and during the first weeks of winter not many persons are able to withstand the temptations held out by its attractive appearance, its appetizing perfume, its cheery warmth, and its strengthening and fortifying powers. It must be remembered that though the chestnut—the 'poor man's truffle' as it has been called—is always considered as belonging to the working-classes, as a matter of fact its flavour is and always has been keenly relished by the upper classes . . ."[126]

---

* Some biblical scholars quibble over whether this was actually the same chestnut tree we know today. Whether it truly grew in Biblical Palestine or not, *Castanea sativa*—sweet chestnut—was definitely known to the ancient Romans. Valuing it highly for both food and timber, they spread it throughout their empire.

Unfortunately chestnuts are rather difficult to find in modern America, since a fungal blight wiped out most of the chestnut trees in this country in the early twentieth century. (Horse chestnuts are still fairly plentiful but produce a less desirable nut.) They remain fairly common in other parts of the world, and I had enjoyed them immensely when I had traveled abroad in both France and Japan. One holiday season Gabriel found some at a grocery specializing in Asian foods in Seattle's International District and brought them home for me. My mouth watered when I saw them.

I put the chestnuts in my great-grandmother's cast-iron skillet and slipped them into the hot oven to roast, thinking I would have them as a sort of appetizer before dinner. I prepared my kale and my mushrooms, set them on the stove, and settled down at the kitchen table with my diary and my fountain pen to write a bit while my dinner cooked.

I had no real idea how long the chestnuts should roast, since I had never prepared them before. In Kyoto, I had bought them prepackaged, wrapped up in little paper sacks sold at the train station, and once from a Japanese pushcart vendor like the ones who also sold roast purple sweet potatoes or baked cakes with sweet fillings. In Paris, the chestnut sellers had roasted the nuts over fires in large metal drums, turning the delicious-smelling treats over and over again with soot-dusted fingers while shouting, "*Des marrones! Des marrones! Des marrones!*" The mouthwatering treats had had decorative cross-hatches cut into their shells. At least, I thought they were decorative.

As I sat writing and absorbed in my diary, the smell of my dinner mingling with the rose-scented ink in my pen, I was suddenly started out of my concentration by a noise like a gunshot. After a brief moment of astonishment I realized that one of my chestnuts must have burst. No sooner did this thought pop into my mind than I heard another gunshot-loud explosion.

Judging that I had best get my chestnuts away from the heat before I lost them all, I opened the oven door. I was astonished by what I saw.

I was prepared to see a couple of chestnuts with cracked shells resting comfortably among their intact brethren. Instead, I saw that all six sides of the oven's interior were covered with a fine, clinging powder resembling nothing so much as tawny snow. I yanked the skillet of chestnuts out of the oven and set it briefly on top of the stove as I marveled at the mess inside. Then it occurred to me that I had best get the remaining chestnuts away from all heat—including the pan holding them. I poured them onto a plate by the sink, then covered the lot with an upside-down bowl.

I felt immensely smug at what I saw as my brilliant foresight about that bowl. I reasoned that if any more chestnuts exploded from the heat remaining within them, the mess would be contained within the bowl and might (I prided myself on my own cleverness) even still be edible. It would, after all, be contained within a hygienic environment.

I was soon to have a good laugh at my own expense over the naive nature of that plan.

I had just turned to examine the astonishingly unidentifiable residue of the former chestnuts coating inside of my oven when yet another shot rang out behind me. I whirled around in time to see the bowl thrown high into the air and come spinning downward. It landed with a resounding crash just as yet another—final—chestnut blew itself into oblivion. The remains snowed down on me and everything else in the kitchen. Later I found fragments of chestnut shrapnel in my hair when I brushed it out for bed.

There are not really a lot of options in such a situation. Cursing would have served no purpose, so I laughed instead. I laughed at the whole comic scene of my kitchen looking like a bizarre ecru snow had fallen indoors, and I laughed at my own naiveté of thinking I was being terribly clever in covering the chestnuts with a bowl. Then I shook my head with a smile and a chuckle and started cleaning.

The incident of the exploding chestnuts was certainly my loudest cooking failure, but at least by blowing themselves to oblivion they had solved the age-old problem of what to do with an unsuccessful culinary concoction. In the case of the candy which my husband called "pure evil," we were not so fortunate.

I knew that caramels were some of the most popular candies in America in the late nineteenth century, so when I found a recipe in an 1888 *Good Housekeeping* for this much-beloved sweet, I became quite excited. The recipe made it sound so simple:

Caramel
   Three pounds of sugar (Coffee A, or granulated), one-half of a pound of baker's chocolate, one-fourth of a pound of butter, one cupful of cream or milk. Vanilla to taste . . .[127]

How hard could it be?

I had made caramel before numerous times using a recipe from the book my grandmother had given me in lieu of cooking lessons. The treat had always turned out deliciously, so I expected a real, nineteenth-century recipe from caramel's heyday to have even tastier results. Three pounds of sugar did seem like a lot, but I reasoned that heat would melt and reduce it. As I walked to the store and invested in a new sack of sweetness, my mouth watered in anticipation of delicious candy.

When I arrived home again, I combined all of the ingredients (except the vanilla, as specified) in a large, heavy saucepan, put it on the stove, and started stirring. When the small amount of butter heated up and browned, the mixture started to resemble dry sand. I kept stirring, expecting the sugar to liquefy any minute.

Any minute now . . .

Cooking can sometimes feel like alchemy, and I knew that foods like hollandaise sauce or egg-white meringues experience a seemingly magical instant when their whole nature changes and they transform from one substance to another. I thought this concoction would undergo a similarly fabulous change. I kept stirring, expecting the solid grains of sugar to melt together into flowing liquid caramel.

Any minute now . . .

I kept stirring.

Any minute now . . .

Nearly an hour later, Gabriel came into the kitchen to ask why the entire house smelled of burnt sugar. I looked forlornly into the giant pan of brown ashes—darker now but no less granular—and kept stirring.

"I kept expecting it to melt," I explained disappointedly. "—But I don't think it will." I pouted out my lower lip.

"No, now it's just burning." Gabriel wrinkled his nose. "Did you try adding any liquid?"

"I put in exactly what the recipe called for," I protested. "But I suppose we could add more cream."

Gabriel retrieved the half-full pint carton and I emptied it into the saucepan. As soon as the liquid hit the sandy sugar, it did something cream should never do. It sizzled loudly. The kitchen filled with a sound like a red-hot poker thrust into a bucket of water. Gabriel and I cast horrified looks at each other.

"I think it's as done as it's going to be," Gabriel suggested. I nodded glumly and removed the pan from the heat.

The extra cream had added enough moisture to change the concoction from a substance resembling dry sand to a mixture resembling silty mud, but it still neither looked nor smelled like something a human would gain any enjoyment from eating. Gabriel and I took turns stirring the stuff for the next hour until we judged it to be cool enough to taste without risking fourth-degree burns.

I dipped a small spoonful from the pan and cast a sideways look at it. "Maybe it tastes better than it smells," I ventured hopefully.

"Maybe—" Gabriel looked doubtful about this.

"Well." I held up the spoon. "Here goes nothin'." The alleged caramel had the consistency of thick tar, and I had to pull it off of the spoon with my teeth. I tried to swallow it like custard, and when this proved impossible, I attempted chewing it like taffy. I soon found my teeth gummed together by a thick, viscous substance that tasted like liquefied charcoal. When I unsealed my mouth and was able to talk again, I reminded my husband of an incident from a previous year. "Remember when I puréed an entire pint of chopped parsley and drank it? Remember how I said it didn't taste good but it tasted like health epitomized?"

Gabriel nodded.

"This doesn't taste good, and it tastes like 'unhealth' epitomized, as ungrammatical as that may be."

Curiosity overcame my husband's better judgment. He ate a spoonful of the concoction. Both corners of his mouth turned violently downward, and after he had managed to swallow he stuck his tongue out. "It reminds me of the *Get Fuzzy* comic by Darby Conley, where the dog eats something and says it tastes like pure evil," he commented.

I looked glumly at the huge quantity of the foul stuff I had generated.

"Here, let's throw it away." Gabriel reached for the pan.

I stopped his hand, rebelling at the idea of wasting so much food. "There are three pounds of sugar, a whole pint of cream, and nearly ten dollars' worth of baker's chocolate in there!" I protested.

"But it's god-awful!" Gabriel remonstrated.

I looked at the pan and sighed. "I'll eat it."

"Why?" Gabriel's astonishment was about on par with how he might have reacted if I had announced a plan to stand on our roof singing show tunes.

"So it won't go to waste," I told him.

"It's already wasted!" Gabriel argued.

"No, I'll eat it." I looked at the mess resignedly. "Charcoal's good for the digestion, isn't it? At least it's sweet."

My husband shook his head at my folly. "Don't try to eat it all at once," he cautioned.

I glowered at the cauldron of unhealth/pure evil. "No danger of that," I assured him.

It took me about three months to nibble my way through the sweetened charcoal. If I called it toasted toffee crunch it became more palatable—but it still wasn't caramel.

Commercially produced caramels go through ebbs and flows of popularity like any other commodity. When I was in college around the turn of the millennium, I noticed a rise in popularity of high-end caramels, especially the ones seasoned with sea salt. For several years, my absolute favorites were the chocolate-covered sea salt caramels produced by Fran's Chocolates in Seattle. Unfortunately, I had to stop this little indulgence when their price went through the roof after President Obama's affinity for them made national headlines in 2008.

While researching various foods and companies from the late nineteenth century, Gabriel and I learned that Milton Hershey had initially made his fortune manufacturing caramels long before he ever tried producing chocolate. After Gabriel and I moved into our Victorian house in Port Townsend, we started paying increasing attention to the origin stories of the foods we were eating, and the idea of Mr. Hershey's caramels pulled at our imaginations with particular ferocity. *What had they tasted like? Were they the silky caramel in a Caramello bar, or were they chewy like a Rolo?* We sighed wistfully over the idea that we would never know. Then one day a very rude seagull steered me toward an answer to our questions.

I was out for an early morning bike ride through town and had stopped at a traffic light on the main street by the water. The buildings on this thoroughfare are always ornamented with an assortment of noisy seagulls, some of which are bigger than ducks, and on this particular day they seemed to be having an especially raucous convention. Just before the light changed, a group of seagulls on the shoreward side of me took off for the water with loud shrieks. Naturally, they did what birds always do when they launch themselves into flight: they dropped their excess baggage.

I recoiled as a rain of watery gray goop poured down from the sky. The man in the truck next to me very rudely cracked up laughing when he witnessed my predicament. I responded with the most venomous look possible and consoled myself by reflecting that he wouldn't be laughing quite so hard when he saw what the gulls had done to the roof and truck bed of his otherwise shiny pickup.

I pulled up my mental map of Port Townsend to find the closest business with a public restroom. I decided that the best choice for my needs was the pharmacy, so I darted over to the building and locked my bike outside.

Luckily I was wearing my most washable outfit (a simple cotton print skirt and shirtwaist, made from fabrics that were reprints of nineteenth-century originals). I managed to clean myself in the bathroom sink without too much trouble, then I headed for the exit via the candy aisle. I hadn't intended to buy sweets that morning, but aerial bombardment by fecal matter tends to put a person in a mood for self-consolation.

I had recently been reading about the caramel company Milton Hershey had started in Lancaster, Pennsylvania, in the late nineteenth century, so when I saw a new variety of caramels with the name Lancaster on the label, the sight stopped me in my tracks. I felt like cheering, and suddenly I was no longer quite so angry at the seagulls. Now we could finally learn the answer to the question that had inspired such endless speculation: What had the caramels tasted like that delighted Victorians all over America and made Milton Hershey's fortune? I bought a bag and was already pulling it open as I left the store.

The soft drops of caramel had a texture like silk charmeuse and a sweet flavor like childhood visions of buttercups. They melted languidly over my tongue into a pool of dulcet richness. I was amazed that such ambrosia had ever retired from the world and delighted that the Hershey Company had brought it back. The Victorian era is never as far from us as people believe it to be, even when it comes to something so ephemeral it vanishes upon the tongue.

Part of why Gabriel and I like the Hershey Company so much is that it has such a wonderful story: For Milton Hershey, the great tragedy of his life had been that he and his wife had no children of their own. To give something back to the world, they opened an orphanage. In 1918, three years after his wife Kitty's death, Milton left his entire personal fortune to the school. To this day the Milton Hershey School still owns controlling stock of the Hershey Corporation.[128] Buying Hershey candy supports orphans! What could possibly give a person a warmer, fuzzier feeling?

Gabriel and I are story people. For us, the whys, wherefores, and whens of a thing add immense depth to our experience of it. Discovering the reintroduction of Lancaster caramels gave us an extra push to explore other store-bought foods from around our period. Partly owing to the Columbian Exposition World's Fair in Chicago, 1893 was a particularly prolific year for new foods in America. Shredded wheat, Cracker Jacks, Cream of Wheat, and Ak-Mak crackers were all introduced to America in that year.

Cold breakfast cereals started entering the market in the late Victorian era and really hit their stride in the Edwardian period. In the years between then and now, many of the recipes have changed, often to incorporate increasing quantities of sugar. Since Gabriel and I moved to Port Townsend, I had been phasing the newer cereals out of my diet and accustoming myself to breakfasts of fruit, soft-boiled eggs, homemade bread, oatmeal, or a combination of any of these. Realizing that shredded wheat had been invented right around our target period—and, more importantly, had remained unchanged since then—inspired me to stock it in our cupboard again. The sensation this gave me probably wasn't so very different from the reaction people must have had when it first became available: It was nice to have a quick, hassle-free, and healthy option as a default breakfast, even if it wasn't my everyday standard.

Neither Gabriel nor I are particularly fond of fireworks but we are, nonetheless, American, and in 2014 we wanted to do something appropriate to celebrate the Fourth of July. Port Townsend wasn't having a parade that year. We're fond of picnics, but that had been our Independence Day default activity for so long that we really wanted a bit of a change. After a great deal of brow-furrowing and making low *hmm*ing noises to each other, I finally came up with the idea to spend the day being aggressively American. In our minds, this involved eating corn on the cob and potatoes (New World foods), burgers for Gabriel, and, of course, root beer.

Some foods are inherent colonizers. They originate in one country, but as soon as a small example of them spreads abroad, global hegemony soon follows. (Brie cheese, Coca-Cola, and sushi are all examples of this—although I wouldn't recommend mixing them.) Other foods are the gastronomic equivalent of hermits: they seldom spread on their own, and when they do they are rarely welcomed outside their native territory.

Cream of Wheat advertisement, 1901.

Gabriel's mom used to arrange home-stays for exchange students at a private high school, and back when Gabriel and I were dating, Barbara invited me to come along to a buffet dinner with an entire class-full of Japanese schoolgirls. About halfway through dinner, a strangled sound of disgust broke out from the middle of the *Nihon-jin*. The other chaperones and I looked over to where a rapid-fire conversation had suddenly broken out in high-pitched Japanese.

One of the pretty raven-haired girls was looking at her drinking glass with an expression of utter betrayal on her face. She handed it to the girl on her right, who took a cautious sip, screwed up her face, and handed it to the girl beside her, who repeated the performance. If the liquid in the glass had been clear, I might have thought they had assumed the cup had water in it, then found that it was in fact white vinegar. The drink in the cup wasn't clear, though. It was brown and foamy.

"Must have found the root beer," one of the chaperones commented with a low laugh.

Hearing this, I turned a quizzical look on Barbara. "Really?"

She seemed embarrassed. "Oh, yeah. The Japanese students usually don't like root beer."

"Only Americans like root beer!" the other chaperone said in a tone that brooked no discussion.

My Canadian-born grandmother never objected to root beer, but I knew that most of the world lumps residents of Canada and the United States under the general "American" category. I filed the statement away for further analysis, deciding to test it at the first opportunity.

The next day was Saturday, which was afternoon archery practice day for the UW team. We had two wonderful coaches, both of them highly British. Nick was a debonair brunette Englishman; Angus was a fiery-haired Scot with a heart of gold but a feisty sense of humor. They seemed a reasonable pair to interrogate about the root beer theory.

"Nick—" I addressed the Englishman as I stepped through my bow to string it. "I'm curious about something. Someone told me that only Americans like root beer, and I'm wondering if it's true." I pulled my bowstring up onto the grooved notch on the leg of my bow.

Nick's arrow slid into the perfect center of his target's bull's-eye, then he lowered his bow with a motion so smooth and suave James Bond would have envied the action. "I like root beer," he said with a grin.

On the other side of the range, Angus's arrow smacked into the center of his own target's bull's-eye. "Only Americans—" The red-haired Scotsman looked meaningfully at the Englishman. "—and *freaks* like root beer!" he declared emphatically.

In the back corner of the range, Tom (the club president and my buddy who would prove such a good correspondent through time) looked up from the lab notebook he had brought to practice and burst out laughing.

In the years since that conversation, I've inquired into the soft-drink preferences of countless friends and found precious few root beer–lovers outside of North America. (There have been a few—but not many.) When Gabriel and I decided to be aggressively American for the Fourth of July, drinking root beer seemed appropriate.

Root beer floats seemed even more American than the unadulterated beverage, so I decided to take things up a notch by concocting one of these frothy ice cream treats. I initially felt guilty about the plan; although I knew root beer had been a favorite beverage in nineteenth-century America and that Charles Hires had jump-started his company by selling carbonated root beer at the Philadelphia Exposition in 1876, I had long assumed that adding ice cream to the treat was an Edwardian innovation. However, when I investigated the matter, I learned to my delight that root beer floats are, in fact, highly Victorian.

The invention of the root beer float is often credited to Frank J. Wisner of Cripple Creek, Colorado, and dated to August 1893. However, an oft-repeated story about him having the idea for his "black cow" drink after seeing a full moon rise over a snowy mountain is probably apocryphal. Even if it isn't, nineteenth-century magazines debunk the idea that Wisner's idea was a novel one.

In 1892—a year earlier than Wisner supposedly imagined his black cow drink—*The Western Druggist* was already assuring its readers that, "The now quite general custom of serving ice cream with soda water is not of so recent origin as is commonly assumed." The publication goes on to explain that Eugene Rouselle had originated the idea in Philadelphia "some thirty-five years ago"—or around 1857. Rouselle, "who kept an elegant establishment on Chestnut Street . . . Philadelphia, and who first introduced bottled soda in the United States," mixed chilled, flavored syrup with ice-cold cream and then added "a liberal quantity" of shaved ice. (He kept a carpenter's plane at his soda fountain to shave the ice.) He then dispensed carbonated water onto the creamy, sweetened mass of ice and served his customers "a most delicious and cooling drink." These were so popular that other purveyors of soda counters attempted to copy Rouselle's model, but his would-be rivals

Hires root beer advertisement, circa 1890s.

felt that his process was too troublesome; it used too much ice, and the cream would often sour. (The article doesn't specify whether the cream was souring because Rouselle's rivals weren't as conscientious about keeping it on ice as he was or because they were mixing it with more acidic syrups than Rouselle's. It seems likely that both problems were encountered at different times and by different businesses.) To make the process easier and more cost-effective, many drug stores started replacing the combination of shaved ice and plain cream with a spoonful of ice cream, and the ice cream soda was born![129]

In August 1891, the Hires Root Beer Company was selling an average of 15,000 bottles of root beer extract per day and estimated that 1,500,000 glasses of their product were being consumed on a daily basis.[130] Root beer syrup wasn't the only option for flavoring in ice cream sodas, but given the drink's beloved status, the purveyor of a soda counter would have been extremely foolish not to stock it.

By 1897, ice cream sodas had taken over the soda trade so thoroughly that druggists were actively discouraging people from buying them in an effort to push their customers toward more profitable drinks. Soda dispenser D. W. Saxe wrote, "In hot weather room is valuable and time is money at the soda counter, therefore the foreseeing and level-headed dispenser will work every scheme possible to serve as many people possible in as short a space of time as he can . . . You can wait on ten customers for still drinks as quickly as one for Ice Cream Soda, and the per cent of profit is more than double . . . Now, then, is it not worth your while to push almost anything but Ice Cream Soda?" Saxe told his readers not to advertise ice cream soda, ". . . for at present Ice Cream Soda needs no advertising." Instead, he advised druggists to concentrate on advertising their still drinks and stated, "It is much easier now to make this change in your soda trade since nearly everybody, young and old, have taken to riding a wheel. Wheelmen of any experience whatever all know that Ice Cream Soda is not the proper drink when riding, and they want something to quench thirst and relieve that dryness of the throat and tongue. There is nothing better for this purpose than . . . Raspberry Cordials or Blood Orange Phosphates, and besides when you once get your customer educated to this style of drink he will want three or four of them in an evening while riding; whereas one glass of Ice Cream Soda and two glasses of ice water is the old rule."[131]

Finding Saxe's commentary was particularly fortuitous. Gabriel actually doesn't like ice cream sodas, but he is definitely an avid Wheelman. (By this

Hires root beer advertisement, 1888.

point he had an antique 1887 high wheel bicycle—but more on that later.)
I went out hunting for a blood orange phosphate, and found them in bottles
in a cooler at our local bakery. Thus we were able to celebrate our holiday in
thoroughly delicious style.

15

A Problem That Didn't Exist in the Nineteenth Century, and a Treat That Did

"Alluring as is the occupation of light gardening to the average woman, yet it is not without its difficulties and its discouragements . . ."[132]
—"Amateur Gardening," *Good Housekeeping*, 1890

Both the biggest difficulty and the biggest discouragement of gardening in America in the twenty-first century can be summed up in a single four-letter word: deer. Bambi is a bastard.

There are actually a higher estimated number of white-tailed deer in North America now than were here before Columbus landed.[133] The farming and logging that destroy habitat for many species actually create ideal conditions for deer: they dislike deep woods and prefer the transition areas between forest and fields. (American Indians used to deliberately burn sections of forest to draw in deer for hunting.) Deer populations have gotten so out of hand in twenty-first century America that on September 2, 2014, deer crossing San Francisco's Golden Gate Bridge caused a traffic jam.[134]

A few days before Independence Day in our second Port Townsend summer, Gabriel decided he would like venison burgers for the holiday. There is only one store in Port Townsend that sells venison, and it is located almost exactly one mile from our house. As we walked there, I started counting the deer we passed along the way. *One, two, three . . .* There are literally hundreds of thousands of acres set aside for wildlife in Washington State, yet these ruminant bums had clearly decided that stealing from humans was easier than living as nature intended. Like enormous tawny vacuum cleaners, they were Hoover-ing up vegetable gardens, lawns, all the tree foliage they could reach, and virtually all the ornamental flora.

At a different time, I had even seen a deer devour an entire hellebore plant, which shouldn't be biologically possible since hellebores are deathly poisonous. Whenever I pass deer eating daffodils (which are also toxic) and juniper boughs, I shake my head. All these plants appeared on a "deer-resistant" list that a nursery where I used to work handed out to gullible customers. The list sold plants, but no deer ever read it.

By the time we got to the store on our pre-Independence Day shopping trip, I had counted no less than *twenty-four* deer actively engaged in demolishing people's gardens. Twenty-four deer aligned along a walk of one mile! I pointed out to Gabriel that this was a rather ridiculous situation on our way to lay down hard-earned dollars for deer meat. However, we hadn't even gotten to the punchline yet. When we went inside the store and found the venison, the back of the package was labeled PRODUCT OF NEW ZEALAND. Apparently modern Americans find it more palatable for their meat to have a seven-thousand-mile carbon footprint than to come from their own backyards.

In the nineteenth century, a deer in one's yard simply meant free venison. However, in the twentieth century, a number of stringent hunting laws were put in place; furthermore, it became illegal for hunters to sell venison. This is even the case if the meat has been legally bagged with an official license. (Indian reservations are some of the last places in the United States where people actually can buy American deer meat, for the same reason people can buy fireworks on Indian reservations that would be prohibited elsewhere. Indian tribes are considered sovereign nations and are legally entitled to determine laws on their own territories.) As of 2013, an estimated 85 percent of the venison sold in the United States came from New Zealand, where captive deer are raised and slaughtered on farms.[135]

Meanwhile, the American deer are running amok. They stand right against the windows of our house and stare in at me while they eat my rosebushes, as if daring me to do something about their behavior. When I run outside with a broom to chase them off, they ignore me until I literally either throw the broom at them or start whacking them with it. Sometimes that doesn't even have an effect. If I go out without the broom, they'll often just turn their rumps towards me and defecate—cocky bastards.

Luckily our fruit trees are tall enough that I can get a decent number of apples and plums off the highest branches—as long as the raccoons don't beat me to the fruit while it's still green. Raccoons have a nasty habit of checking for ripeness by taking one bite out of a fruit, throwing it away if it's still sour, then repeating the process over and over again. Sometimes they strip an entire tree this way. After a long spring and early summer of eagerly anticipating homegrown fruit, going outside to find a whole tree's efforts wasted on the ground is enough to make anyone reflect on how nice it would be to have a raccoon fur collar.

I manage to sneak in a few herbs under the cervine radar, but I've long since decided that it's a losing proposition to grow vegetables in a neighborhood where the deer outnumber the squirrels. I console myself by foraging in the local woods, relishing the array of wild foods available in the Pacific Northwest. If the deer are going to invade my territory and steal my food, turnabout is only fair play.

Some of the wild foods of the Pacific Northwest are familiar all over America, while others are unique to this region. It's tempting to think that all the plants that grow wild have been here since time immemorial, but this is far from the case. The Northwestern woods may seem timeless, but in fact they constitute their very own history lesson.

Strolling along trails in the Washington woods where paths cleared by feet have allowed light to angle into the undergrowth, a small trailing vine drapes itself over the evergreen bushes like tinsel on a Christmas tree. *Rubus ursinus* is the only blackberry native to the Northwest; its fruits are sweet and potently flavorful but modest in size, being only about as large as the nail on a woman's pinky finger. Northwestern tribes have long gathered these berries for food, either eating them immediately after harvesting or drying them for winter storage. They also used the leaves and roots to treat diarrhea, menstrual problems, and a variety of other medical issues. The Stl'atl'imx and the Coast Salish tribes told a story about the plant's origins that might have something to do with the way the thorny vines seem to chase the plants' flowers and fruit, or with the resemblance of the berries' juice to fresh blood. The traditional myth holds that a woman with a cruel husband fled up a tree to escape him. Her blood fell upon the earth and the blackberry sprang up.[136]

Rubus discolor or Himalayan blackberry has no such myth about its origins; its introduction is a matter of historical record. The huge, arching brambles that appear anywhere with the barest scratch of earth (from abandoned lots to cracks in sidewalks) were introduced to North America in 1885 by Luther Burbank—the botanical wizard who invented rainbow corn, elephant garlic, Russet Burbank potatoes, Shasta daisies, crimson California poppies, and a wide array of other plants that have become ubiquitous throughout America.[137] The blackberries descended from Burbank's seeds have gone feral in a big way. Every year in late summer, crowds of people swarm around bramble patches, gorging themselves on the huge, juicy berries and bringing home gallons more, yet there hardly ever seems to be a dent in the bounty. No matter how many humans and animals devour them, by early autumn the air turns heady with the wine-scent of thousands of remaining berries fermenting under their own thorns.

Thirty years before Burbank's blackberries started enveloping the West Coast like something out of H. G. Wells's *The Food of the Gods*, US Army doctor Rodney Glisan was stationed in what was then still part of the Oregon Territory. Writing in his journal on July 25, 1855, he recorded: "Of fruits we have the salmon-berry, thimbleberry, and sal-alle berry. The latter resembles in appearance and taste a large variety of the huckle-berry, and affords a very delicious dessert. The thimbleberry is almost exactly like a raspberry in size and appearance, but grows on a larger and less prickly bush."[138]

Salmonberries and salal berries were both important foods for various Northwest Coast tribes, although in different ways. Salmonberries (which resemble raspberries but are salmon-colored) are too watery to preserve by drying, so they were eaten fresh. Since they are among the earliest wild fruits to ripen (from May to June), they must have been a very welcome treat. In some tribes, salmonberry patches were owned by specific individuals or families.[139] Salal berries could also be eaten fresh (members of the Kwakwaka'wakw tribe garnished the fresh berries with oolichan grease and served them at feasts); however, salal had the added advantage that it was storable. Salal berries resemble blueberries and—as Glisan noted—huckleberries: All three are members of the heather family. However, salal berries are significantly drier than their botanical berry cousins. Aboriginal peoples of the Northwest Coast dried them into cakes for winter storage.[140]

When baking with fruit, I far prefer salal berries to blueberries in both muffins and pancakes. The flavors of the berries are very similar, but whereas blueberries tend to explode in the heat of cooking, salal fruits maintain their integrity. Another difference is the color: blueberries baked into foods translate into splashes of purplish-red in the finished product, but salal berries (which are practically black when raw) turn an eye-popping blue so bright it almost looks artificial. My first experiment making salal berry tarts turned out disappointingly dry, with the sugared berries shriveled up far below the edges of their pastry cups. However, a bit of creativity solved this problem in a most delicious manner: I made a batch of my favorite custard recipe from Mrs. Beeton's Book (the same custard described in chapter eleven) and topped up the tarts with it. The result was so tasty that it became a summer staple.

Many wild foods have their charms, but the dearest one to my heart—my favorite fruit in the whole world—is the thimbleberry. Imagine the sweetest strawberry you've ever tasted, crossed with the tartest raspberry you've ever eaten. Give it the texture of silk velvet and make it melt to sweet juice the moment it hits your tongue. Shape it like the ages-old sewing accessory that gives the fruit its name, and make it just big enough to cup a dainty fingertip. That delicious jewel of a fruit is a thimbleberry. They're too fragile to ship and too perishable to store, so they are one of those few precious things in life that can't be commoditized, and for me they always symbolize the essence of grabbing joy while I can. When it rains in thimbleberry season, the delicate berries get so damp that even the gentlest pressure crushes them, so instead of bringing them home as mush, I lick each one off my fingers as soon as it is picked. These sweet berries are treasure beyond price.

Going out to gather thimbleberries on dewy summer mornings is an activity that has acquired almost sacred connections in my mind. Moving through the woods to spot the jewel-bright berries seems a link to the region's deep history, yet at the same time those luscious fruits represent all that is sweet and ephemeral about summer. All the spiderwebs are coated with dew and stand out like a thousand silk handkerchiefs dropped among the wild rose bushes. Some webs are so heavily laden with moisture that they hang in curves like little fairy harp strings, and I could almost be convinced that if I gently strummed the gossamer strands with my fingertips, I would hear notes of fairy music.

There is a plethora of hummingbirds in the woods around Port Townsend, and when I hear their tiny little squeaky songs I pause, searching the trees above me for the jewel-like dainty creatures. I can usually spot them, despite their diminutive size. Whenever I go berry picking, I wear a fringed sunbonnet that I brought back from Japan, where farm-women still wear the classic items. To hummingbirds, it resembles a huge version of the trumpet flowers adored by the nectar-lovers. They fly right up to me and hover just a few feet away, evaluating this perplexing vision that—almost—seems to be the largest single food source the little creatures have ever seen. When they realize their mistake after a

Watching a hummingbird. Photo courtesy Estar Hyo Gyung Choi, Mary Studio.

few moments, they zip away, and I marvel at the sparkling iridescence of their flight.

Thimbleberries are small and grow with relatively wide spaces between them so it can take hours to gather a single cupful, but this is meditative time, prayer time. From my first sight of their delicate five-petaled flowers in late spring (like snow-colored wild roses on plants without thorns), I contemplate how fleeting some of life's joys can be and how very precious that makes them.

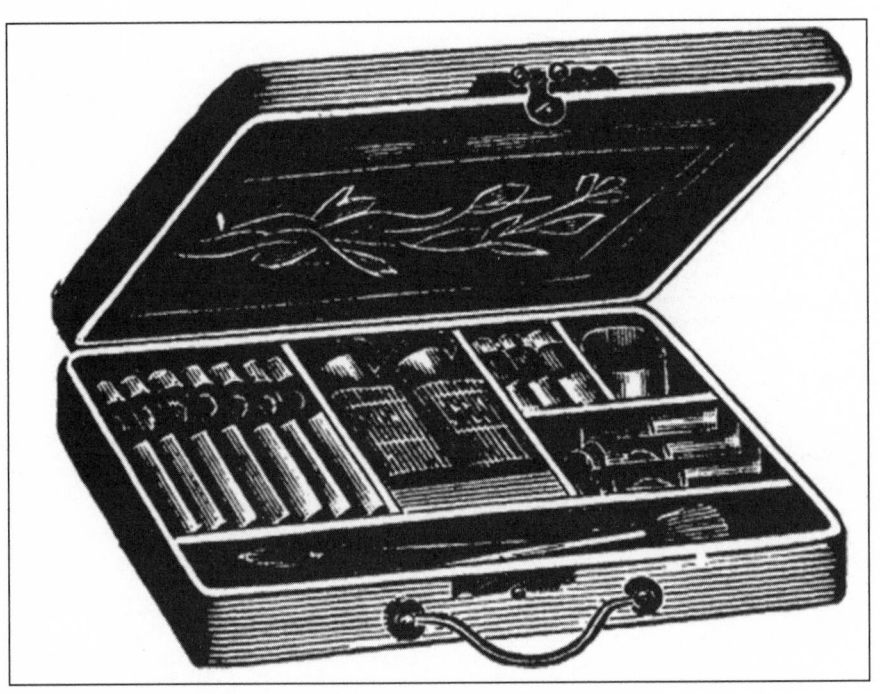

Amateur's oil painting outfit from the 1895 Montgomery Ward & Co. catalogue.

16

Portrait

"To sit for one's portrait is like being present at one's own creation."
—Alexander Smith, 1863[141]

As mentioned at the start of this tale, Gabriel and I had been in his hometown visiting his mother for a while before we moved to Port Townsend. During a trip to the grocery store one afternoon, I was stopped in the checkout line by a distinguished-looking elderly gentleman. He complimented my outfit in a cultured British South African accent and explained that he was a painter. "Do you think you might be willing to sit for a portrait sometime?"

I hesitated. I certainly wanted to take him up on his offer; sitting for a painting was one of those experiences about which I had always fantasized. However, I was broke and I knew portraits weren't cheap. Painters needed paint, canvases, and an entire range of other materials, even before the long hours of work that went into a painting were taken into consideration. In college, I had known artist friends who had sold commissioned paintings for thousands of dollars.

"We pay sixty bucks!" The elderly man smiled at me.

They would pay *me* to paint my picture? I was so astonished at this inversion of my thoughts that I bit the inside of my lower lip simply to keep my jaw from falling open.

"I'd love to!" I pounced on the opportunity.

Several weeks later, Francis (the painter) picked me up from my mother-in-law's house in his sparkling Jaguar, and we drove to his studio a few miles away. A small group of painters were assembled inside and they greeted me with a warm enthusiasm I found incredibly charming. I felt myself blushing and was grateful that the studio's proximity to the water added a coolness to the room. The chill air, I hoped, would mediate my complexion a bit and help keep my skin from turning too crimson.

Besides not wanting to create an undue challenge to the artists' supplies of red paint, I had a second reason to appreciate the refreshing air: I was dressed rather warmly. When I had met Francis in the grocery store, I was en route to see a friend on the other end of the island. Accordingly, I had been dressed for a thirteen-mile walk in brisk autumn air. When Francis brought up the subject of a portrait, I offered to wear other clothes than those I had met him in. I had more ornate choices within my wardrobe. However, he had been quite insistent that I come in exactly the clothes he had seen me, and so here I was in my wool skirt and sturdy wool cape.

When I arrived in the studio, some debate went on among the painters regarding the best position and props. After some discussion they decided that, in the interest of showing off my corseted waist for the portrait, I should forego my cape during the sitting. This pleased both my vanity and my internal thermostat. It would have seemed a shame to hide my figure, and my wool skirt and silk petticoats kept me at just about the perfect temperature without any extra layers. Once the veteran artists were satisfied as to my placement on their modeling bench, they used masking tape to mark reference points on the floor (delineating the edges of my feet), the seat (showing exactly where I was sitting), and my skirt (marking the placement of my folded hands). The purpose of this, they explained, was so that I could return to exactly the same position any time we took a break. The modeling would last several hours and they wanted all the variables to remain constant to maximize their ability to capture all the details. Francis advised me to choose a point of reference to keep my gaze consistent, so I looked for a point on which I could focus my attention. The optimal position for natural light (so valuable for art) dictated that I be facing away from the picture window and toward a clean wall. At first I thought it would be impossible to refocus my gaze into exactly the same position vis à vis the broad, immaculate surface, but then I noticed a tiny smudge of paint against the tidy expanse. I directed my sight toward this and held the focus. Every twenty minutes for the next four hours, the painters gave me permission to stand up and help myself to cookies and other refreshments at the side of the room, then I stretched a bit and returned to my tape marks, again focusing my eyes on the minute little serendipitous smudge on the wall opposite.

Being painted was a tremendously flattering adventure. It is difficult to imagine a more complimentary experience than sitting in a small room for four hours while a group of accomplished artists brushed my portrait and occasionally made comments about how beautiful I was. For someone who had spent all her adolescence as an awkward outcast, who had never had a date until college, it created an amazing feeling of prettiness. When I returned to my mother-in-law's home that afternoon, I was fairly dancing.

A few months later, the charming experience was repeated. The artists had been so pleased by my disinclination to fidget during my first sitting that they invited me back to model again. This time, they wanted to recreate a classic work of fine art: "Nana" by the Victorian painter Édouard Manet. The piece had been considered slightly scandalous in its day, but a modern audience might be amused to hear that the controversy surrounded not a lack of garments, but the presence of them. The Victorians were accustomed to classical images of goddesses and other deities shown completely nude. Art historian Michael Hatt points out that:

> Throughout London, throughout Britain, there are Victorian sculptural nudes wherever one looks, be they plaster, marble, bronze or stone. This may seem surprising; popular myths about the Victorians continue to circulate, branding them as the very epitome of prudishness . . . These [sculptures] are objects that have somehow become invisible to us, unnoticed a century on in our own visual landscape.[142]

In fact, Queen Victoria herself had a habit of giving nude sculptures as birthday gifts to her beloved husband, Albert.[143] The shock factor of the mortal (albeit fictitious) Nana arose from her flaunting of her corset, stockings, and knee-length pantalets. (In chapter 5 of her book, *The Corset: A Cultural History*, fashion historian Valerie Steele explains how, to a nineteenth-century viewer, a corseted woman's form can be far more erotic than a nude one.)

Manet's Nana, her hair beautifully swept up and pinned with a row of crystals, stands in front of a mirror with a powder puff in one hand and a lipstick in the other. As fate would have it, I happened to own an ornamental comb similar to the one in Nana's hair. I had worn it for my wedding ten years previously and, like most brides, I had archived the artifacts pertaining to my marriage ceremony with a diligence verging on obsession. The comb with its entwined string of Austrian crystals lived in the same acid-free archival box that held my wedding dress and other accessories from that day. I brought the comb out of its private place and wrapped it in tissue to bring with me. Lacking an actual powder puff, I cut a small segment off a feather boa from my sewing supplies and twisted the marabou into a loose knot. The result wouldn't have passed overly intense scrutiny, but it looked enough like a powder puff from a few feet away that I judged it would be passable enough for the painters. The one thing I didn't have was any sort of loose clothing that could be quickly thrown on and off in the rests between modeling—a fact I was rather to regret in the chilly air of the studio. I did have my cape—a simple, waist-length affair of felted navy blue wool—and in the planning stages of the operation I deemed that this should be more than adequate.

I started to have second thoughts about this choice when I walked into the studio on the scheduled morning and realized that—even fully clothed—it was rather colder than my memories of it. However, I put this out of my mind as I greeted the kind members of the painting group and the warmth of their welcome pushed the chill of the room out of my mind. Francis ran into his house to borrow a lipstick from his wife (I don't use makeup myself, and a lipstick is slightly harder to mock-up than a powder puff), and we were ready to begin.

There was some discussion about what they all perceived as the difficulty of Nana's pose, which I listened to quietly but with a slight degree of amusement. As before mentioned, Manet's Nana is simply a woman standing in front of a mirror, holding some minor articles of toilette whose weight is so negligible as to be practically nonexistent. The painters kindly told me I could rest every fifteen minutes instead of every twenty, and for a significant portion of the first fifteen-minute set, I amused myself by reflecting on how easy my pose was compared to others I had seen in paintings in the Louvre on various visits to Paris. Eugène Delacroix's *Liberty Leading the People* features a bare-breasted goddess, her right arm raised high above her head to extend a huge tricolor French flag and her left hand holding up a long rifle with fixed bayonet—all this with her weight posted on her bare left foot as she steps over an obstacle. Théodore Géricault's *The Raft of the Medusa* shows even more subjects with their arms raised high, as an entire raft-full of shipwrecked sailors wave frantically toward a distant ship. (That is, the ones who are still alive wave frantically: Whoever modeled the numerous corpses in the scene presumably had the easiest time of it.) The scenes are ones of frantic activity, with all the subjects captured in mid-motion. This makes the portraits exciting for their viewers, of course, but must have been excruciating for the models. Even assuming that the painters economized on modeling time by capturing their posers in quick sketches before setting to work in earnest on the oil painting, I can't imagine that any sketch would seem quick enough to people in those positions. (*The Raft of the Medusa* does show one living man sitting down and staring into the distance at the bottom left-hand corner of the painting. He is generally explained by art critics as a man who has completely lost hope, but the cynical portion of me wonders if he might have simply been a model who got fed up with waving.)

After our four hours of painting and modeling were over, I chatted with the artists a while, ate more cookies than—doubtless—were good for me, then spent the rest of the afternoon loitering in the café attached to the local grocery.

I rather thought that would be the end of it, but a few weeks later, Gabriel announced that Francis had come by the bike shop earlier that day and informed my husband of his intention to make a gift to us of his painting of me.

"Really?" I asked, astonished. I had no experience at all with commissioned portraits, but I supposed they must be worth hundreds or even thousands of dollars depending on the artist. The idea of getting one as a free present was astonishing. "The modeling was fun on its own!"

Gabriel affirmed his earlier statement, and the next evening he came home carrying a large, rectangular package, loosely wrapped. We took off the covering and I stepped back, admiring the painting. I had only seen the work in progress before, not the completed product, and I folded my arms as I looked at it, thoroughly impressed. "Wow!"

The elements painted from life—me, the accessories I held, and the mirror—were close to photographic in their attention to detail. The rest of the background had been copied directly from Manet's original, and so exact was the duplication that if the section had been cut away and placed next to the same section of the Frenchman's work, I would have been hard-pressed to say which was which.

"Most excellent, isn't it?" asked Gabriel, beaming at the portrait.

"I'll say!" I concurred. I walked side to side, admiring it from different angles.

"Have you decided where you want to put it?" my husband asked.

I rubbed my chin. "I've been really wondering about that." I gazed at the beautiful portrait of myself—in my knickers and copying the modeling pose of a courtesan. "It's not really appropriate to hang it in the parlor, is it?"

"Sure it is!" Gabriel told me with a beaming expression. "That's exactly where a painting like this goes!" He held it up against one parlor wall, then another. "I just wondered where in here you wanted to put it."

I laughed and shrugged in amused acquiescence. "All right." I did like the idea of hanging my portrait in the parlor. Besides, I was showing considerably less flesh in the picture than a bather on a modern beach. I told myself that its reference to fine art excused the slightly scandalous nature of the pose. We debated where it would look the best in the room but not be in direct sunlight (which fades paintings), and ultimately hung it on our largest wall. Thus it was that I came to have a portrait of myself (the quality of which I would challenge any professional to match) hanging in my parlor at a point when I couldn't even really afford bedding flowers for the front yard yet.

The same group of painters had Gabriel pose for them twice, as well. They found his green antique frock suit delightful and went wild over his antique high wheeler. The sixty individual spokes in the bicycle's huge front wheel gave them a bit of a challenge—but more on the bike later.

An interesting inversion of my modeling for the painters happened when a photography student contacted me asking if I would pose for a photograph of a nineteenth-century painting. She asked for my advice on which painting we should copy, and I must admit the puzzle had me stumped for a while. I enjoy paintings but they are by no means my forte, and it took a bit of research to locate some appropriate images. Luckily, although artwork may not be my strong point, research is and it was a project I enjoyed immensely.

Part of the challenge was that, for the project to work, we would have to locate as many elements of the original painting as possible. I knew from my experiences with the painting group that painters often use supplementary props in place of elements that are not available, like when I used a piece of the feather boa in place of a powder puff. In a photograph, though, the final image would be exactly how we presented it. This meant that I would have to find a painting that featured a woman who looked like me, wearing a dress like one of mine, in a setting like something I could find in Port Townsend. This was a lot of variables to arrange, but I saw it as a worthy challenge.

I have wonderful memories of visiting Monet's garden at Giverny when I studied in France, but his impressionistic style is hopelessly fuzzy to someone looking for details. Mary Cassatt's paintings were promising but she usually painted women in pairs or with children, whereas I would be modeling solo. I had some dresses not too far off from some in Renoir paintings, but his murals are famously crowded. In the end, we decided to copy Charles Edward Perugini's *In the Orangery* because the scene is an uncluttered one (a woman holding a book and reading) and I had an appropriate dress for it.

The photographer came to our house for tea the day before our shoot to arrange details. She enjoyed the sound of our mechanical clock in the background—"The heartbeat of a Victorian home," I told her with a smile. The next day, I met her near a fountain downtown and we accomplished our shoot—although not before a passing radio journalist stopped and asked if he could interview me for his show. Victorian style seems to be applicable to all sorts of media!

Cartoon from *Life* magazine, April 27, 1916. Vol. 67, No. 1748, p. 790. The caption reads, "Dinner in the suburbs: The sacred hour in which your friends know they can reach you by telephone. An idea to save getting up from the table."

"Only the worst is, that this beautiful invention for talking miles off,
won't feed people in the long run, my dears, any more than the old
invention of the tongue, for talking near, and you'll soon begin to think
that was not so bad a one, after all."

—John Ruskin, 1878[144]

17

Communication Parallels

"America cannot fail to live more in Europe, and Europe more in America . . . the world is fast becoming a vast city."
—The Success of the Transatlantic Cable Etc,"
The Times, July 30, 1866[145]

In a teashop one day, I overheard two mothers at the table next to mine complaining about their daughters' cell phone use. Their lamentations were fairly typical ones: the devices interrupted other activities, they distracted the daughters from their families . . . The women complained about how difficult it was sometimes to tell if someone was talking to them or to someone else in a different place altogether.

I smiled to myself over how similar their comments were to editorials written over a century earlier. Some of their complaints could have come directly out of the citations discussed in a book I had just finished reading, *The Victorian Internet* by Tom Standage. In this excellent work, Standage discusses how the telegraph opened a world of speedy communication—and increased communication challenges.

I considered suggesting Standage's book to the two women in the café, but doing so would have been an admission of eavesdropping. Admittedly, they were talking so loudly and our tables were so close together the only way to avoid hearing them would have been to clamp my arms over my ears and hum loudly to myself, but such behavior would lack dignity. Etiquette suggests a certain feigned deafness in such circumstances, so I kept my own counsel and occupied myself with writing reflections in my notebook. After listening to their increasingly hopeless and bitter lamentations—and considering the whole time how close their comments were to those of a little over a century before—I set down my pencil and took a long sip of tea. What I heard next nearly caused what a cartoonist would call a "spit take."

"We're the first parents ever to have to deal with this!" wailed one of the mothers. "There's no one to turn to for advice!"

I gulped hard, hid my choked expression with a napkin, and hurried into the bathroom, where I coughed a combination of laughter and milky black tea into the sink. Luckily I managed to avoid soiling my dress, and after a bit of spluttering, I cleared my windpipe. By the time I had washed my face and exited the lavatory, the a-historical mothers were gone.

When the telephone was introduced, people saw it as something that could potentially invade their privacy in ways never before imagined or dealt with. More than a century later, people are still dealing with this quandary—the only surprising thing is that they consider this a new development!

The story of the telephone begins in the late 1870s. On March 10, 1876, Alexander Graham Bell penned a letter to his father describing his first effective experiment in remote communication. ". . . The success is this," he wrote. "Articulate speech was transmitted intelligibly this afternoon. I have constructed a new apparatus operated by the human voice. It is not of course complete yet—but some sentences were understood this afternoon." He went on to describe with great excitement how his assistant, Mr. Watson, had complied to his request, "Mr. Watson—come here—I want to see you," after hearing it through the first telephone speaker. (Watson had been in a different room out of hearing range by ordinary means.)[146]

After this historic first telephone communication, Bell and Watson played around with the efficacy of their device. "Every note was audible" when Watson sang an air, but when he read aloud from a book, "the voice came from the electro-magnet in a curious half muffled sort of way. The sense was not intelligible but [Bell] caught a word here and there such as 'to'—'out'—'further.' The last sentence however [Bell] heard very plainly and distinctly. It was 'Mr. Bell, do you understand what I say?' [They] tried other sentences, 'How do you do' and etc., with satisfactory results."[147]

Judging from Bell's description, that first telephone conversation was rather more coherent than a number of calls I've muddled through myself. Certainly it was more rewarding than waiting on the line for a caller to travel into a place with better reception—only to realize that it's not a friend in a tunnel at all, but an electronic recording in an automated call center with faulty wiring.

In June 1876, Professor Bell displayed his first (short-distance) telephone at Philadelphia's Centennial Exposition. Bell's incessant hard work at improving the apparatus led to dramatic improvements. By March of the next year, he had created a version that successfully transmitted the human voice 143 miles from Boston to North Conway, New Hampshire. When *Scientific American* discussed this spectacular feat, the journal pointed out that Bell and his assistant (unnamed in the article, but presumably the Watson of the first historic experiment) had successfully transmitted their voices through a wire whose resistance had been artificially amplified to 40,000 ohms. This was greater than the resistance of the entire length of the cable that was already linking telegraphs in America to corresponding devices in Europe.[148] (The first transatlantic cable had been sent and received nearly twenty years earlier, on August 5, 1858. A plethora of challenges faced the 2,050-mile cable, stretched as it was over a notoriously turbulent sea.[149] That first version was only in operation one month, but by the time a second—far more successful—cable was run across the Atlantic in 1865, demand for its service was so great that it earned more than five thousand pounds sterling in revenue.[150])

By the end of the nineteenth century, newspapers were printing articles about the subject of taking a telephone to bed, and magazines were printing articles recommending a telephone as an appropriate gift for a distressed widow. (The idea was that other ladies would visit her in order to use her phone for ordering deliveries from merchants—and hopefully stay a while and keep her company; and that clerks would use the phone to call their bosses and pay her a small fee for the service.)

Even in its early days, there was controversy about this invasive invention, as well as a number of amusing jokes made at its expense. A particularly entertaining one appears in *Adventures of an Old Maid*, a humorous book written in 1881. A deacon arrives home one day looking "oncommon [sic] sober." His wife and her friend fear that his dark mood is the result of a catastrophic bank failure, but he snaps at them that there are other troubles in the world besides money troubles. He goes on to tell them of an awful performance he had just witnessed that made him feel "like death." While in a grocery store having lunch, he saw a young man who was the oldest son of a widow and the mainstay of his family. "He steered straight for the back end o' the store, and leanin' up agin the wall, begun to go through with the silliest lot o' performances I ever see. If he hadn't been more'n six year old, I should a thought he was makin' believe at some kind o' child's play! He pertended to be talkin' to somebody, hollered 'hullo!' and 'all right!' and a whole mess o' stuff, then laughed as hearty as could be, at his own nonsense."

The deacon concluded that the young man must be either drunk or insane, and he and his wife both lament that such a misfortune is likely to kill the man's poor, widowed mother. After a moment's reflection, the visitor suggests that the man might have been "talkin' through a telefone—one o' them talkin' machines, you know."

When I read the story for the first time in 2007, to me the funniest part was how similar the deacon's response was to my own reaction the first time I saw someone walking down the street talking on a wireless headset. Everything comes around in cycles—even tendencies of technology to make sensible people resemble lunatics.

From the time telephones were first installed in people's homes and through to the present day, a major issue for people has been how invasive the device can be. Coming to a home unannounced and expecting to be let inside for an indefinite period of time is a privilege most Americans reserve for friends, family, and neighbors. Even within these privileged groups, there are numerous individual exceptions. I certainly know plenty of people who don't relish the prospect of visits from certain relatives. We allow them this privilege and welcome them into our sacred space because we trust them to perceive whether we are in a position to extend hospitality. If the house is strewn about with work in progress, a good friend will see that we are busy and keep their pleasantries short. In the nineteenth century when it was more common to pay calls in person to casual acquaintances, middle- and upper-class women would often set a specific day and time to receive callers—say, Tuesday afternoons from 2 to 4 p.m., or Thursdays from 1 to 3 p.m. This would frequently be printed on calling cards underneath one's name.

In contrast, telephones invite invasion at increasingly odd hours. Anyone with access to a telephone can disrupt dinner, sleep, or any other intimate activity without recognizing how intrusive they are being. When cellular phones came into vogue, the list of activities that could be interrupted by telephonic devices expanded even further. The advertised promise of a cellular telephone is its claim to increase communication; however, its tendency to have exactly the opposite effect is made painfully clear by a sight all too commonplace in the twenty-first century. When I see a pair of young lovers out together and absorbed in each other, I smile at their union. When I see the same two people drawn apart by separate conversations with individuals who aren't even present, I shake my head sadly.

18

Chatelaine

"Spriggy was consulting her tablets, which hung from her chatelaine.
'Would Tuesday do?'"
—*A Victim of Circumstances*, 1901[151]

I first really learned about chatelaines when Gabriel and I visited a pair of acquaintances who collect antique purses. About halfway through showing us their collection, the wife asked if I knew what a chatelaine was and added that I absolutely should.

My adrenaline kicked in and I froze in my seat like a rabbit in headlights, realizing I was caught in one of those embarrassing moments in life when some-one else's "common knowledge" category overlaps with the "not a clue" portion of my own mental library. The word *chatelaine* was remotely familiar to me in a hazy way. For some reason, it was bringing up obscure memories of novels with medieval settings.

"Um . . . yes?" I proffered vaguely, setting down the antique teacup from which I had been sipping. I fervently hoped that she wouldn't ask any more detailed questions and force me to concede my own ignorance.

"This is a chatelaine purse," our hostess continued, bringing out a pretty little bag in a quite different style from the others she had shown us. It was flat with a hinged top and hung from a sturdy chain on an ornate clip.

"Oh!" I exclaimed, immediately charmed. "I've never seen one with a clip before!"

Our hostess blinked in surprise and gave me a slight frown. "That's what makes it a *chatelaine* purse," she explained slowly.*

---

*Her tone reminded me of the one I used to adopt when I'd worked near a city park in a rural area and tour-ists would come in asking, "What's 'The Grand Forest'?" "Well," I always used to say, "It's this forest—and it's sort of grand."

Busted! So much for my bluff about knowing what a chatelaine was. I reflected it was probably fortunate that I don't play poker. My tremendous sense of embarrassment squatted in the front row of my mind's theater, gnawing on the foot I had metaphorically shoved in my mouth.

Soon though, fascination had also pushed aside chagrin. Our hostess demonstrated how the little purse clipped onto the wearer's waistband, and I was as hooked as the purse. I immediately saw the utility of a bag that would hang from the waist, completely hands-free—and I wanted one.

For me, certain nineteenth-century items inspire the same sort of raw, unadulterated feelings of covetousness that the latest electronic gadgets evoke in my contemporaries. Showing me that chatelaine purse was a bit like showing an obsessive petrolhead the latest model of Lamborghini.

Illustration of a woman wearing a chatelaine purse. From *Frank Leslie's Illustrated Weekly*, August 24, 1893.

When I went home and a bit of research unearthed a picture of an actual chatelaine—the item that had inspired those purses—it was like seeing next year's Lambo with all the options. What I had seen at our neighbor's house was just a purse. (Admittedly, it was "just a purse" in the same way that a Lamborghini is "just a car.") An actual chatelaine, however, was on an entirely different level of excellence. A chatelaine was to the Victorian woman what a smartphone is to her twenty-first-century counterpart: a personalized device with tools for every circumstance.

My research did make me feel slightly better about my initial association of the word *chatelaine* with vague impressions of medieval settings. The tradition of these items is very old indeed—and has a complicated story. Etymologically speaking, the word *chatelaine* itself can be traced back to a castle. Linguistically, *castellanus* (medieval Latin for castle) begat *castelain* (Old Northern French for the governor of a castle) which later became *châtelain*. No French word is complete without a gender, so the male *châtelain* (a man who governs a castle) picked up an "e" in its feminine form: *châtelaine* (the woman who governs a castle, a manor, or other great house). English speakers love to pickpocket words from the lexicons of other languages but we don't generally care for jewelry on our vowels, so when the term was smuggled over the Channel, the circumflex was dropped from the "â."

The running of a castle requires keys. If issues of security are no concern, there are far cozier, cheaper, and generally more pleasant ways to arrange one's domicile than by piling stones into a drafty perimeter. When security is a concern, a person has a natural desire for locks. Locks on the gate kept out Vikings, and locks on progressively smaller spaces, from weapons storage to spice boxes, kept out progressively pettier thieves.

A lock with no key is nothing more than an ornamental impediment to use, and losing the keys to a castle would land its governor in a world of trouble. Presumably manors are slightly less prone to Viking attack than the castles that preceded them, but nonetheless losing the keys associated with a grand manor or estate would still be a distinct embarrassment. No one really wants to go bashing open their wine cellar door with an ax or smashing their delicately filigreed jewel box apart with a rock. Yet, as anyone who has come home to a locked door on a dark night can attest, keys have an uncanny ability to hide themselves in the last place their owner will look. In this way, they are rather like the more meandering sort of mongrels, and since leashes work tolerably well for dogs, it seemed a sensible enough idea to apply the same theory to keys.

It became customary in those far-off days of noble lords and fair ladies for the woman who held the keys to a manor to carry them in a cluster on her waist. This curbed the keys' tendency to wander and kept them handy. At the same time, the tinkling, jangling bundle served as an obvious indicator of who—quite literally—held the keys of power in a given household. The term *chatelaine* started shifting from the woman who held every key to a house to the bundle of keys that symbolized her authority.*

As keys became more commonplace among increasingly lower and lower classes of society, the uppermost classes wanted something a little flashier and less quotidian to hang from their waists and represent their position. In the eighteenth century, keys disappeared from the waist displays of upper-class women and were replaced by flashy jewels.

---

*The authors of *Chatelaines: Utility to Glorious Extravagance* point out that waist-hung appendages in general can be traced back to around 2000 BC but that the word chatelaine can't actually be documented as a reference to these bundles until April 1828. After the nineteenth-century's explosion in the popularity of chatelaines, however, the term came to be used retroactively in reference to similar bundles from earlier times.

Housekeeper with simple chatelaine, circa 1890s.

By the nineteenth century, women realized that dangling jewels from one's waist doesn't really serve much function beyond getting them inconveniently caught on things and tempting pickpockets. People's thoughts turned once again to ideas of utility.

A Victorian chatelaine is essentially a tool belt of a highly personal nature. Picture a Swiss Army knife crossed with a charm bracelet and you'll start to get the idea. Nineteenth-century chatelaines are highly customized to suit the needs of their individual owners; the two elements they all share are the clip, which hangs them from their owner's waist, and a series of chains hanging from that clip to tether various accessory tools.

Even the clips were beautiful. The simplest chatelaines worn by housewives in the lower-middle class might be little more than a clip with an unassuming geometric pattern, but they grew progressively more elaborate as one's budget increased—while never losing their functionality. Most chatelaine clips from the nineteenth century are made of base metal worked into shapes and patterns appropriate to jewelry. Flowers and classical motifs were especially favored. Particularly valuable chatelaines could be plated with silver or even gold, inset occasionally with semiprecious gems.

From the clip that hooks into the wearer's waistband dangles a number of chains, and each chain ends in a tiny clip that hooks into a tool. The tools on a woman's chatelaine give a casual observer an immediate insight into that individual woman's daily life, since these are an indication of which items she uses on a constant basis. (They are often sewing-related.) The tools are quotidian but seldom plain, and the makers of chatelaines often followed William Morris's very good advice that a person should have nothing in their life which they do not know to be useful or feel to be beautiful—but preferably both together.

Besides sewing tools, there were other feminine items. Elaborately crafted perfume bottles for chatelaines were especially prized. In August 1890, the English noblewoman Maud Berkeley wrote in her diary about a whist tournament at her club where the players competed for two chatelaine scent bottles. "We all played our hardest for such a desirable offering," she reported. The winning pair of players was made up of a man and a woman; when the man waived his half of the prize, his feminine partner "carried off both bottles in triumph."[152]

Chatelaine tools often cleverly disguise themselves as ornaments or hide within more decorative pieces. Thimbles pass themselves off as fairy buckets or are carried in hinged containers resembling nuts—like Shakespeare's elves, they "Creep into acorn cups, and hide them there."[153] There is often a supernatural

Wealthy woman with chatelaine. Special thanks to the Paul Azoulay collection for permission to use this image.

element to the art motifs, showing off classical deities or medieval fairy folk— or at the very least highly ornamental flower patterns that a sprite would be happy to call home. Scissors pose as tiny daggers or at least rest in sheaths; pin cushions appear as little wheels (literal "pin wheels") or in any number of other fantastic shapes.

There were whistles (often shaped like tiny animals) for chatelaines, mechanical pencils, glove hooks, mirrors, corkscrews . . . Theoretically, there is no maximum limit to the number of tools a chatelaine can hold. To increase its capacity, all one has to do is keep adding splitter rings to the chains off of other splitter rings, like following the genealogical chart of a particularly fertile family of rabbits. In practical terms, however, there are a few natural problems to this idea. No sane woman wants to wear a tool belt so long and complicated that it drags along the ground behind her like the chains on Marley's ghost—there would be the obvious tripping hazard to consider, and besides, one would need a significant portion of Scrooge's fortune to finance the acquisition of all of those intricate tools.

In 1873, Walter Thornhill, royal jeweler to Queen Victoria, created a silver chatelaine for a woman named Olive (her last name has not been recorded). In accordance with the ideas of both artistry and personalization, Thornhill decorated every tool accompanying Olive's equipage with an olive in realistic colors. Olive's chatelaine must truly have been remarkable; the tools manufactured for it comprise such a lengthy list there seems to be no option unexplored. There was a perfume bottle shaped like a bugle horn; a watch; a pencil case; a pedometer; a case containing two pairs of scissors; a heart-shaped flask with a cup; a glove hook; a mirror with a locket; a whistle; a fan made of Brussels lace mounted on tinted mother-of-pearl with silver mountings; a silver-cased knife including "a number of useful instruments" (presumably what would now be called a pocket knife or multitool); a paper-knife; a silver memorandum book fitted with a telescoping pencil; a portrait album matching the memorandum book; a silver-framed morocco bag; a match-safe shaped like a little barrel; a miniature almanac; a small case containing an ivory brush and comb; a white silk umbrella with pink silk lining, an ivory handle, and silver mounts; an embroidered parasol, also with an ivory handle and ivory mounts; a purse; and a telescope. There was also an étui (a sewing kit) in the shape of a policeman's lantern: an olive was enameled on the crystal of the lantern, and the étui was crafted in such a way that turning the cylinder that held the sewing tools would result in the owner's choice of a green, red, or white background behind the crystal. But still, Olive's collection was not yet complete! The matched set of tools for her chatelaine (each ornamented with her symbolic olive) also included a seven-barreled Colt revolver with a silver butt, silver sheath, and matching cartridge case.[154] These tools accompanied a leather "Norwegian" belt with an enameled buckle and silver fastenings to which Olive could attach her accessories. Clearly, she would have only worn a small fraction of this collection at any given time. Obviously, the umbrella and the parasol were intended for different conditions. Since the memorandum book had its own high-tech pencil, there would have been no reason to wear the pencil case along with it—and so on. However, the astonishing list of Olive's equipage certainly illustrates the amazing variety of tools that women could collect on their chatelaines.

Researching chatelaines and seeing pictures of them expanded my raw, gnawing desire for one like reading cookbooks expands hunger. I wanted a chatelaine so badly that I truly believe I went a bit mad over the idea for a time. When we visited the Craigdarroch Castle Museum in Victoria, British Columbia, Gabriel pointed out a chatelaine displayed hanging from the skirt of an antique dress on a mannequin in the sitting room. It took all the will-power I possessed to keep myself from jumping over the barricade separating me from the exhibit. I pictured myself prone on the floor, crying to a group of startled tourists and museum volunteers, "It's mine! Mine at last! You'll pry this chatelaine out of my cold, dead, lifeless fingers!" But I knew, of course, that it would be taken from me eventually (even if the action required break-ing every carpal bone in both my hands). I very reluctantly left the coveted item behind.

Antique chatelaines that still possess all their original tools (or tools that can pass as original to the piece, even if there's no proof and in some cases dealers might fudge the point a bit) are immensely more collectible than chat-elaine tools and clips sold separately. In terms of value to collectors, it is a case where the whole truly is greater than the sum of its parts. Entire chatelaines are expensive, but disassociated pieces were within my reach. Once I realized this, it simply became a matter of watching various online auctions and waiting—and a lot of patience. After a great deal of observation, I found a clip crowned with an art-nouveau morning glory (symbol for affection in the Victorian language of flowers), a memorandum book* embossed with orchids ("a beautiful lady"), a pair of sheathed scissors shaped like a tiny dagger (a reference to the bladed weapons carried at the waist in medieval times), and a pincushion shaped like

---

* A memorandum book accompanying a chatelaine can also be called an *aide-memoire*; literally, "memory aid."

a book. Given that the vast majority of my waking hours are divided between sewing and writing, when I saw a pincushion shaped like a book, I knew it had to be mine. A similar scenario played out when I saw another book-shaped chatelaine accessory a few weeks before my birthday: in this case it was a vesta, or match-safe.

Vesta (with a capital "V") was the Roman name of Hestia, goddess of the hearth. As I moved through my home every day and tended lamps and candles, I had reason to reflect on her role as guardian of the home, and on the accessory that bears her name. I thought of the connection most especially when I filled, cleaned, and lit our Perfection heater. (Incidentally, some types of matches are called vestas as well, again after the connection with fire.) I had trained myself to compulsively always return a box of matches to its usual spot after use so that it would be possible to find it again in the dark, but I couldn't help reflecting that it would be very convenient to have matches close at hand whenever I wanted them. This is exactly the reason for hanging a vesta on a chatelaine, so when I saw a book-shaped vesta that matched my pincushion, I dropped a frank hint to Gabriel about my upcoming birthday. Sure enough, the desired item arrived right on time.

After I had assembled the various components of my chatelaine, it became a constant component of my wardrobe while at home. (When I venture outside I exchange it for a chatelaine purse. For a while, every time I sewed a new dress for myself, I would use the scraps of fabric left over to make a matching purse that could hang from a clip on my waist.) When people come to visit and something comes up in conversation that we want to remember for later, quite frequently they'll reach for their cell phones at the exact same moment that I reach for the memorandum book on my chatelaine; then they'll turn on their phone while I pull out the little pencil that doubles as a closure on the notepad holder. (The pencil slots into two little loops on the left side of the case to keep it shut when not in use.) My guests will peck at keys while I write myself a note, and if this is their first such experience, they'll generally note the similarity and remark that their cell phones are their chatelaines. I'll concede that there are definitely similarities: Both are small, portable objects designed for utility. Both have been available in a wide range of manufacture, from the very simple to the wildly extravagant. Both can have additional components (applications and tools) added to their basic format, and after a certain point, they can both become increasingly unwieldy if too many of these are accessible at the same time. Most of all, they are both quotidian items that people use to express their individuality and attach a vast amount of sentiment to. I only take issue with the metaphor when people try to claim their device is superior to mine because theirs can make calls. This is my cue to smile smugly and point out that mine can make a fire, snip a thread, or pin a dress—and theirs can't.

Fashions are like the waves of the sea: they go out and come in. Something one generation considers the ultimate expression of absurdity might be considered normal by people in a different time and place—and they, in turn, will have their own strong opinions about the older fashions and what they consider ridiculous. In the long view of human history, it seems that virtually every fashion is destined for repetition given enough time. For example, the pompadour hairstyle (named after Louis XV's mistress, Madame Jeanne-Antoinette de Pompadour) was popular among eighteenth-century French nobility, then disappeared for a while when the French Revolution came and "a French fashion of bobbing heads held sway for a few months."[155] It was revived across the western world in the late nineteenth and early twentieth centuries: fashion icon and First Lady Frances Cleveland was often photographed wearing her hair in a pompadour, and the artist Charles Dana Gibson drew such beautiful women in such bouffant hairstyles that many people now know the pompadour as "the Gibson Girl hairstyle." It went out for a while again in the 1930s and '40s and came back as a man's fashion in the 1950s. (Elvis Presley's slick pompadour was probably one of the most famous hairstyles of mid-twentieth century America.)

Bell-bottom trousers (long familiar to the naval world) were wildly popular in civilian fashions of the 1960s and '70s. In the 1980s, they were considered the lowest depth of gaucherie. Then in fall 2013, a fashion column described flared jeans as "super stylish."[156] In and out, the waves just keep coming and going.

The custom of wearing beautiful items at the waist never entirely dried up in the world. Both Scottish men and Norwegian women still have items very similar to chatelaine purses as part of their traditional national dress. For the Scots, it is the sporran, the waist-hung bag that should be familiar to nearly anyone who has seen a man in a kilt and that is, very slowly, starting to creep into some people's wardrobes as a modern fashion accessory. The Norwegians wear their traditional waist-purse as part of a woman's *bunad*, or folk dress. (Incidentally, the Norwegians are so serious about maintaining the historical integrity of their traditional clothing that their ministry of culture appoints a National Bunad Council to set strict regulations enforcing authenticity.[157]) The high-end Norwegian goldsmith Sando[158] still makes and sells jewelry-quality "Lady of the House keys" to be worn with the *bunad*, and they hold the same symbolism now that they have since medieval days—a woman's power and authority over her home. So the traditions never entirely vanished; they just ebbed low in mainstream popularity for a while. The tides of fashion inevitably turn, though. I would love to see a fresh high tide of chatelaine-wearing sweep over modern America.

LADIES' 6 SIZE 14K SOLID GOLD STEM WIND WATCHES.
For Prices With Elgin, Waltham or Hampden Movements See Table Below.

Style B3. 2 Diamonds, 3 Rubies, any name, furnished in one week's time. Case only. $27.30

Style C3. Raised ornaments, 1 Diamond. Case only, $28.00.

Style D3. Fancy engraved, 1 Diamond Case only, $25.00.

Style E3. Plain polished, 1 Diamond. Case only, $24.00.

Style F3. Heavy Raised Ornaments. Case only, $24.00.

Style G3. Fancy Engraved. Case only, $20.00.

Style H3. Fancy Engraved. Case only, $22.50.

Style J3. Fancy Engraved. Case only, $20.00.

Style K3. Fancy Engraved. Case only, $22.50.

Style L3. Fancy Engraved. Case only, $19.00

Style M3. Fancy Engraved. Case only, $19.00.

Style N3. Fancy Engraved Case only, $19.00.

Catalogue No.	Prices of Complete Watches.		Style B3	Style C3	Style D3	Styles E3 & F3	Styles H3 & K3	Styles J3 & G3	Styles L3 M3 N3
19027	A	7-Jewel Gilt Exp. Bal. Elgin, Waltham or Hampden Mov't	$32.25	$33.02	$29.95	$28.95	$27.45	$24.95	$23.95
19028	An 11	" " " " " " "	33.63	34.40	32.10	31.10	29.60	27.10	26.10
19029	An 11	" Nickel " " " " "	34.18	34.95	31.88	30.88	29.38	26.88	25.88
19030	An 11	" " " " " " Jewels in Settings	35.00	35.77	32.70	31.70	30.20	27.70	26.70
19032	A 15	" " " " " " "	38.30	39.07	36.00	35.00	33.50	31.00	30.00
19033	A 16	" " " " " " "	39.30	40.07	37.00	35.96	34.45	31.95	30.95
19034	A 17	" " " " " " "	49.30	50.07	47.00	46.00	44.50	42.00	41.00
19035	A 15	" " " " Montgomery Ward & Co.'s Mov't with Special Guarantee Certificate	35.30	36.00	33.00	32.00	30.50	28.00	27.00
19036	A 16-Jewel Nickel Chronometer Bal., Montgomery Ward & Co. Mov't, with Special Guarantee Certificate		42.30	43.00	40.00	39.00	37.50	34.95	33.95

Montgomery Ward & Co. Movements are made to run. They are the best value we can offer. We send a written guarantee with each movement, and every purchaser is insured satisfaction.

We charge for engraving initials 2½ cents per letter for script style; 5 cents for Old English.

19

Watches

"Quite naturally, Mr. Selby prized this watch in proportion to its intrinsic value and admirable time-keeping qualities. He never tired of displaying to his friends the peculiar construction and superior workmanship of his rare treasure. He would press a spring and remove the outside case, laying it aside with a smile, as much as to say 'There, already, is the full value of one of your cheap American watches!' Then he would pry open the inner case with his penknife, and with the greatest care lift upon its hinge the plate bearing the movement, and point admiringly to the jeweled chronometer works. 'Did you ever see a movement like that?' he would exclaim; and then, as his friends crowded around, he would let the works back into place, declaring that he could trust no man's breath except his own amongst such delicate wheels and springs."
—"Mr. Selby's Lost Watch," *Good Housekeeping,* June 7, 1890

The Victorians did not, by any means, invent the pocket watch; by our favorite period, variations of the device had already been in the world for about four hundred years. A letter written by an ambassador in Milan and dated July 19, 1488, mentions three watches intended to be parts of "costly garments decorated with pearls." Over four centuries, timepieces slowly improved in their accuracy. Their timekeeping fluctuated less and they became less affected by changes in temperature or in movement. (In the early days of pocket watches, the same watch might keep different time depending on whether it was worn by an active horse-rider or a more sedentary individual.)[159] What the nineteenth century did for the pocket watch was make it widely available in an accurate format, even to people of relatively humble means.

Precise timekeepers had long been important to navigators in determining longitude, but for average people on land, a few minutes' more or less accuracy in a watch made very little difference—until they had trains to catch. Trains and accurate watches became so intimately associated that companies specifically presented their best products as railroad watches, even when they weren't necessarily used on trains. Horological historian George E. Townsend considers the period of "true" railroad pocket watches to have stretched from 1866 to 1969, with 1893 representing a turning point in regulation of these watches. Previously, some railroad companies (especially the larger ones) had specified particular watches they wished their employees to use, while others were content with "any watch that keeps the correct time" or "any seventeen jewel watch." When the greatest tragedy of a late train involved someone being late for a meeting, a hodge-podge of watches was good enough. Unfortunately, vehicles of massive momentum sharing the same tracks on tight schedules could result in far worse consequences than a businessman's irritation.[160] On April 19, 1891, an engineer's slow watch resulted in a disastrous train wreck in Ohio. A fast mail train and the Toledo Express were traveling opposite directions on converging courses, a common practice with railroads. The schedules called for the express to pull onto a siding and allow the fast mail train to pass, but one of the engineers' watches on the express was four minutes slow and the train didn't make it to the siding in time. The two trains collided head-on and nine men were killed.[161] As a result of this sad occurrence, in 1893 all railroads operating in America adopted a set of standard requirements for the watches carried by their workers. Among other specifications, official railroad watches were required to deviate no more than thirty seconds per week, be size 16 or 18 (1.7 inches to 1.8 inches across the mechanisms), be labeled with arabic (not roman) numerals, and be adjusted to temperature 40 to 95 degrees Fahrenheit.*[162]

One of the best summaries of historians' view of the effect that railroads had on timekeeping was expressed in a 2002 thesis: "It seems to have become almost mandatory for scholars describing modern time keeping and organization to assert that before the extension of the Victorian railway network, every English town followed its own time."[163] Increasingly accurate watches allowed schedules to run on ever-tightening grids of time, but the devices would have been useless without standardized time zones. Four standard times zones were instituted for the United States on November 18, 1883, and Britain was instrumental in standardizing global time zones in 1884.[164]

Prior to the nineteenth century, watchmaking had been done by jewelers or other specialty artisans. (In England, watchmakers would sometimes become so

---

*Temperature extremes can affect the accuracy of a mechanical watch when the metal expands or contracts.

specialized that different men would make different parts of a watch and carry it from man to man for each stage to be completed.[165]) In the nineteenth century, watches—like so many other useful items of everyday life—started being mass-produced in factories. (America was especially known for being "the home of mass production."[166]) This shift in manufacturing practices greatly reduced the price of the average watch at the same historical moment accurate timepieces were becoming increasingly important. These two factors combined to shift people's attitudes toward watches. They were still status symbols, but in a situation very similar to what would happen with cellular telephones in the early twenty-first century, they became so taken for granted that simple ownership was no longer enough. People started caring about specific models and exterior presentation.

In the late nineteenth century, catalogs frequently sold watch cases separately from their mechanical workings. The case is the ornamental exterior of a watch; it can be made of gold, silver, or a cheaper and frequently more durable metallic alloy. (These last often mimicked silver and had names alluding to it: Silveroid, Silverode, Silverore, Silverine.) Enamel had been another option for watch cases in the eighteenth and early nineteenth centuries, but it became increasingly less common as the Victorian era progressed. Most of the gold cases weren't solid gold, but were brass sandwiched between two thin layers of gold. A guarantee accompanying the watch stated how many years (ten, fifteen, twenty, or twenty-five) would go by before the brass started showing through the gold.[167]

Watch collectors devote entire books to the differences in mechanical workings of various watches. One of the most fundamental components for novices to remember is that, as a general rule of thumb, the more functional jewels a watch's mechanism contains, the more accurate it will be. (The railroad watch specifications of 1893 dictated that a train worker's timepiece have least seventeen jewels.) In the nineteenth century, these jewels were usually sapphires or rubies too small or too flawed to be used in jewelry. Modern watchmakers use synthetic gems. These jewels essentially act as bearings and bushings for the very small gears and cogs in a watch; because crystal is so much smoother than metal and doesn't wear down as easily, jewels greatly reduce the friction within a watch and therefore increase its accuracy. (Obviously, setting extraneous and nonfunctional jewels into the movement doesn't increase the accuracy of the watch—although it has been tried as a marketing tactic.[168]) High-end watch mechanisms also include technical features too numerous to be listed here.

To really flaunt their status, a Victorian didn't have just any watch, just like a twenty-first-century person doesn't buy just any cell phone. A Victorian man with social aspirations would desire a twenty-one jeweled, railroad-grade movement watch in a solid gold case hanging from a solid gold chain with fobs representing his particular interests and associations.

While timepieces became increasingly important in running railroads, they also became indispensable in daily life. As people moved into cities and worked in industrial jobs, punctuality and awareness of time became larger issues. In earlier eras and more rural communities, most people's need for punctuality was limited to church and special events. When more exact timeliness became possible, it very soon became expected.

In one of my earliest childhood memories, I am standing in a bank's vault with my grandmother while she accesses her safety deposit box. There can't have been much in her box, as it was the smallest variety the bank rented, and whatever it did contain has long since passed from my mind—except one precious item. It might have been the fact that she told me it would one day belong to me that caught my memory, or perhaps it was simply a young girl's magpie attraction to something shiny and pretty. That one gleaming item, with its subtle shades of colored gold and its dainty design of a single bird among flowers, nestled into my memory and remained long after a vague impression of paper documents had flown from my mind: the watch. It was passed down to the Almas of the family; my grandmother Alma Sarah had inherited it from the ancestor whose Christian name she had been given. As her namesake Sarah Alma, it would eventually come to me.

I now know it to be of about average size for a lady's pocket watch of the late nineteenth century: thirty-three millimeters across its dial, which makes it a size 6 by the way these things are measured. In terms of price, it was about mid-range for a watch of its time, which still made it a quite valuable item. The 1895 Montgomery Ward catalog lists the style of a watch case very similar to mine at a cost of $24. The mechanical workings for this model would run between $28.95 and $39, depending on how advanced they were. So the entire watch was worth around $53, or a little more. To put this in perspective, $24 would buy one dozen pairs of ladies' button boots from the same catalog. A half-dozen ready-made ladies' Newport wool suits with satin linings went for $35.70.[169]

My grandmother's family were hard-scrabble farmers in Alberta prairie country, so poor that Great-Grandma Helen made her children's underwear out of flour sacks. This watch must have represented a particularly valuable item to them. In an interesting example of how the financial value of something can change over time, today it would be worth less than a single pair of new shoes. For me, though, it is absolutely priceless.

My grandmother's watch is, in fact, too precious to me for use on a daily basis, so when Gabriel and I started wearing Victorian clothes and using Victorian technology regularly, he and I each acquired a daily-use pocket watch from eBay. His never worked, and the local jewelers were unable to repair it. Mine worked for about a year and a half after being cleaned by a jeweler and then fell into a coma about which the jewelers could do nothing.

In May 2013, Gabriel traveled to New Jersey to celebrate coinciding special occasions: his cousin's wedding and his grandmother's ninetieth birthday. (We had both been invited, but it wasn't practical for me to take the requisite time away from my businesses at that particular point.) Deciding to make optimal use of the trip, he brought our nonfunctional pocket watches with him and sought out a New York watchsmith while he was in the area. The night after he had found such a craftsman, he called me from his uncle's phone to relate a fascinating story.

Gabriel had read of a watch repairman in Manhattan, so he took the train from New Jersey and sought out the craftsman. In the crowded, narrow alley New Yorkers call Diamond Row, he found a tiny shop run by a single elderly man behind a folding counter. While my husband was waiting his turn, he was privy to a most entertaining encounter. A handsome young Israeli (whom Gabriel described as resembling a young James Dean with a yarmulke) examined and ultimately purchased a mechanical wristwatch valued at $18,000, which was bartered down to $17,250 and paid for in crisp American cash. The bills were so fresh, in fact, that the watch seller commented upon their newness. "Yes," replied the buyer with a twinkle in his eye, "I just made them yesterday!"

After witnessing the casual exchange of a sum that beggared the fiscal value of my engagement ring, Gabriel was a bit sheepish about his own transaction. He was quite touched when the watch seller set him at his ease and accorded him every bit as much respect as he had given the man who had just paid out the value of a small automobile in cash.

The verdict on our two watches was mixed. They had been eBay finds and we hadn't known much about their provenance, but after examining them the watch repairman was able to tell Gabriel that his was a working-class man's watch from a small maker. We had more or less surmised this. Mine, on the other hand, was a far more interesting creature: a British brand name adorned an American-cased watch with Swiss mechanisms. Gabriel and the watchsmith agreed it was interesting enough to merit repair. (Gabriel's watch, however, was not. The parts for it had long since ceased to be available, and the only way to repair it would have been to replicate every necessary part from scratch. It was far more cost-effective to simply buy a different watch whose parts were easier to acquire.)

The really intriguing part came when the watchsmith explained the leading threat to mechanical watches in the modern world: cell phones. This is not some metaphorical threat about new technology replacing old or a case of people ceasing to wear or carry watches because their mobile telephones have digital chronometers built into them. No, this is a very real, literal threat. Cellular telephones (and many other electronic devices) physically assault and injure mechanical watches.

The watch repairman was very glad to hear that Gabriel and I do not carry cell phones. To illustrate his point, he used a simple Boy Scout compass to demonstrate how the watch had been damaged by magnetic fields. When he slowly ran the compass in a circle around my watch, the needle pointed to the timepiece as north, no matter which direction it was held. Those who recall their elementary school science classes can easily deduce what this means: at some point, the watch had become magnetized.

When I was a young girl, I was fascinated to read in one of my books that small bits of metal can be turned into magnets themselves by being rubbed against a strong enough example of one, and I subsequently spent an entire evening happily magnetizing every pin and needle in my sewing box. I was amused to see the little sharps sticking together and lifting each other. This amusement turned to frustration when I tried to create my own compass (as my book told me I could) by floating a needle on the surface tension of a shallow bowl of water. My book hadn't mentioned sticking the magnetized needle into a cork first and I only succeeded in sinking every needle I tried to float.

Navigating the magnetic minefield the world has progressively become, my watch came under the influence of a significant magnetic field. During my ownership of the watch, it had never kept great time, so it was probably already suffering from magnetic effects when I bought it. Something since then had caused it to cease working altogether. Since I don't carry a cell phone, the most likely culprits were probably the various metal detectors I'd passed through at airports and public buildings. After exposure to these magnetic fields, the tiny, vulnerable metal workings of the fragile watch had been corrupted. They had turned magnetic themselves, and instead of moving in the neat, regulated ticking motions by which a mechanical watch keeps orderly time, the gears were sticking together in clumps as tenacious as the clumps of needles and pins in my childhood sewing box.

As the knowledgeable watchsmith was explaining this, a man who seemed the stereotype of a quintessential New York banker came up to the counter. He was in a blue pin-striped suit, and he carried a brand-new iPhone in the same hand whose wrist wore a $50,000 Patek Philippe watch that, besides telling time, also displayed a perpetual calendar and the phases of the moon. This watch should have been superlatively accurate, but the banker complained that the calendar was stuck on Wednesday and that it wasn't keeping accurate time. The watchsmith patiently explained that the watch had been magnetized (probably by the iPhone), and it would have to be disassembled and each piece demagnetized separately. He illustrated his point with the same Boy Scout compass trick he had showed Gabriel, then clamped the watch in a horological equivalent of an EKG machine to display its ticking heartbeat on a paper tape. He pointed out the irregularity in the markings caused by the magnetization of the tiny parts of the watch's mechanism. Then he explained that he could fix the watch, but that as soon as the watch was brought back into close proximity with a strong magnetic field (like that of a cell phone), it would start having problems again.

The businessman gave the watchsmith a put-upon look. "You're saying I have to send it to Switzerland?"

"No," explained the patient watchsmith. "I'm saying that if you hold it in the same hand as your iPhone, it's going to happen again no matter who fixes it this time."

The businessman took another call on his cell and walked out of the store. With a sad shake of his head, the watchsmith turned back to Gabriel. After some deliberation, Gabriel chose to buy a watch with a similar case to the nonfunctional one he had brought to the shop. The new/old watch (from 1895) is a seventeen-jewel American Waltham railroad grade that fits very well with our middle-class social standing. The mechanisms are all fairly standard, so it will be easy to repair and maintain. He left my watch with the watchsmith to be serviced and repaired.

As a result of the conversation with the watchsmith, Gabriel tracked down a special type of fabric to use as a lining in the watch-pockets of his suits. It has a texture similar to heavily starched silk, but is actually made of a very fine metallic mesh. The mesh acts as a Faraday cage to block magnetic fields.

Several months after Gabriel's New York trip, we presented an educational talk about Victorian life for a group of homeschooling children. They were particularly fascinated by Gabriel's watch, and when we told them about how pocket watches had progressively shrunk in size as technology improved, the kids' parents had a good laugh about how similar this was to what they had seen happen with cell phones. Playing off this metaphor, I pointed out, "Yes, and the fobs on his watch chain are a bit like his apps!" The whole room cracked up.

20

Science Matters
and Outdoor Outings

There is pleasure in the pathless woods,
There is rapture in the lonely shore,
There is society, where none intrudes,
By the deep Sea, and music in its roar;
I love not Man the less, but Nature more.[170]

—Lord Byron, 1889

The most common images of the nineteenth century are of parlors and factories, but it should be remembered that life was blooming and burgeoning
outdoors as well as indoors. In addition to the technological innovations in the
world of business, nineteenth-century science also experienced a vast expansion
of the way people understood the natural world.

Charles Darwin (whose *On the Origin of Species by Means of Natural
Selection* was first published in 1859) is doubtless one of the most recognizable
names in Victorian science, but the *Beagle* voyager was scarcely unique in his
explorations. Botanist Matthias Schleiden and zoologist Theodor Schwann
had pioneered cell theory in 1838, the same year Queen Victoria was crowned.
In 1856, excavators in the Neander Valley in Germany unearthed a humanoid
skeleton that would spark debates scientists are still having: at first some said
that these bones were the remains of a deformed modern human, then in 1886
the discovery of more Neanderthal skeletons in Belgium led researchers to the
conclusion that they represented a separate species.[171] (Current research suggests
a bit of truth in both these theories: a 2014 study concluded, "Anatomically
modern humans overlapped and mated with Neandertals [sic] such that non-
African humans inherit ~1 to 3% of their genomes from Neandertal [sic]
ancestors."[172])

Gabriel looking for fossils.

British historian Dr. Sarah Whittingham has called natural history "a national obsession among the upper and middle classes of Victorian Britain"[173]—and this was the case in America as well. If the eighteenth century had been the Age of Reason, perhaps the nineteenth could justifiably be called the Age of Comprehension. In the 1880s, bicycle magazines pointed out that one of the many benefits of this new machine was that it could take its riders to new and exciting places for hunting scientific specimens ranging from pond microbes to beetles and butterflies. Books for women and girls included instructions for taxidermy along with tips about collecting mosses and seaweed.[174]

The idea of taxidermy being a popular hobby for Victorian ladies rather surprised my buddy Tom when I mentioned it. (Tom is the dear friend who proved so amenable to answering my letters with emails.) He's a research scientist who has personally dissected more species of creatures than most people would even recognize. He looks upon the flesh-eating beetles in his laboratory as pets. He has a far more open-minded approach to death than most people I know; he was just shocked at the idea of Victorian ladies doing taxidermy because he had always heard that they were squeamish.

I pointed out to him that it's kind of funny that modern stereotypes simultaneously hold caricatures of both the squeamish Victorian woman who faints at the sight of dead animals and the Victorian woman who was chained to the kitchen. These ideas aren't very compatible images in an omnivorous society. Up into the twentieth century, small food animals were often sold whole or even still alive. (In many countries, they still are.) The live ones could either be killed on the spot at the time of purchase or taken home squawking. Really, it must have seemed a natural step for young women who'd grown up gutting birds for the dinner table to start disemboweling them for decorative purposes, especially since decoration, whether of the home or of wearable things like hats, was very solidly in the woman's sphere. At the end of the nineteenth century, the American millinery industry employed around 83,000 people—and most of these were women.[175] Preparing and arranging bits of dead birds represented a significant portion of their livelihood.

A few of my neighbors own bird feeders they keep well-stocked, and several of my other neighbors are owned by very active and happy domestic cats. The results of this combination are exactly what one would expect. Personally I hate to see anything go to waste, so I wrote to Tom asking for taxidermy tips for small birds to put some of the cats' leavings to use. I was able to try out his advice when, some time later, Monsieur Chat came calling and presented me a hostess gift of a dead house sparrow.

I have been a vegetarian since I was eight years old so I've had less intimate experience of dead animals than most people, but I took a scientific attitude toward the project and followed Tom's instructions. When I got the bird's body out of its skin, I was highly amused at how closely it resembled a roasting chicken in miniature. A first attempt at any form of art is liable to be a muddle, and I'm afraid I made a bit of a hash of the sparrow; but I managed to preserve the wings and they made a rather nice addition to my autumn bonnet.*

For my part, I would argue that Victorian ladies were far less squeamish than their twenty-first-century counterparts. It is difficult to imagine a modern popular woman's magazine describing the mating habits of spiders in graphic detail, but in 1889 *The Cosmopolitan* did exactly that. Pictures accompany the article, illustrating everything from the various steps in locomotion for European water spiders to zoomed-in details of an *epeira* spider's fangs and claws (magnified vastly larger than their actual size) to an illustration of the sexual dichotomies of the male and female jumping spider![176]

So much for Victorian women being squeamish.

For our tenth wedding anniversary (traditionally the tin anniversary in the way that the twenty-fifth is silver and the fiftieth gold), Gabriel gave me a gift that tied into the scientific aspects of the nineteenth century in a most remarkable way. The shiny tin cylinder had a hinged front, and at first I wondered if it might be some sort of display case related to my massage business—for essential oils or lotions, maybe.

"It's called a vasculum," Gabriel explained as I cocked an eyebrow quizzically at the item, trying to puzzle it out. It was thirteen inches in its longest dimension and had slightly curved ends that bulged a little less than half an inch beyond this. Its small side was a narrow oval. My sewing tape, stretched around the outside of this oval, would measure sixteen inches in circumference, but a hard ruler would only measure its diameter as four inches in one direction, six in the other. It was shorter than a poster tube, but at the same time much broader than one.

---

*Readers in England should be advised that in their native country, house sparrows have legal protection—although no one tells this to the kitties—so using them as decorations might raise some questions. In America, sparrows are an introduced species and are considered invasive because they compete with our own songbirds for food and nesting sites.

As I inspected the case, Gabriel grinned broadly, obviously delighted and barely able to hold in the answer to the riddle.

"Vasculum." I quietly repeated the word he had used, trying to parse it out. *It sounds like vascular . . .* I pondered. "Doesn't it have something to do with 'nourishing,' in Latin?"

I would later learn that I had been stretching the connection in the wrong direction. "Vasculum" and "vascular" are indeed related, but linguistically speaking, I had mistaken the branch for the root. *Vasculum* is Latin for "vessel," and is, in fact, the parent word from which English derives *vascular*—since the vascular systems of animals and plants are made up of vessels that carry blood and other fluids.

Gabriel, who was still grinning broadly, couldn't keep the puzzle's answer to himself any more. "It's a specimen collecting case!" he said proudly.

He explained that vascula originated in the 1700s as a way for scientists to collect and carry specimens while doing fieldwork. (Fans of the 2003 movie *Master and Commander* might remember seeing an eighteenth-century vasculum carried by the ship's doctor in the scene where he is collecting plants and animals in the Galapagos Islands. Gabriel bought my vasculum from the same tinsmith who made the prop for the movie.[177]) By the nineteenth century, their popularity had grown far beyond the realm of professional science, and vascula were popular accessories for amateurs (and even children) to use for collecting wildflowers and other items of scientific interest. The nineteenth century had a particular fad for Pteridomania, or "fern fever." It was very fashionable to collect live ferns from forested areas, carry them home in a vasculum with a damp cloth, moss, or moist bit of cotton against the roots, and replant the botanical curiosity in one's home garden or as a potted parlor specimen. The same was done with wildflowers, and orchids were especially sought after.

Personally, I've never been able to cosset any outdoor plant sufficiently to accommodate its survival indoors. The difference in temperature and humidity was always too much any time I tried it—even with a plant as stalwart as a dandelion. Fashions, however, seldom bear a very strong relationship to simplicity. If any readers do feel like trying their luck, they should be careful of where they gather specimens; regulations about digging things up on federal land are much stricter than they used to be. At the end of the nineteenth century, legal authorities were already starting to crack down on such things in England. In Devon in 1896, two "fern stealers" were sentenced to four and six weeks' hard labor.[178]

On my tin wedding anniversary, I smiled at the pretty, shining vasculum my husband had given me. "I thought you could use it for picking berries,"

Gabriel said, smiling. He held up a forefinger. "There is a slight element of a project to it," he warned.

I groaned inwardly. I've been wary of Gabriel's ideas for projects ever since he gave me an antique cape with more than two thousand beads on it—all of them popping off like confetti, since the silk thread that originally held them on had long since disintegrated. The only needle that would fit these tiny beads was hardly wider than a human hair. The cape was beautiful, but I had feared that I might go either insane or blind by the time I finished repairing it.

Gabriel showed me a piece of rough material like flat rope and pointed at the tabs on either end of the vasculum. "You'll want to sew on the shoulder strap. I would have done it ahead of time, but I wasn't sure how long you wanted it to be."

I smiled at him, grateful the project was a simple one that would take less than five minutes of labor. I fetched a strong needle and thick linen thread from my sewing kit, and while I completed the task, we imagined the fun we would have with this newest acquisition.

The vasculum would prove to be a remarkably useful item, even for quotidian activities that don't involve scientific specimens. For example, it makes an excellent purse. The metal structure is excellent protection for any material put inside it, which makes it quite useful for transporting small posters or fragile items. Even nineteenth-century fern hunters used to carry their sandwiches in their vascula.[179] And when it comes to outdoor activities, the lovely tin case really comes into its own.

"PALÆONTOLOGY (Gr. *palaios*, ancient; *onta*, beings; *logos*, discourse) is the science which treats of the living beings, whether animal or vegetable, which have inhabited this globe at past periods in its history. It is the ancient life-history of the Earth, and if its record could ever be completed, it would furnish us with an account of the structure, habits, and distribution of all the animals and plants which have at any time flourished upon the land-surfaces of the globe or inhabited its waters . . . All natural objects which come to be studied by the palæontologist are termed 'fossils' (Lat. *fossus*, dug up)."
—Henry Alleyne Nicholson, *A Manual of Palæontology*, 1889[180]

My buddy Tom enjoys sharing his specimen collection as much as Gabriel and I love to show off our antique clothing. Tom's research has taken him up and down North America from Alaska to Mexico, around the globe, and from Egypt to South Africa. After seeing a horse brain in a jar on his bedroom shelf, I decided I could no longer be surprised by anything in his collection. When a particularly beautiful fossilized scallop caught my eye, he mentioned that it had come from a beach not too far from my house. I immediately knew it was a place I must visit.

Gabriel was as excited about the idea of fossil hunting as I was. Tom had warned us that the tides on the beach we would be visiting were rather extreme, and that we would want to time our visit to do as much fossil hunting as possible while the tide was out. Accordingly, we looked up a tide table and scheduled our trip for an occasion when Gabriel's day off would coincide with a particularly low tide during daylight hours. While we eagerly waited for the day to arrive, we each prepared for it in our own way. Gabriel sent away for a rock hammer, and after it arrived in the mail, I sewed a leather holster for us to carry this useful tool. To give either of us the option of carrying it, I put two notches in the holster's belt—one corresponding to Gabriel's waist, and the other to my own.

Naturally I planned on bringing my vasculum when we went fossil hunting. Tom highly approved of this idea. He had mentioned we should bring some fabric to wrap around any fossils we found so they wouldn't chip by banging against each other; so as the day for our expedition approached, I raided my scrap box. The biggest piece of fabric in it at that point was my first berry-picking dress, worn thin as tissue paper. I had made it two years previously, and in that time I had dragged it through so many brambles and washed and rewashed it so many times that the original fabric still remaining between its many patches and swathes of darning sundered like cobweb at even the slightest pressure. Its useful life as an actual garment was clearly over, and it was too fragile to turn into quilt squares. As padding material, however, it would be perfect.

It had taken me days to sew the dress two summers before, and I had spent countless hours since then maintaining it in various ways—washing out sweat, dirt, and berry juice; darning holes; re-stitching seams—but it had served its purpose. With very little sentiment, I ripped the product of all of this work into pieces ranging from the size of a napkin to the size of a dishtowel. It was like tearing tissue paper, and the garment, which had taken countless hours to create and maintain, took less than thirty minutes to reduce to fragments.

Gabriel and I had a somewhat lengthy discussion about the appropriate clothing to wear on a fossil-hunting expedition. I obviously didn't want to shred any of my delicate town dresses climbing over beach boulders, and wearing a tea-gown (which would have been the Victorian equivalent of showing up at the beach in a nightie) would have been silly. Besides, my tea-gowns wouldn't have stood up to the rocks either. My wardrobe held two practical choices, both made of canvas duck (a sturdy fabric also used for tents and mattress ticks). I could wear my hiking dress or the thorn-proof blue-and-white striped dress I had made to pick berries in. I had sewn the hiking dress using a photo of Fay Fuller's hiking outfit from 1890 as inspiration. She had worn this dress when she became the first woman to summit Washington's tallest mountain, Mt. Rainier.[181]

I had made the work dress (the striped one) by copying an antique dress in our collection from around 1900. Gabriel had given the original to me the previous Christmas and had written the intriguing clue, "An everyday item," on the package's tag. When I sat down to study the dress and create a copy of it, I found that this example of rough clothing incorporated one of the most brilliant methods I have ever seen for dealing with the tedious task of measuring pleats for a skirt: a thick piece of string had been drawn through every other stripe and pulled tight to gather it. Thus, not only did the stripes help to camouflage the various stains inevitable on a workdress that sees hard use, they also served as an intrinsic portion of the pattern. Since the stripes were all of equal width, using them as a gather-guide was a brilliant way of making regular pleats without requiring the tedious task of measuring every quarter-inch. I love the finished visual effect of pleats but detest measuring them out, so seeing this shortcut constituted a true "Eureka!" moment for me. These little lessons from the past, held in stasis by artifacts, are exactly the reason Gabriel and I enjoy collecting authentic antiques so much.

Gabriel pointed out that the work dress's stripes made it the more beach-appropriate option. The tradition of wearing striped clothes at the seashore has a long and salty history. English and Dutch paintings have depicted sailors and seafarers wearing stripes since the mid-seventeenth century. The shirts worn by low-ranking members of ships' crews were knitted jersey worn for warmth—and the jersey fabric produced by the European hosiery industry was predominantly striped. (This is due to technical reasons related to the way in which jersey is produced.) In terms of safety at sea, in the days before "safety orange" or "DayGlo yellow" garments were possible, stripes were of added benefit to help visibility in the unfortunate case of a man falling overboard. They also fit in with other visual elements of life aboard ships: striped flags had been common on sailing ships since classical and medieval times.

When civilians started taking seaside holidays, these visits were regarded as a time to leave behind their formal, everyday clothing and wear something they wouldn't mind getting dirty. By the end of the Second Empire in France, striped clothing was the popular choice for seaside visitors in Normandy, and from there the fashion spread to the coasts of England and Belgium. In the Belle Époque, stripes were de rigueur in beachside clothing. This was partly for modesty, since uniformly pale garments turn sheer when soaked with water.[182] See-through clothes were grudgingly tolerated in pre-Victorian society: during the Madison administration, Betsy Bonaparte (Napoleon's American sister-in-law who was notorious for appearing at social events almost naked) went to at least one Washington, DC, dance in nothing but a skimpy muslin dress deliberately dampened to render it transparent. (The assembled crowds were given a full view of the fact that she wasn't wearing any underwear.)[183] However, Betsy was an exception even within her own crowd, and by the late nineteenth century people had rather more taste. Wearing stripes to beaches provided a certain amount of camouflage even if one's clothing got wet.

At forty-eight degrees northern latitude, the frigid waters of the Pacific Ocean are not particularly fun to go cavorting in, and I didn't plan on getting any wetter than I absolutely had to. Consequently, I wasn't very concerned about transparency, but all the other historical reasons for stripes on the beach were in favor of my work dress, so it won the clothing contest. I used a stiff brush to clear the skirt of various burrs it had picked up while berry picking and eagerly anticipated our trip.

When we first arrived at the fossil beach, the tide was still two hours from its lowest point. The terrain was profoundly rocky, and traveling parallel to the sea was really more like bouldering than walking. It was one of the steepest beaches I had ever seen, barring those that were outright cliffs or bluffs. This made for a very dramatic unveiling as the water receded. At the tide's highest level, it was possible to be trapped between the onrushing waters and a steep cliff, and as we traveled parallel to the hill, we saw ropes dangling from high points to help unwary adventurers escape from such situations. I know people who would probably elect to exit by such a route even if they weren't blocked off by water, but I prefer my movements to remain more two-dimensional.

We started onto the beach two hours before low tide so that we could travel out a reasonable distance before the waters' lowest ebb. We wanted ample time to explore, hunt for fossils, and then still have a reasonable getaway time without resorting to the escape ropes.

The very first thing we noticed when we went down to the beach was a remarkable quantity of sea urchin shells. Gulls and other creatures had been feasting on them, leaving their empty carapaces behind. There were fresh urchins—bright purple like a Roman emperor's imperial toga—with their spines still poking out at all angles, and older ones from which the spines had dropped—bumpy orbs bleached to a dull ivory. I set two aside on a log at the beach head for retrieval when we returned.

Gabriel, target-focused and keen as always to make distance, rushed ahead as I slipped and clambered my way over the slimy rocks. The stones were more slippery than oiled eels. Progress was slow over the treacherous footing, but we soon arrived at a spot on the fossil-rich beach that looked promising.

Tom had told us to look for roughly spheroid sedimentary rocks. I had my vasculum and we brought a wire basket for Gabriel to use while collecting, but somehow I wound up carrying both of them. While Gabriel forged ahead with an intensity of purpose that made him seem far more like he was going for a land-speed record than hunting for anything, I filled the basket with promising-looking rocks. When I had too many to keep carrying, I called for Gabriel to wait for me. He had the rock hammer.

"Let's bash these open and see if they're worth carrying," I told him, handing over the heavy basket.

He unholstered the rock hammer and commenced pounding away at the stones, his expression as happy as a little boy's. We both experienced an excited anticipation as Gabriel worked at cleaving the rocks. It was a sentiment somewhat like opening presents at Christmas, but with an aura of gambling in it as well. We didn't know what we would find—if anything.

The first rock broke open after a few blows, revealing a homogenous core identical to its exterior. "Nothing in this one," observed Gabriel.

"Well," I said philosophically, "that's one we don't have to carry."

The next stone revealed a similarly blank interior.

"Empty!" I proclaimed, rolling it away.

Candidate number three was flatter, a more splintery rock than the others we had tried. It broke along its grain, showing tiny specks like detritus frozen in ancient mud.

"Micro-fossils," observed Gabriel.

I regarded the size of the rock—about four pounds—and debated the hassle of hauling it around versus the actual merit of the tiny specks of fossilized mulch. "I don't think that one's really worth carrying," I observed.

"No," agreed Gabriel, casting it aside. "We'll wait until we find some better ones."

I left him merrily cracking open rocks and I carefully picked my way toward a huge stone formation that jutted out into the retreating ocean. From a distance, I thought it was covered with bird guano or irregular rock bits, but as I climbed onto rocks that were deep underwater at any time except low tide, I realized my mistake.

"It's covered with mussels!" I called up to Gabriel, beaming. "Solid mussels! There must be thousands of them!"

Depending on the level of the tide, the outcrop was sometimes a peninsula, sometimes an island, sometimes an underwater mound. It was thickly encrusted with a solid coating of blue and white teardrop-shaped shellfish. They were the biggest mussels I had ever seen, each one the length of my hand or bigger. Their numbers were beyond counting, and what little space existed between them on the rocks was solidly filled with enormous barnacles.

I stepped gingerly at first, worried they might crack under my weight. However I soon found I had no cause for concern. The dense mass of thick shells supported me with the solidity of concrete. They weren't slippery like the seaweed-covered rocks, and I gained confidence from my surer footing. I wandered out farther toward the retreating sea.

The tide's current level put the massive rock formation in its island stage, and I found a place where the saltwater channels surrounding it were narrow enough to step across. I climbed up and over the formation, enjoying its tide pools and delighting in the tiny red crabs and huge green sea anemones filling these trapped collections of water.

Meanwhile, during my distraction by the living shells and tiny animals, Gabriel had found more microfossils. When I rejoined him, he showed them to me. Some of these were large and interesting enough—and collected in a small enough piece of surrounding stone—to merit the trouble of carrying the rock out with us. I carefully wrapped it in one of the old dress scraps I had brought with us and put it in my vasculum.

Gabriel and I wandered different ways again, and at length my husband called out. When I looked toward him, he was holding both arms in the air triumphantly. "Success!" he cried.

I made my way toward him as fast as the slippery footing on the upper beach rocks would allow.

"Find something good?" I asked when I was close enough to voice the question in a civilized tone instead of shouting it.

"Yeah!" he proclaimed, holding up a heavy stone nearly the size of his own head. Sticking out of one edge was a bit of fossilized scallop shell. "Now, if I can only get it out of there." He worried at the rock with the hammer, trying to break off a manageable chunk containing the scallop fragment. Misdirected force broke off part of the shell, but at length he salvaged a piece worth carrying home. This, too, I carefully wrapped in another old scrap of berry-picking dress and put in my vasculum.

After a while, Gabriel developed blisters from overenthusiastic use of the rock hammer, so I took it from him and took my turn at smacking things. I found another prize-worthy section of micro-fossils along with a fossil clam, and at length we saw that the tide was beginning to turn. We steered our feet back toward the place where we had entered the beach, exploring tide pools and investigating rocks as we went.

The bigger rocks sheltered dozens of scurrying crustaceans hurrying for cover when I upended their shelter. I told Gabriel that I may not have learned to hunt fossils, but I had certainly learned how to hunt crabs. There were limpets everywhere, as well, and I found the best way to remove the tenacious univalves from a promising stone was to use the prying end of the rock hammer. There were chitons too—prehistoric-looking things that yet lived and moved. It was intriguing to see so many living shellfish juxtaposed against their fossilized ancestors.

We climbed up above the tideline and laid out our lunch on a bench. Our picnic was copied from a meal in one of our favorite books, *Possession* by A. S. Byatt. The novel is a wonderfully romantic story of two couples—one pair in the nineteenth, and one in the twentieth century. The Victorian couple are poets, the later pair are researchers studying them, and throughout the book their stories become increasingly parallel and intertwined. (Should it surprise anyone that Gabriel and I enjoy the book so much? He had first read it aloud to me a few months before our marriage. He read it to me again in anticipation of this trip, because the Victorian couple in the story were amateur fossil finders.) Our picnic copied one brought by the modern couple to a beach where their Victorian counterparts had hunted fossils: "Fresh brown bread, white Wensleydale cheese, crimson radishes, yellow butter, scarlet tomatoes, round bright green Granny Smiths, and a bottle of mineral water."[184] As we nibbled away at our feast, we watched bald eagles soaring overhead. It was the perfect conclusion to an ideal outing.

The next day, I wrote a short letter about the trip to our friend Cathy, a professional geologist. Cathy said I reminded her of Mary Anning, a nineteenth-century fossil hunter. I had heard about this woman but knew little about her—so of course I started researching. She proved to be an extraordinarily fascinating figure.

Mary Anning (May 21, 1799–March 9, 1847) would ultimately be called the Princess of Paleontology by German explorer Ludwig Leichhardt, but she was born in direst poverty.[185] She was the daughter of Richard and Molly Anning—a poor carpenter and his wife who lived near a jail in Lyme Regis, on England's southern coast in the county of Dorset. Richard did what he could to augment his carpentry income, habitually journeying out to the fossil-rich seashore near Lyme to hunt fossils. The interesting stones (called "curiosities" by local Dorset residents of the time) could be sold or displayed outside to draw attention—and hopefully business—from visitors passing through the area. As a small child, little Mary enjoyed accompanying her father on these expeditions to seek out the pretty stones, but these happy outings were not destined to last long. When Mary was only ten years old, her father died after falling off a cliff.[186]

The family's economic situation was always precarious, but after Richard's death, it became absolutely dire. Stalwart little Mary, however, had a character as strong as the stones she hunted. Young as she was, she took it upon herself to help support her brother and their widowed mother. Starting with an ammonite she was able to sell to a visiting lady for a half-crown, Mary set about earning a livelihood through fossil-hunting.[187] (Some people have even suggested that stories of Mary inspired Terry Sullivan's famous tongue-twister, "She sells sea-shells by the seashore."[188])

While Mary was still a child by modern standards, she and her brother made a discovery that would fossilize Mary's fame in geological circles*:

---

* Accounts vary as to exactly how old Mary was when she found the ichthyosaur. The Chambers say she was only ten; Goodhue reports her age as fourteen. There is also some dispute as to which of the siblings saw the creature's bones first: Nineteenth-century writers such as the Chambers and Isabel Thorne give all the credit to Mary and only mention her brother as someone who benefited from her geologic labor. Writing in the twenty-first century, Goodhue reports that the brother found the creature's skull and Mary searched an entire year before finding the remainder of its skeleton. Davis gives the brother all the credit for the find.

One day her eye trained by long practice detected some bones sticking out of the side of the cliff. With her hammer she traced the outline of some huge monster, whose existence had never before been recognized; she employed men to dig away the earth that was around it, and at length the entire skeleton was made clear. From the end of the jaw to the tip of its tail it measured thirty feet, the socket of the eye was as large as a huge saucer. It was like a creature made up of parts of many other animals, the head shaped like that of a lizard, the teeth were those of a crocodile, the trunk and tail resembled that of an ordinary quadruped, but it had the paddles of a whale, the ribs of a chameleon, and a long slender neck.[189]

Mary's remarkable find was the first example ever discovered of an ichthyosaur. This dolphin-like reptile lived contemporary with the dinosaurs—and Mary found it two decades before the word *dinosaur* even entered the English lexicon![190] She sold the "crocodile" (as many then called it) to Squire Henley, the lord of the local manor and owner of the property where Mary had found the fossilized skeleton. In exchange for her find, Henley gave Mary twenty-three pounds sterling—enough money to feed her family for more than half a year![191] Selling the treasure to Henley was somewhat of a neat trick since she had dug it out of his own land, but the squire was known for his generosity[192] and, young though she was, Mary could be quite forceful when it came to getting what she needed to support her family.

Squire Henley donated his purchase to Bullock's Museum of Natural Curiosities in London, and when that collection was disbursed, The British Museum purchased the ichthyosaur Mary had found. A nineteenth-century scientific journal later reported:

It quite engrossed the attention of the scientific world. The great geologists, Buckland, Delabeche, Sir Everard Home, Birch Conybeare, Cuvier, and the élite of that body in this [England] and other nations, were for six years deep in the study of the contribution from the young girl of Lyme-Regis. Mary Anning, now called with great respect Miss Mary Anning, furnished drawings of fragments, supplied deficiencies in published accounts, and proceeded to discover plesiosauri, pterodactyles, and fish more numerous than the present sea produces. Only look round the cases of the British Museum, and you will see that the grandest specimens were found by Miss Mary Anning.[193]

Mary never had any formal schooling; she taught herself everything she knew by reading every book about geology she could buy or borrow, by her fieldwork of digging fossils from rocks, and by corresponding with scientific authorities.[194] She had the humblest origins imaginable, yet the fossils she hunted were displayed in the British Museum and the geological museum at Cambridge University and were bought by the Bristol Institution for the Advancement of Science.[195] Besides the ichthyosaur, Mary was also the first finder of the plesiosaur,[196] Hybodus (prehistoric fish with hooked teeth),[197] at least four species of ammonites, Icthyoduralites (prehistoric shark bones),[198] and pterodactyls—those flying dinosaur-contemporaries so beloved by the brushes of artists and the imaginations of children.[199]

Mary's biographer, Thomas W. Goodhue, credits her with sparking "the very first fossil frenzy."[200] When my husband and I went hunting these bits of ancient history, we really were following in this nineteenth-century geologist's footsteps, as our friend told us. Countless others had done the same. From the Philpot sisters—a trio of affluent ladies whose interest in Mary's "curiosities" prompted them to befriend her and then to start their own fossil collection[201]—all the way up to modern professional scientists like our lady geologist friend, myriad people have been links in the chain Mary helped forge.

An illustration on the cover of an 1869 children's magazine[202] shows Mary as a small, sturdy girl with windswept hair and rustic dress, standing on a high ledge of stone. Her right hand holds aloft a rock hammer, while her left passes a coiled ammonite down to her father, who wears a striped mariner's shirt and holds a basketful of fossils. A feature article about her in the magazine for tots wraps up with the inspirational conclusion:

> This short account of a life is written to show other children what has been done by one of themselves, who made use of the talents entrusted to her, and who by diligent observation not only secured an honest livelihood for herself, but aided in establishing the foundations of science whose records contain all that is known of the condition of the earth in the countless ages before men were created.[203]

This stirring call to arms (or rock hammers) is practically the biblical injunction, "Go, and do thou likewise"[204]—and people did!

A later portrait of Mary shows her as an adult woman in a round bonnet and long woolen dress, her ubiquitous rock hammer still in her right hand. Her left forefinger points at a fossil ammonite, and curled up next to it is her dog, Tray, whom she trained to guard her finds for her while she fetched her tools.[205]

There is something captivating about the story of a little girl who refused to be broken by either tragedy or poverty, and thus grew into a woman who made amazing contributions to the world's scientific knowledge. I often contemplate what I would say to various historical figures if I had the miraculous gift of a conversation with them; in Anning's case, I know exactly what I would tell her. It's an expression that didn't exist yet in the nineteenth century and therefore would require explanation, but I can't possibly imagine a more apt phrase to address this gumption-filled woman than simply, "Mary, you rock!"

21

Strength and How to Obtain It

"It is the brain which develops the muscles. Physical exercise must be commenced by degrees, first bringing into play one muscle, then two, then three, and so on, being careful all the time to put the mind into every movement."

—Eugen Sandow, 1897[206]

Anyone who claims the Victorians were prudish need only glance at portraits of bodybuilder Eugen Sandow to be instantly cured of their misconception. The most famous photographs of Sandow show him in classical settings wearing gladiator sandals and a plaster fig leaf—nothing else. Sandow built his muscles to mimic ancient Greek sculptures of gods and heroes as closely as possible; he even took measurements of the marble muscles of statues to more precisely sculpt his own thews to match them. Born Friedrich Wilhelm Mueller in East Prussia in 1867, Sandow began his career as a strongman circus performer and professional wrestler. By the late 1880s, he was earning fame in London music halls for his feats of strength and he had adopted a stage name more pronounceable to Anglophonic tongues.[207] He was often called Sandow the Magnificent for his remarkable physique, and many of his shows involved him simply flexing his amazing muscles for the admiring (and doubtless drooling) crowd. He went on to write a number of books advising people how they could follow his example and build their own bodies. The 1890s saw an enormous surge in popularity for strenuous athletic activity, and Sandow was a major figure in the latest craze.

The late nineteenth century (from about the 1870s onwards) was an interesting turning point for the way genteel people viewed physical exercise. For a long time, sweating and strenuous activity had been seen as the way working-class people earned their daily bread. It wasn't something people engaged in for fun. There were a few exceptions; for example, fencing was viewed with favor because of its martial connections. Equestrianism was likewise enjoyed by the upper classes, partly due to military associations with cavalry and partly due to stewardship traditions of landed gentry. By and large, though, as long as bodily toil was associated with lower-class labor, people didn't choose to exert themselves unnecessarily. This attitude shifted when large numbers of the poorest classes moved from agricultural labor (with its full-body workout routines) to factory jobs (which were tedious, but less energetic). When sculpted muscles were no longer a sign of backbreaking employment, they could become a sign of affluence among the leisured classes.

I first learned of Sandow when Gabriel decided to follow the workout routine developed by the father of modern bodybuilding. Being a devoted wife who likes to encourage my husband's interests, I acquired an 1897 edition of

Victorian bodybuilder Eugen Sandow, late nineteenth century.

Sandow's book *Strength and How to Obtain It* and gave it to Gabriel as a gift. Unfortunately, like most extant copies of this rare book, it was missing the fold-out anatomical chart and exercise diagrams, but Gabriel still found it highly useful for recreating Sandow's routines.

The daily exercises he adopted are rather remarkable to watch. He begins with bicep curls using fifteen-pound weights. (Sandow was the first bodybuilder to base his routines on anatomy.) Then he lifts the weights repeatedly over his head; this is followed by moving the weights outward from the chest at arm's length in a swimming motion. Then he lifts the weights upward from his sides in an alternating fashion. Push-ups follow (familiar though these are to a modern audience, Sandow had to describe them in detail to his nineteenth-century followers).

Midway through the routine come the exercises I find most extraordinary to observe. Gabriel places his weights on the floor by his feet, then squats quickly to grab them. Leaping up in a fluid motion with the weights grasped in

SANDOW'S OWN COMBINED DEVELOPER

*E*VERY MAN, WOMAN AND CHILD who wants strength and health should know of this invention of Eugen Sandow, the highest authority on physical culture. Far superior to any other system of home-exercise in simplicity, scientific correctness, convenience and efficiency — officially chosen from all others by the **Imperial Government in Great Britain** for training in army, navy and police. It is a wall-exerciser, weight-lifting machine, chest-expander and dumb-bells, all in one, yet occupies less space than a coat hung on the wall. Practically indestructible. No pulleys. No weights. No oiling. No danger. Adjustable to strength of man, woman or child.

Price, $5.00,

delivered, including anatomical charts with full directions in Sandow's celebrated system of physical culture, and free course of instruction at our exercising rooms, open day and night.

Send for *free* illustrated Booklet B.

SANDOW DEVELOPER CO.
(A. LEWIS, Manager),
125 West 37th Street, corner Broadway, New York.

Advertisement for exercise equipment, circa 1890s.

each hand, he rotates his body around a quarter of a circle with lightning speed and shadow boxes an imaginary opponent. Then he quickly squats back down to the floor and the amazing performance is repeated.

Sandow recommends these actions be performed in front of a full-length mirror so that the mind can focus on the control and development of the muscles. Modern gymnasiums have enough reflective surfaces to rival Versailles's Hall of Mirrors for exactly the same reason. However, I did veto Gabriel shadow boxing the mirrors on our antique armoire. We put a cheap second-hand mirror in the linoleum-tiled room for his exercises.

Less aggressive squats follow the shadow boxing routine, then side bends complete the drill. The entire workout takes my husband about twenty minutes and has definitely given him a more Victorian physique. I highly approve—and enjoy it!

Sandow's routine was intended to fit into busy middle-class Victorians' everyday lives. His devotees included many average people, as well as famous figures such as Sir Arthur Conan Doyle. In *Strength and How to Obtain It*, Sandow recommends specific exercise regimes for children of both sexes aged seven to ten, ten to twelve, and twelve to fifteen years old, for girls aged fifteen

Some of Sandow's pupils, from *Strength and How to Obtain It*.

to seventeen, boys the same age, girls aged seventeen and upward and boys likewise. He advocated measuring various elements of the body both before and after a physical regime had commenced, to chart progress.

The father of modern bodybuilding was not alone in this; in fact, his methods are very similar to those of Harvard physician Dr. Dudley A. Sargent. In 1883, when Sandow was still an unknown sixteen-year-old boy, Sargent had already been encouraging students to undertake gymnastic regimens for nearly twenty years. Describing the doctor's methods, a journalist for a cycling magazine reported:

> He subjects each of his pupils to a private examination, taking into account the relative proportions of the different parts of the body; the undue development of certain muscles, and the enfeebled condition of others; the comparative size of body and limbs; with a variety of facts concerning personal history, bone and muscle measurements, and acquired or inherited tendencies to chronic or functional disease. He can thus judge at once of the needs of the person under advice, and prescribe the general regimen and the kinds of apparatus necessary in his case. He does this with great minuteness, and with great resulting success in securing harmony in function and symmetry in development.[208]

The Victorians saw the rise of physical culture at the end of the nineteenth century as a harkening back to the golden age of ancient Greece. In 1883, a writer for the sporting magazine *Outing and the Wheelman* compared Greek exercises to contemporary examples. He declared that "health is 'the power to work long, to work well, to work successfully'; that health is our first wealth, the capital to be used as a basis in all our mental and spiritual processes." He claimed that exercising the body was a way to enhance the functions of both the mind and the soul; and went on to state that "we have something . . . to ask that the Greeks did not possess or wish for. We value the health, happiness, and usefulness of our maidens as well as of our youths. We would ask as much for the one as for the other."[209] Modern America's emphasis on fitness owes its entire existence to these Victorian interpretations of Greek physical refinement. Cultures twist to meet other cultures and history folds back on itself in fascinating ways that can rival a Sandow routine.

Bicycle ads from *The Youth's Companion* Boston, June 14, 1888, No. 41. Note that the prices quoted are for small boys' bicycles. The models for grown men usually ran from $100 to $125, with additional charges for extras like nickel plating.

22

An Ordinary Bicycle

Illustration from *The Wheelman* magazine, June 1883, p. 167.

"Truly this is an age of enterprise and adventure. We may refer to the
wheel as a product of the former and a means for the latter."
—W. H. Butler, 1883[210]

My husband's first love was a bicycle, long before he had the slightest clue of
my existence. He was already working at a bike shop when we met, and his side
of one of our first telephone conversations detailed a spoke-by-spoke account of
building a wheel. Like many infatuated eighteen-year-old girls before me, and
doubtless many more until the last syllable of recorded time, I made my very
best effort to convey utter fascination. At the time, though, the subject held

not the least interest to me whatsoever; at that point in my life, I couldn't even ride a bicycle. Given Gabriel's preoccupation with cycling, it was somewhat inevitable that he should teach me, but he tried not to be pushy about it for fear of scaring me off. He gave me my first riding lessons when we had been dating a little less than a year. Three years later, he built a bike for me as a Christmas present and I caught "wheel fever," as an 1890s woman might have said.

An interesting fact that deserves to be much better known than it is—and certainly merits better appreciation by motorists than it enjoys—is that modern roads were not made for cars. It was the work of nineteenth-century wheel-men that resulted in the well-paved roads that automobiles later thuggishly pushed cyclists off of. Lobbying for better roads, the wheelmen pointed out the advantages to business and commerce in allowing for freer movement of goods to market, and also pointed out that easier travel improved quality of life for inhabitants of both cities and rural areas alike. As famous nineteenth-century cyclist Karl Kron expressed the situation in 1883:

> The bicycle is an index to the existence of good roads just as certainly as the good roads themselves are an index to the existence of a high degree of civilization in the locality possessing them . . . If the highways of Hampden County had not been greatly improved from their condition of thirty years ago [i.e. the early 1850s], it is hardly probable that the last three years would have witnessed the phenomenon of an increase of local bicyclers from three to four hundred. Were the roads of the region as poor now as in 1850 Springfield bicycling would not be much of a power to conjure with—would not supply the machinery for creating so great an exhibition as that which lately attracted thousands of strangers to the city . . . The men who drive horses may not always greatly love the men who drive wheels (though, of the numberless things which "frighten horses," it would be hard to name one which causes fright less frequently than the bicycle), but they always do have a great liking for good roads and they ought clearly to see not only that good roads will develop bicy-cling in any given locality, but that the increase of bicyclers there will tend to make the good roads better and more numerous . . .[211]

When we started incorporating more and more aspects of Victoriana into our everyday life, Gabriel absolutely itched for an antique bicycle from the 1880s. The distinctive Victorian cycle with its one large wheel paired with a much smaller wheel has several different options of nomenclature. In the nineteenth century, it was termed an ordinary bicycle—or just an Ordinary. Some nineteenth-century writers capitalized the "O," others didn't. The term *Wheel*—which also means a bicycle—has a similar issue. When a person stands next to an Ordinary bicycle, the huge front wheel is such a dominant feature that it's easy to understand why the whole machine was often simply called a Wheel (sometimes capitalized, sometimes not) and why cyclists called themselves Wheelmen (again with capitalization optional but common). For clarity, in this narrative Ordinary and Wheel (capitalized) refer to the entire bicycle; when lowercase, the words have their more familiar meaning.

The term *Ordinary* was preferred by serious cyclists of the late nineteenth century and continues to be the most popular appellation among enthusiasts of the machine. Purists considered the Ordinary to be the true bicycle, and the safety bicycle (a cycle with two wheels of the same size, like most modern bikes) to be a watered-down, sissy version of the "steed of steel." The name *high wheeler* refers to the placement of the rider high atop the large wheel, while *penny-farthing* is a reference to the relative sizes of the wheels (somewhat reminiscent of the relative sizes of a British penny versus a farthing coin).

Incidentally, as long as we're on the subject of nomenclature: antique bicycle enthusiasts usually reserve the word *velocipede* to refer to draisines (hobby horses scooted along the ground with the feet) and the earliest generation of pedal bicycles from the 1860s. To a real enthusiast of the machine, referring to an Ordinary bicycle as a velocipede can sound a bit like referring to a 1980s Ferrari as a horseless carriage—the term is general enough that (strictly speaking) it may be technically correct, but it makes a person sound like sort of a git.

Ordinary bicycles of antique but still rideable condition are fairly rare and difficult to acquire in modern times. Most of the Victorian examples fell prey to the metal drives during the two world wars of the twentieth century and were melted down.

Fortunately, a few Ordinaries are still around. They're few and far between, but they exist. When we had been in Port Townsend about one year, a friend helped Gabriel acquire an 1887 Singer Challenge Ordinary from an auction in upstate New York. (The Singer bicycle company had no associations with the Singer sewing machine company, although they were contemporary with each other.)

With the acquisition of the Ordinary, our adventures really began!

Perhaps the most common (and certainly the most basic) question about a high wheel bicycle is that of why one wheel is so much larger than the other. The answer to this is very simple indeed: the larger a wheel's circumference, the more distance it covers with each rotation. Ordinary bicycles have neither chains nor gears, and their cranks are attached directly to the larger of the two wheels. For every rotation of the rider's legs, there is exactly one rotation of this wheel: the larger the wheel, the faster it goes. In 1883, the average size of wheels used by riders in reported runs for a one-hundred-mile record was fifty-two inches. The fastest rider to complete what cyclists now call a century did it in nine hours, forty-seven minutes—eight hours, thirty-five minutes of riding, with a one hour, twelve minute rest.[212] Many modern riders of high-tech safety bicycles would be hard-pressed to manage such a feat!

After we had been in Port Townsend a couple of years, Gabriel arranged a high wheel bicycle race as part of a local spring festival. He had some trouble finding other high wheel riders, and less than a week before the race was scheduled to occur, we were still worried we might have to cancel it. He did find one other rider, though—and two competitors does constitute a race—so the event went ahead as planned. Seeing the other rider, Dash, arrive at the designated place on the race day, I concluded my husband had the race in the bag. Gabriel's Wheel was noticeably larger than his competitor's; for every rotation made by their legs, my husband would be traveling farther. I made an impetuous declaration to spice up the race for the spectators—I boldly declared that the winner would receive a kiss!

The race was taking place at Fort Worden—a former military base that is now a state park. (In the late twentieth century, it served as the setting for the 1982 film *An Officer and a Gentleman*, starring Richard Gere.) I explained the race to the assembled audience: three laps of the fort's parade ground, starting and ending directly in front of the commanding officer's quarters. I waved a silk flag to start the riders, and they were off!

Gabriel pulled in front quickly, but Dash was right behind him. After they rounded the first turn, Gabriel pulled ahead again and shot into a considerable lead. A long straightaway, then a turn, then another straightaway—I cheered as Gabriel passed me and the other spectators while Dash was still back at the last corner of his first loop.

Halfway around the second loop, something went wrong. Gabriel was still moving—and quickly—but he wasn't gaining speed at the rate he had been. I would later learn that he had severely cracked a crank—the part of a bike that connects the pedal to the wheel. As the two riders lapped the parade ground for a second time, though, all I or any of the other spectators knew was that Dash was gaining on my husband.

"Go Gabriel!" I cheered as they passed the watching group.

Behind me someone sniggered. "You might have to kiss a younger man!"

As the gap between the racers narrowed, I somewhat regretted my impetuous declaration. At least Gabriel isn't the jealous type, and I reflected that the scenario wasn't far from what happened in plenty of Victorian games. In *The Sociable*, a book of parlor and outdoor games originally published in 1858, kisses are involved in twenty-five of the fifty-six forfeits suggested when someone loses a round of play.[213]

Despite the broken crank, Gabriel was only behind Dash by the barest hair's breadth when the two racers completed their final lap. Still, the winner was undeniable, and my dear husband was a good sport about it when I stepped up to pay his forfeit. He even stayed in good humor when the gathered spectators insisted I repeat the kiss for a better photo opportunity.

Remington bicycle advertisement, 1897.

23

Woman's Cycle

"You know when I left school, last month, I was simply bicycle-mad—
had the fever in the very worst way."
—"Rosalind A-Wheel," *Godey's* Magazine, 1896[214]

Unfortunately for me, the woman's machine that corresponds to a man's high wheel bicycle has become an even more endangered species than the Ordinary. Except for some very rare anomalies, women didn't ride high wheel bicycles. There are a few extremely good reasons for this. In the first place, a wheelman's legs straddle the enormous front wheel and there is no conceivable way to keep a skirt out of the huge spokes. (There were only a handful of female Ordinary

An Ordinary's cranks come straight off the hub. Image courtesy Matt Choi, Mary Studio.

riders in the entire world, and they tended to be stunt riders or circus performers who wore bloomers on their Wheels.) In the second place, when someone rides a high wheel bicycle, their crotch is right at eye-level for pedestrians, and most pantalets—the standard "drawers" for Victorian women—are split right down the middle. This is extremely convenient when using lavatory facilities; access is simply a matter of pushing layers of fabric out of the way instead of undoing any fasteners, so toilet use is actually less complicated for a woman in Victorian clothing than for a man in trousers. However, it does make women particularly disinclined to hoist themselves up to "flash" level. (Incidentally, this is also the reason that ascending stairs is one of the times etiquette dictates a gentleman should precede a lady.) Thirdly—and most importantly—Ordinary bicycles are sized to the length of a man's leg, like a pair of pants. There's no devious plot behind this; it's just a simple physical necessity. The cranks of an Ordinary come straight off the hub, so the wheel's radius has to correspond to its rider's leg length.

If the wheel is too big, the rider won't be able to reach the pedals; too small, and his knees will get caught underneath the handlebars on every upstroke. A tall man and a short one can't ride the same Wheel. Since most women are

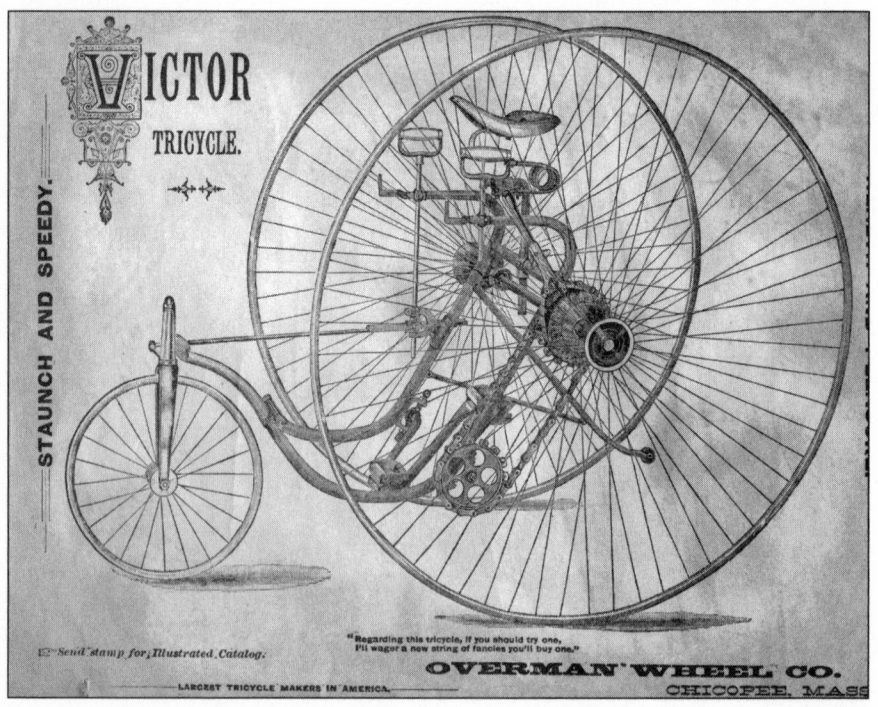

Victor tricycle advertisement, 1883.

more petite than the majority of men, they tend not to fit the average sizes of Ordinaries. (The female stunt riders had Wheels specially made for them or rode Wheels built for boys.) What women in the 1880s did ride (and what I someday, in my wildest dreams, aspire to own) were high wheel tricycles!

Besides being more seemly and practical for women, high wheel tricycles also had greater carrying capacity than their two-wheeled brothers, which made them very useful for cycle touring. Some men preferred tricycles over bicycles because of this, and also for reasons of comfort and stability.

Tricycle-riding was greatly encouraged for ladies; medical man George E. Blackham rode a tricycle himself and loaned it to his sisters. He declared, "I should be glad to see this delightful and invigorating exercise become popular among the ladies of this country. It would be greatly to their advantage, and to the advantage of the coming generation, if our young girls could increase their appetite, improve their digestion, strengthen their muscles, purify their blood, and steady their nerves, by this pleasant and profitable exercise in the open air and sunshine."[215]

The manufacture of high wheel tricycles required an incredible amount of high-precision machine-work. Unfortunately, this meant that even in their hey-day, these wonderful vehicles were so expensive that only rather affluent people could afford to buy them. They were always rarer than their two-wheeled counterparts (which weren't terribly common themselves), and survival bias worked overtime against these beautiful machines. In storage, Ordinary bicycles at least have the benefit of being somewhat two-dimensional, but high wheel tricycles take up an awkward amount of floor space. Depending on the model, they might not even be able to fit through a standard door. A few of the rarer designs were arranged with their two small wheels in line with each other, which does allow them to pass through ordinary portals. The more standard arrangement, though (where the rider sat between the wheels), was too wide to fit through a door without removing a wheel. An unfortunate result of this was that, as they fell further and further out of fashion, these amazing machines were often moved to increasingly less desirable shelter: from carriage house to stable, from stable to barn, then to a field or backyard where they fell to rust. When the metal drives of the two world wars came along, what remained of these glorious machines—some of the highest technology of their day—were melted down for scrap. The exceptionally rare and scattered survivors cost as much as a new car. I do hope to own one someday, but it will be quite a while.

In the meantime, I've been contenting myself with a safety bicycle: a bike with two wheels of the same size. Safeties first came into vogue in the 1890s thanks to advances in pneumatic tire technology. Smaller wheels meant that

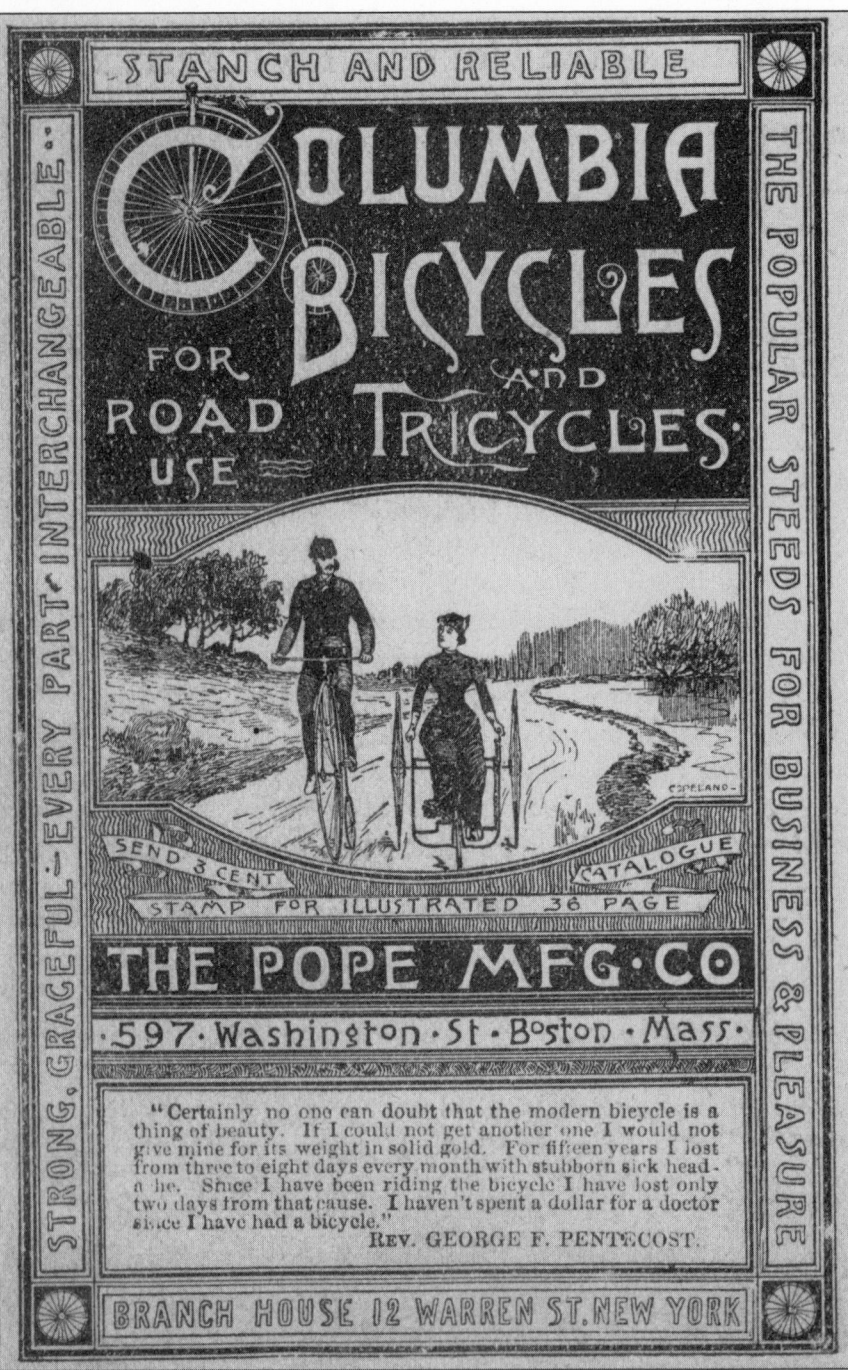

Columbia bicycles and tricycles advertisement, circa 1880s.

safeties required less metal and were easier to build than Ordinaries, so when the popularity of the smaller bicycles started to escalate, economy of scale allowed them to become drastically cheaper than their high-wheeled counterparts. Cycling shifted from an elite pastime to a democratic sport and became increasingly available to the middle and working classes as well as the rich. The lower and more skirt-friendly wheels meant that bicycling (as opposed to tricycling) became as attractive to women as to men.

When the safety-bicycle craze broke out in the 1890s, cycling was so popular among women that even fashion magazines devoted significant page-space to the sport. *Godey's* published bike-related articles dealing with everything from advice on the best cycling clothing to discussions of the social implications of the wheel for the fairer sex. A bicycle could provide an excuse for a new wardrobe; possibilities ranged from cycling outfits cut on the bias (a technique that allows fabric to stretch) to cycling corsets, which were cut slightly higher over the hips than standard stays. A special corset isn't really necessary for cycling any more than specialized shoes are required for walking. (Personally, I always wear the same corset for cycling that I wear for all my other activities.) However, sports gear is always eminently marketable. People may not need special shoes for walking, but they'll certainly buy them. The situation was the same with corsets and cycling.

Bicycles were seen as the vehicles of the future. By riding a "steed of steel," a woman showed that she was modern, progressive, and technologically savvy. Like dancing, riding a bicycle was a physical art that exhibited grace while facilitating social interactions. Bicycles gave their riders a common frame of reference—men and women could discuss the best roads and the latest innovations and show off their gear to each other, as well as their skills.

Lady journalist Mary L. Bisland declared:

If in an assemblage of women today we should be asked to name the most precious acquisition by the sex in this century, the majority of shrilly-sweet voices would be lifted up—not in favor of the approaching privileges of the ballot, O earnest lady suffragist; nor yet, Minerva, in advocacy of the advantages of higher education. Those are great and glorious blessings, but there is something women of every class have learned to prize as a shorter road to freedom than wide, welcoming college doors, or open gateways to the polls. In possession of her bicycle, the daughter of the nineteenth century feels that the declaration of her independence has been proclaimed, and, in the fullness of time, all things will be added to complete her happiness and prosperity . . . What is true of nations is

Advertisement for cycling corset, 1897.

true of sexes—that without physical strength no victories can be won. For a time . . . the growth of intellectual efforts, and the ambitions and professions adopted by women, threatened to allow their minds to out-run the growth of their bodies. The opening of new and almost purely sedentary employments for women, and the increase in educational exac-tions, threatened dire results for the physical conditions of our girls and matrons. Where their grandmothers, with broom and duster and stirring kitchen spoons, used to work up a capable amount of muscle, scientific methods have minimized household duties to the merest formalities, and even the gymnasium failed to counteract the steadily increasing epidemic of nerves . . . Right at this crisis . . . two wheels, a saddle, and a pair of pedals came to the rescue . . . Were the gift given us to look a bit into the future, what should we probably find the middle-of-the-twentieth girl wearing on her wheel—bloomers, very short tunics, or troserettes and similar abominations in the sight of grace and sweet femininity? Not if she is the direct descendant of her nineteenth-century grandmother, who here in these United States, spite of talk to the contrary, and in spite of the efforts of fashion, still sticks to her traditions and her skirts. Long may they wave, the petticoats in modest ankle-length folds of brown cloth or gray, since those are the best colors for cycling![216]

Bisland calls the bicycle "the very mainstay of health and pleasure to that great factor in modern life, the bread-winning woman . . . Her bicycle is her first thought, her sweetest refuge. Once in her saddle, the world of petty cares runs behind her like the road she travels." She goes on to explain that the speed and motion of a bicycle necessitates focus, thus banishing humdrum worries. At the same time, the extra oxygen delivered to the blood by exercise in the open air and sunshine not only improves health, but brightens one's entire outlook upon the world. From her 1896 perspective, Bisland imagines the future: "[I]t is hardly an exaggerated fancy that paints the women of two thousand and fifty, every one taking her bicycle as much a matter of course and necessity as food and clothing. Why should she not, when already the bicycle has established a wonderful democracy among women, who ride it winter and summer, rain and shine, for ills and for pleasure?"[217]

Why should she—or I—not, indeed?

When we moved to Port Townsend, I still had my 2001 Raleigh that Gabriel had built for me when we were dating. He proposed looking for an antique bicycle for me. (Those from our period are about the same price as a

Gabriel and me with our bikes. Image courtesy Matt Choi, Mary Studio.

new, mid-range bike.) However, I didn't want to worry about the cumulative effects of one hundred and twenty years of entropy every time I went for a ride. I intended putting my bike through all the same activities women cyclists of the 1890s had done on theirs: jaunts around town, quotidian errands, and long-distance touring. I wanted my bike to be a young sporting partner up to a few challenges, not a venerable supercentenarian I would have to cosset (no matter how many races she had won in her day).

Gabriel, in his role as my favorite cycling authority, discussed the possibilities with me. At first we considered a Pashley, a British bike from England's longest established bicycle manufacturer. Their roots only go back to 1926, though, and I wanted something more appropriate for the 1890s—the Victorian "cycling craze." After long discussion, we decided the best bike for my purposes would be a Royal Dutch Gazelle. The Gazelle company was started in 1892 and they've been making quality bikes ever since, some of which have changed very little. In 1992, they were awarded the title Royal by Holland's Princess Margriet, and on April 7, 1999, Crown Prince Willem-Alexander added the final touches to the ten millionth Gazelle produced.

My particular model is a Gazelle Tour Populair. The frame geometry is virtually identical to that seen on ladies' bikes of the 1890s. It's what cyclists call a drop frame: the top tube snugs down along the bottom one instead of forming a diamond shape. This means it's more skirt-friendly than a diamond frame and also easier to step through. (Some men prefer drop frames for the latter reason.) The bike has a few features that strike people as modern, but they're actually far older than most people realize. *Godey's* was already describing bicycles with kickstands and electric lights in 1896.[218] The drum brakes on my Gazelle are a technological innovation going back to the 1880s high wheel tricycles I covet so much. (I may not be able to have a high wheel trike yet, but at least my bike uses their brake technology!)

In the shape of my pretty little Gazelle I acquired, as Mary Bisland would have said, "the Pegasus on which the sex will one day ride into the fulfillment of all its dreams of universal health and beauty."[219] It was time to start riding!

Cover from *Metropolitan* magazine, November, 1896.

24

My First Adventure in Cycle Touring

"The world is a new and another sphere under the bicyclist's observation. Here is a process of locomotion that is absolutely at her command, a little light machine of steel and rubber that she can lift in her arms, that has greater staying powers than a horse, that is all her own, and at her will must halt or advance, speed like the wind or jog on at an even pace. The magic carpet possessed no higher virtues."
—Mary L. Bisland, 1896[220]

I first learned about National History Day through a newsletter from the state historical society. It's basically the humanities equivalent of a science fair: middle and high school pupils around America do projects on a given theme and compete at regional, state, and national levels. The newsletter said that regional contests were fast approaching, and it seemed the coordinators were in need of volunteer judges.

I had such a grand time judging History Day the first two years after I learned about it that when a call for judges came up a third year, there was no question in my mind I wanted to help. The only question was where—and this issue was easily answered when I saw that the Northwest regional was being held in Bellingham. Not only is Bellingham a charming city ornamented with a great dose of history from precisely my favorite period, but my old buddy Tom had just moved there, so I could stay with him. Best of all, it was the perfect excuse to try something I had been pondering for years: my first adventure in cycle touring!

The distance from Port Townsend to Bellingham is about 65 miles each way, making for a round trip of 130. Personal opinion of this distance varies widely between individuals—serious cyclists consider it a nice, easy ride, while non-cyclists splutter in amazement that anyone could go such a distance under their own power. Both groups, however, would be daunted by the fact that I had no intention of leaving my corset at home. Late nineteenth-century women had special riding corsets, but I would make do cycling in my everyday one.

I had personally never done a bike trip nearly this long before, but that didn't seem like any reason I shouldn't. The late February weather grew warmer and warmer as we turned to the March page of the calendar, and the cycling fever had me increasingly in its grip. I decided to have a go at it.

In preparation for the trip, I made myself a cycling outfit based on a *Godey's* fashion plate of sportswear. Technically it was a tricycling outfit, but the combination of plaid skirt, white shirtwaist, and gaiters remained fashionable cycling attire for women well into the era of safety bicycles. The skirt was significantly shorter than my everyday walking skirts (which come down to my ankles to trap a bubble of warm air around my legs), but appreciably longer than the hiking skirt that goes over my trouserettes. It comes a little lower than midway between my knees and ankles and has a brilliant feature I picked up from an 1896 *Godey's* article. Ordinarily, a Victorian walking skirt has a wide strip of canvassing along the bottom of the skirt to weigh it down in breezes and give it

The fashion plate I copied to make my cycling outfit.

the proper drape; alternatives to canvassing that served the same purpose were horsehair and tailor's weights. *Godey's* recommended that cycling skirts be lined with strong leather.[221] Leather has a distinct advantage when weighing down cycling skirts; it's heavier (and therefore more effective) than canvassing and more comfortable against a rider's calves than lead weights.

I didn't quite have time to finish an Eton jacket to match the skirt and gaiters, but the jacket from my hiking outfit served the purpose well enough and the Eton jacket could wait for later cycling adventures. A few days before my trip, Gabriel brought home some period-appropriate ride food (dried fruit, mixed nuts, and a hard cheese) for me from the same store where he buys our ice. I didn't have much luggage since weight is always an issue when cycling, especially when covering long distances. After I finished ranking the papers I was evaluating and adding commentaries for their young writers, I mailed the essays ahead of myself to Tom's place so I wouldn't have to carry them.

The items I would be carrying—maps, a nightgown, extra socks, a notebook, and of course the food—all went into the Brooks panniers on the back of my bike. (John Boultbee Brooks started making horse harnesses and general leather goods in 1866. In 1878, he got into cycling after the death of his horse, and the company shifted their focus. Today the Brooks company manufactures some of the best quality saddles and panniers in the world. The particular panniers on my bike are made of waxed canvas.[222])

In a dilemma well-known to all travelers, various miscellaneous sundries had to wait until the morning of departure to be packed. Obviously I needed things like my hairbrush and toothpaste to make myself presentable before I left, and letting water sit in a metal canteen overnight gives it a metallic tang I preferred to avoid.

On the morning of my departure, packing these incidentals took longer than I had expected. When Gabriel wandered, bleary-eyed, into the kitchen, I was experiencing a mild case of the running-late nerves.

"You said I should leave at six?" I asked him, confirming a point of discussion from the previous night. Port Townsend is located on the Olympic Peninsula, and Bellingham is on the mainland of Washington State. To get from one to the other, I would have to take a ferry from a dock near my house to Whidbey Island, ride up Whidbey, take the Deception Pass Bridge (ranked thirteen out of nineteen in *Travel and Leisure* magazine's list of the world's scariest bridges[223]), then cross another bridge from Fidalgo Island to the mainland. The ferries only run every few hours, and missing the first one would significantly delay my whole trip.

"Mmm-hmm." Gabriel yawned and nodded. "What time is it?"

"Pretty darn close." I darted up to the bathroom to brush my teeth, and as soon as that was accomplished, rushed back downstairs. As I turned the corner at the base of the staircase, I grabbed the waxed-canvas cape portion of Gabriel's Inverness from the hook where it hung with the rest of the coats. The weather report said I would have a dry trip to Bellingham, but it was expected to rain on the day of my return to Port Townsend. A waxed canvas cape is basic Victorian rain gear. It was bulky, but it would be well worth carrying if the weather turned inclement as predicted.

"Thank you for letting me borrow this!" I told my husband, draping the cape over a chair and sitting down to button on my gaiters. The time-crunch combined with my impending adventure made me a little nervous. When he saw I was having trouble buttoning my gaiters, my sweet husband knelt gently before me and buttoned my right gaiter while I fumbled with the left. I was deeply touched; despite the pressure of time, I paused long enough to kiss his forehead.

He smiled up at me. "Did you remember the buttonhook?" We were currently working without one. Buttonhooks aren't, strictly speaking, essential for gaiters. (On the contrary, button boots are nearly impossible to fasten without a hook.) Even when not required, though, they do facilitate the job.

"The traveling one's packed, but we have others." I rushed upstairs again. Survival bias works overtime on buttonhooks. In a toiletry set, the mirror will be broken or lose its silver over time, the brush will drop its bristles, and the comb's teeth will be broken, but the buttonhook will survive. They are practically indestructible. They became obsolete when functional buttons on shoes and gloves fell out of fashion; doubtless some of the plainer buttonhooks were melted down over the years for the sake of the metal they contained, but countless numbers of them were spared for the sake of their handles. Their handles are often ornamental—either by being made of a decorative material such as mother-of-pearl or by being artistically fashioned to resemble anything from dragon scales to flowers; these were often pretty enough to spare the scrap of metal (the hook itself) from the crucible. Buttonhooks were a de rigueur item in ladies' sets of various kinds from vanity sets to traveling *étuiles*, and they tend to be one of the last items remaining from these collections. We had acquired our traveling buttonhook early on as an impulse buy at an antiques store. It had charmed us because it folded so neatly from an open position where one end was a shoehorn and the other end was a buttonhook. I wanted a shoehorn anyway, and since this two-in-one item was priced lower than a cup of coffee, it seemed a worthwhile deal. My vanity set had come with a buttonhook whose handle was etched with flowers to match the handles on the nail file and the various brushes, then my *étuile* had come with another buttonhook—this one with a mother-of-pearl handle to match the various tools in that set. I like these because they complete their sets, but I've truly lost track of how many buttonhook offers I've turned down from people who wanted to give me unmatched examples. There really is a limit to the number of buttonhooks one woman can use!

I grabbed the long-handled buttonhook from my vanity set and hurried back to the kitchen where Gabriel was still yawning. I handed him the tool, and while I fastened my left gaiter, he returned his attention to the tightest buttons over the bulge of my right calf. He had virtually given up on these before as unbuttonable, but now—

Pop! The hook snapped them into place with a facility as easy as the snapping of fingers. "My god," Gabriel marveled. "That was easier!"

We laughed together at the difference, and I smiled down at my husband. "That's what they're for," I told him.

As Gabriel finished buttoning my gaiters for me, I draped his waxed-canvas cape over my shoulders. "Even if it doesn't rain, it'll be nice to have this for extra warmth this morning."

"And if it does rain," Gabriel added. "It'll totally save you!"

I stood up, smiling. "How do I look?" I asked.

Gabriel grinned back. "Like you're ready to go!"

He lifted my heavily loaded bike down off the porch and I did some last-minute rummaging in my panniers. I suddenly found myself fretting I might have forgotten something essential.

"You already packed, my dear," Gabriel assured me. "You'll do fine." He gave me a fond kiss. "Have a good time!"

And with those words, I was off on my great adventure.

The ferry from Port Townsend to Ebey's Landing on Whidbey Island can trace its lineage back to 1877.[224] The boats have changed a bit over the years, but the ferry route is virtually identical.

I arrived at the Port Townsend ferry terminal and paid my fare, then politely asked what the procedure was for bicycles on this run. (I had ridden onto the ferry between Bainbridge Island and Seattle in the past, but each dock and each ferry has its own separate peculiarities.) The man who took my money in exchange for a fare ticket waved me toward the pedestrian ramp and told a ghoulishly fanciful story about bikers getting flattened by semitrucks. I followed the wave and ignored the story. Such people are lucky that most cyclists are too tasteful to turn the tables. I wondered how he would have responded to a comparably ghastly story about a trucker murdering ferry-booth operators.

I was the only cyclist at that early hour and I walked onto the boat along with the pedestrians. While the foot-passengers climbed the stairs, I pushed my bike to the forward of the car deck and secured it by a rope tied to the wall for that purpose. I could have pushed it up a ramp to a sheltered deck of the boat, but I was happy to watch the sun rise in the open air. After the cars had finished loading and the ferry got underway, I reached into my pannier and pulled out a jam jar filled with hot tea. I sipped my way through the creamy liquid and watched rosy fingers stretch through the clouds ahead of the ship.

A man at the tail-end of middle age came out of his car to join me in admiring the view. He asked if I was associated with "the guy who rides the big wheel bike" and I explained that, yes, my husband has a high wheeler. The man then asked the usual queries about how Gabriel gets up onto the seat, and I patiently explained the logistics of High Wheelers 101. Then he posed a question that completely threw me for a loop. "I saw you a few months ago stopped in the traffic circle with a car. One of those bikes got run over, didn't it?"

"Huh?" I am asked bizarre questions on a regular basis, but this was even stranger than most. "Uh—no!" *What on Earth is this guy talking about?* I wondered.

"Are you sure? 'Cause—"

Excepting cases of obvious concussion, "Are you sure?" is not a remark that should accompany a query into whether one has been hit by a motorized vehicle. I am fairly certain most people would notice—and remember—an event like getting run over by a car. I definitely know I would.

"—I saw you stopped and talking to someone."

I laughed. People stop us to talk all the time! I thought back to the last ride I had gone on with Gabriel that had taken us through the roundabout at the edge of Port Townsend. We had indeed pulled off to the side of the road—but it had nothing to do with a collision.

"Someone wanted to take our picture," I explained. I often wish we could charge five dollars or so to everyone who wants to photograph us—we could have retired quite some time ago. I chuckled at this man's perception versus the reality of the situation. "She waved us down so that she could photograph us for a contest." I honestly might have forgotten the whole incident if not for the arrival in the mail a few weeks later of an 8x10-inch glossy picture with an attached note saying she had won second prize.

"Oh!" exclaimed the man on the ferry. "Well, I'm glad you were all right. Those bikes look so dangerous!"

It is always interesting for me to see the ways in which people's assumptions influence their perceptions. People can go wildly off course if they start out with an error from the beginning of their reasoning. Based on this fellow's comments, it wasn't hard to work backward and deduce how his mind had turned a photo shoot into a traffic accident. First, he assumed bicycles are dangerous (a tediously reiterated mantra among motorists). Second, he assumed the only reason for pulling out of traffic must involve a collision. Ergo, in a perfectly innocent situation, he saw a life-threatening disaster because he expected to see one. I sincerely hoped he hadn't told anyone else about the imaginary accident. Rumors get started very quickly—and they can be incredibly irritating once they're entrenched.

The man on the ferry wished me luck on my travels and returned to his vehicle as the vessel approached the dock. I spent a few more minutes watching the rosy-fingered dawn creep over the horizon, then went again to stand by my cycle as the boat's ropes were tied off.

I left the ferry with the pedestrians and found myself at a fork in the road as soon as I got off the boat. I pulled off to the side of the road to consult my maps and directions while the motorized vehicles offloaded. I was at the very start of my journey, and already I was facing my first challenge. The directions in my hand told me to go left; the road sign in front of me said to go right.

When in doubt, Highway 20, then Chuckanut Drive. Gabriel had drilled the directional mantra into me before I had left home. Moreover, I knew that the one infallible landmark—the one I could not possibly miss—was Deception Pass. The bridge over that formidable body of water was the only way off the north end of the island. (Islands tend to simplify navigation by limiting options.)

The huge, impossible-to-miss official roadsign in front of me bore two arrows, both of them pointing right. One was labeled, HIGHWAY 20 (right), the other, DECEPTION PASS (also right). I looked down at the printed page of directions in my hand and read, "Turn left." *Hmm* . . .

I take pride in my skill with words, but my efforts at interpreting visual symbolism invariably yield abysmal results. Maps tend to be little more than pretty pictures to me. (Social studies was my most mediocre subject as a child because I failed all the geography tests but aced all the history exams.) Nonetheless, I pulled out one of those squiggly lined pieces of (theoretically practical) artwork and tried to parse some sense out of it.

I remembered someone had once told me that a map should always be "laid to the ground"—aligned with the surrounding territory. In other words, if Street X is on the left of the person holding the map, the map should be turned so that "Street X" is on the left of the map. Unfortunately that was not possible in this particular case; none of the visible road signs matched any of the labels on the map. Even with the map, I was in the same conundrum I had been without it.

I grumpily shoved my bundles of maps back into my pannier, irritably wondering if they might resolve themselves into a more comprehensible form later in the trip. Just as I did this, a roar from the semitrucks offloading from the ferry startled a heron that had been resting in the nearby wetland. It soared up from the mist and was briefly silhouetted against the glowing bright tones of the sunrise.

"Oh!" I exclaimed, momentarily distracted from my navigational issues. "How beautiful!" I watched it for a brief time, then shook my head and returned to the problem at hand.

"I don't suppose you could tell me which way to go?" I called out irreverently toward the majestic bird's retreating form. It continued on its way and soon vanished.

"Didn't think so," I mused with a wry smile.

When in doubt, Highway 20, Gabriel's voice repeated in my mind as I looked up at the arrow pointing right.

"Well," I said aloud to the misty morning air. "I'm in doubt. Highway 20 it is." I slid back onto my bike's leather saddle and headed right.

Just as the last of night's shadows were edging away from the sun's emerging rays, an owl flapped silently across the road and disappeared into the collection of deciduous trees on the opposite side of the highway. I smiled at it, then grinned even wider when I saw a hawk leaving the same clump of woods the owl had just entered. It perched atop a telephone pole and settled in for a hopeful vigil.

"Night shift going off, day shift coming on—raptor-style," I chuckled to myself.

The road eventually left the woods and crossed scenic fields dotted with red barns and wooden fences. The terrain seemed straight out of a child's drawing of an ideal farm. I took my time through the beautiful country, stopping frequently to admire the view and to nibble at the collection of nuts and candied ginger Gabriel had put together for me. In this poky, lackadaisical fashion, I came to the town of Oak Harbor when my watch read nine a.m.

Only nine a.m.! I thought, feeling immensely pleased with myself. *I'm making great progress!*

I stopped at a small café to use the restroom and fill my canteen. Inside the building, I was rather taken aback when I saw a clock that read ten a.m. I was shocked for a moment, then it dawned on me that daylight saving time had just ended a few days previously. We had changed our clocks at home, but I had forgotten to set my watch forward! I felt somewhat sheepish and rather less smug about my own speed of progress, but not too crestfallen. I still had plenty of time to reach my destination.

A woman who had seen me lock my bike outside the café came over to chat with me, and I told her about my mission.

"Oh, you've got a perfect day for it!" she declared with a bright smile. "I'm a cyclist too, and I've ridden that route lots!" She looked outside at the clear sky and brilliant sunshine. "You're gonna have a great view!" she predicted. "The only hairy bit is the bridge."

I reflected privately that I was worried about that myself. Deception Pass Bridge is 1,487 feet long, about 180 feet above the water line (more or slightly less, depending on the tide), and only 22 feet wide. Every day, 15,000 cars cross it.[225] These figures might sound a little dry, but look at it this way: for over a quarter of a mile, two lanes of traffic pass each other on a space that would be too narrow to hold the Statue of Liberty's tablet placed lengthwise. The bridge is higher in the air than the distance between Liberty's base and her torch.[226]

"But all you have to do," the veteran cyclist assured me, "is take the road!"

"Take the road," in cyclist parlance, means to merge with traffic and enter the line of cars and trucks instead of paralleling them on the side of the road. It's perfectly legal, of course, and is the only way to ride a narrow road with no shoulder like the Deception Pass. It was exactly what Gabriel had told me I should do.

Still, I had my doubts. Compared to merging a bicycle into a bottleneck on a state highway, the bridge's dizzying height seemed like a minor concern.

"I was planning to walk along the pedestrian path," I told the cyclist in the café, hoping I didn't sound too cowardly. There are very narrow walking paths on the sides of the bridge, mostly used by motorists who park at one end or the other and get out to take pictures.

"Well, you *can* do that," the cyclist said hesitatingly. Her tone didn't seem to indicate disapproval so much as it expressed that the action described was one she wouldn't care to do herself. "But it's hard to get your bike onto that path. We just always take the road. It's *fine!*" she assured me. Several hours later,

I would understand why she had been so dubious about the idea of taking a bike on the pedestrian path.

I left the café and continued on through farm country that reminded me of the chalky pastel drawings my Great Aunt Della used to sketch on sandpaper back in the early twentieth century. Over the course of hours and many pedal strokes, this gradually shifted to the rugged terrain suited to an inland passage. Soon the road signs confirmed what the geography hinted: DECEPTION PASS STATE PARK, BRIDGE AHEAD, SEVERE SIDE WIND.

As signs go, SEVERE SIDE WIND isn't exactly on par with "Abandon hope ye who enter here," but it didn't exactly calm my nerves either. I was still uneasy about the bridge that soared 180 feet in the air.

I thought back to the cyclist at the café. "Take the road," she had told me. "Everyone's actually very considerate!"

I drew in sight of the bridge and the bike lane started to disappear. *Take the road?* I thought. *I don't think so!*

My previous experiences with "taking the road" in high-traffic areas had generally been to avoid random obstacles in the bike lane ranging from broken glass to dead animals in varying stages of decomposition, or for the very simple reason that the bike lane had ended—as it was doing now. "Taking the road" even in these urgent cases had, as often as not, been confronted with high-decibel profanity bellowed out of car windows—obscenities of a sort that would surely make death-row inmates blush. Still more unpleasant were the tailgating motorists who would deliberately zoom as close to a cyclist as possible, at the highest speed possible, so that the drafted air from their passage created a min-iature cyclone and made an already challenging situation worse. Unpleasantly vivid memories of such experiences flashed through my mind as I neared the Deception Pass Bridge, one of the last places in the world where I wanted to take the road.

I saw the pedestrian path and prepared to dismount and walk across. Then I met with an unpleasant shock. Some time had gone by since I had been to Deception Pass, and I had forgotten a few things. For example, I had forgotten about the stairs.

On the southern end of the bridge's northbound side—exactly the place where I wanted to enter the walkway—the pedestrian path dead-ends abruptly, cut off from the road by a fence that rises to the level of a tall man's waist. Inside the fence is a walker's exit down a long and convoluted set of stairs that follow the cliff, circumvent the bridge by going underneath it, then come back up the other side. Someone must have decided that a quick, illegal dart across the highway was a little too tempting to people facing all those stairs, and the end of the walkway was tightly fenced. If I had been on a lightweight road bike without panniers, I might (theoretically) have hoisted the machine over the fence and scrambled after it, but my Gazelle weighs fifty pounds, even without luggage. Trying to lift that much weight more that waist high in the middle of a highway, then somehow try to follow it over the rail myself without going over the *other* rail (the one marking a 180-foot drop) was even less enticing than my other option. My other option . . . the one I hadn't wanted to do.

I guess I'm taking the road, I realized.

The nearest car nudged to the left, opening space for me to merge. Seeing the gap, I threw my full weight and all my power into pedaling. People travel considerable distances to admire Deception Pass but—for the moment at least—my full attention was absorbed by the road. My peripheral vision registered the panoramic beauty on either side like Odysseus's men noting the beautiful sirens on the mythical rocks, but I willed my focus to stay entirely on the road.

Back on one of my earliest rides with Gabriel, when I was nineteen and he was teaching me how to ride a bike for the first time, I had run into a post precisely because I was staring at it and worrying. As I had picked up my bike and gotten back on it, Gabriel had explained the concept of target fixation: where the eyes go, the muscles in the body tend to follow, whether or not the mind intends them to. I had absolutely no desire to repeat the target fixation lesson and run myself off the Deception Pass Bridge the same way I had bumped into the post as a teenager. The fall would have been a considerably longer one.

I avoided looking at the mountains, the sea filled with seals and waving kelp, and the rushing waters far below. I focused instead on the road, pushing hard to make my pedal strokes as powerful as possible while auto traffic built up behind me. A hard push, and soon I was over the bridge and onto Fidalgo Island. I pulled off the road and into a scenic overview area with a bench.

Despite all my anxieties about crossing Deception Pass, it had actually proved a very small and easy step in the journey. The drivers had already been slowing down, irrespective of my own presence. Speed limits were lower on this section of highway than elsewhere, and besides, they were admiring the view. If anything, they seemed to consider me (with my 1890-style cycling outfit and my bike with a frame geometry that has basically remained unchanged since around the same time) to be part of that view. I breathed a deep sigh of relief and looked around at the scenery I couldn't spare attention for while on the road. A panorama of seawater spread out on either side of the narrow passage crossed by the bridge. Far, far below, boats passed under the iron structure, small as bathtub toys.

All morning, I had been planning to have lunch when I reached Deception Pass. When I arrived there, however, I was extremely surprised to realize I was not particularly hungry. Before leaving on the trip, I had expected to be constantly pulling food out of my panniers every few miles to replace the energy I was burning. Virtually at the halfway point now, I found my lack of appetite to be truly bizarre. I hadn't eaten since a small taste of trail mix twenty miles back, but I had no desire to eat—a situation that shocked me. Despite this, when I did take out my food at the Deception Pass scenic overlook north of the bridge, I was at once overcome by a strong desire to wolf down the whole supply. I felt like the proverbial ravenous dog that almost takes off its master's hand at feeding time—although now it was my own hand.

Eating wolfishly, I made—what was to me—a shocking dent in my food supply in a very short time. Later in Bellingham, I would ask my buddy Tom about this odd lack of appetite punctuated by an overwhelming compunction to consume all the food available as soon as it came in sight. (Tom has university degrees in cellular and molecular biology and biochemistry—as well as a range of other science-related topics—so it seemed a natural question to ask him.) He explained that the body has two different nervous systems. In this case, I was driving my conscious nervous system with a desire to press on so strongly that it overrode my instinctual nervous system's desire to feed—as long as I was still moving. When he explained it this way, I remembered my lessons in school about the sympathetic versus the parasympathetic nervous system—the difference between the "fight or flight" reflexes and the "rest and digest" ones. I just hadn't realized while riding that my body would mistake a pig-headed desire to make good time for a pressing need to run away from a ravenous tiger.

Well-fueled from my stop at Deception Pass, I pressed on with renewed vigor until the road crossed the Swinomish Indian Reservation about twenty miles from the pass. Soon after I entered tribal land, I spied something lying on the side of the road that certainly is not an everyday sight.

It was a huge chunk of a raptor's wing—the length of my arm, and such a dark brown that it was nearly black.

Judging by its size and color, it could only have come from a bald eagle— probably one that had been trying to snatch an easy roadkill meal and had been smashed by a fast-moving vehicle. There was no sign of the bird's body or its other wing; likely they had been carried elsewhere by the momentum of the guilty vehicle. I guessed it was probably a semitruck. If anything smaller had struck such an enormous bird, I would have expected a car with a broken windshield and a hysterical driver in the ditch along with the disembodied wing.

In a slightly surreal emphasis of my bald eagle analysis, the wing was lying right in front of a wooden sculpture of a bald eagle, and behind this was a mural of the same bird.

I pulled my bike off to the side of the highway and stared at the tableau: eagle wing, wooden eagle, eagle mural.

"Really?" I asked the question out loud to the cosmos in general. I looked from wing, to mural, to sculpture again. "Really?"

Some coincidences are so extraordinary that a person encountering them can't help but feel either they've somehow dropped into the middle of a folktale, or else Fate is staging a practical joke at their expense. Immediately after entering the Swinomish reservation, I had come across an item of major significance to American Indians. As if to underline the importance of the discovery, there were not one but two pieces of artwork emphasizing the situation. I looked around, thinking the only thing missing was—*Oh yes, there it is: a place of spiritual worship.* Just around the corner from the wing was a small, white church.

The situation felt a bit like discovering a bag full of money. It didn't seem right to leave it lying at the side of the road, but I knew I couldn't keep it either. Monsieur Chat's house sparrow was one matter; a dead eagle was something else entirely. House sparrows are an introduced, invasive species in the United States; bald eagles are the national bird and have rather draconian legal protection. Possession of eagle feathers by a non-Indian without a permit has been a violation of some fairly major federal laws since the twentieth century.

Still, I didn't want to just leave the wing in the ditch. Given the context, I reasoned that someone at the church would likely know what to do with it. There were cars in the parking lot, so I knew someone must be there. I picked up the enormous wing and shook my head at the whole bizarre situation.

The wing was the length of my arm. Even if my bike's panniers hadn't already been full, there was no possible way to ride with it. Instead I carried the huge chunk o' raptor in one hand and used my other hand to push my bike to the church. The main building was locked so I knocked on the office door of the annex. A small, slightly plump woman on the elderly side of middle age opened the door.

"Good afternoon!" I greeted her.

"Hello!" Seeing a neatly dressed young woman standing in front of her step, she gave me and my bicycle a bright smile.

"I realize this is highly unusual—" I began.

She nodded, smiling brightly at my plaid skirt and starched white shirt-waist, and indicated that I should continue.

"—But I was cycling past and I found this chunk of an eagle's wing outside your church." I held up the portion of dead bird.

The woman's expression froze, then became slightly disgusted. She took a tiny, almost imperceptible step backward.

"It's just not the sort of thing a person sees every day," I continued, looking down at the wing.

"No," she agreed in a quiet, worried voice. "No, it's not." She took another small step backward.

"I was just wondering, since we're on tribal land, if someone in your congregation might be able to see that this gets to someone it would have significance for." I held it out to her and she took another small step backward.

"I really wouldn't have a clue . . ." Her voice (quiet to begin with) drifted downward into the inaudible range.

I frowned down at the wing. I would have delivered it to the tribal center myself but doing so would have taken me miles out of my way, and I was already worried about arriving at my destination before dark. "I know that eagle feathers are spiritually significant to a lot of native tribes—"

It suddenly occurred to me that I was standing at the vestry of a Christian church, asking the secretary to support paganism.

"—Or maybe you could give it to one of the local science teachers," I ended lamely. I wasn't entirely certain about the legality of this. The hypothetical science teacher would need a dead animal salvage permit from the Department of Fish and Wildlife. Still, it seemed better than leaving the wing in the ditch, and at the suggestion of it going to a scientific use rather than a heathen one, the church woman's face relaxed considerably.

"That's a good idea!" she said, her smile partially returning. "Just, er—leave it behind that bench over there."

I did as she instructed, then set out on the road again. As I glided my bike along the highway, I reflected how uncomplicated the whole dead bird scenario would have been in the Victorian era. If I had found an eagle's wing in the nineteenth century, I could have simply plucked out the best feathers and had some rather extraordinary additions to my next hat.

Several miles down the road from the church, I saw the Swinomish Casino. Reasoning that someone there must have a way to contact the tribe's cultural center, I followed several convoluted detours to get off the highway. I looked in

Photographic portrait of young couple; the woman is displaying a very fine feather in her hat.
Circa late 1880s.

vain for a bike rack, then left my bike (along with all the possessions I had with me, which were in my panniers) unattended outside the establishment.

The first casino employee I found was chatting on a cellular phone. I smiled at him to get his attention then waited while he finished his conversation. I occasionally gave a nervous glance back at the door, thinking about my bicycle. I don't even leave my bike outside on my own porch; when not in use, it normally lives inside my kitchen next to the ice box. Parking it unlocked out of my sight in unfamiliar territory made me distinctly uneasy.

When the man finished his cell phone conversation, I explained the situation with the eagle's wing. The expression on his face seemed to slightly doubt the sanity of the corseted blonde woman in a Victorian cycling outfit telling him about a dismembered fragment of a dead bird, but he thanked me politely enough. I felt as if I had done my civic duty, so I continued on my way.

Directly after the casino came the scariest bridge in the world.

I had worried about crossing Deception Pass and needn't have. I barely knew about the bridges over the Swinomish Channel—I had seen the crossing on my map but hadn't given it much thought. If I had known what I was in for, I might have reevaluated the whole trip.

The Twin Bridges (one northbound, one southbound) that cross the Swinomish Channel are seventy-five feet above the waterline,[227] and feel much, much higher. Seeing them loom ahead of me on the highway, I quickly looked around for any other possible way to cross the brackish channel, but the only other option seemed to be swimming it.

In cold numbers, a seventy-five foot fall might seem less intimidating than the 180-foot dive that is possible off the Deception Pass Bridge, but I'm pretty sure that either one would render a person equally dead. The Swinomish Channel (a canal through a bunch of mud flats) is not scenic like Deception Pass, and no one was slowing down to admire the view. I don't believe they were even obeying the speed limit. The huge volume of traffic, including an inordinate number of semitrucks, zoomed past me with a clear determination to get to its destinations as quickly as possible. Taking the road was not an option; I didn't want to wind up like the eagle.

The bike lane—such as it was—on the northbound bridge was an extremely narrow path strewn with loose gravel and broken glass. To one side was the seventy-five foot drop into the Swinomish Channel, to the other a stampede of huge vehicles. Each semitruck that whooshed past—mere inches away—created a fresh whirlwind so dramatic it was difficult to even keep my cycle upright. Never in my life have I been so utterly convinced I was going to die, but I kept pedaling!

Up—up—to the top of the bridge!

"Oh, God! Oh, God! Oh, God!" I don't blaspheme very often, but on this occasion I couldn't stop. No humans could hear me over the thunderous traffic, and I don't think a benevolent deity would begrudge absolution in such a circumstance.

"Oh, God!"

Whoosh! Zoom! Whoosh—

"Oh, God! Oh, God!"

Zoom! Shriek! Whoosh!—

A long, agonizing straightaway—

"Oh, God . . ."

Whoosh! Whoosh!

Over the hump and down—

"Oh, God! Oh, God—"

Down, and . . .

Safe on the other side!

"I'm alive!" I shrieked, hardly able to believe my own statement. I panted a few times, kept pedaling, and started to sing. "I'm the man who broke the bank at Monte Carlo!" The landscape shot into crystal clarity all around me as I experienced a wild adrenaline rush. It felt great to be alive!

After I left Swinomish land, I passed through miles and miles of agricultural fields. One was full of wild swans—so many that I thought at first I must be passing a very large goose farm. I felt a sort of quiet awe when I realized the true nature of the elegant birds. The rest of the fields were filled with cows, cows, cows.

The sun was sinking by the time I hit the mountainous portion of Chuckanut Drive, so the forested, hilly terrain was extremely dark as I made my way uphill. Completed in 1896, Chuckanut Drive was the first road to connect Whatcom county with points farther south. Previously, travel in northwestern Washington had been most often done by canoe, steamboat, sailing ship, or train. The road enabled local people to sell their goods in Bellingham and return home the same day—a major improvement on when it had been a multiple-day trip! With such improved ease of travel, people soon started traveling the road to enjoy its scenic beauty as well as more utilitarian purposes.[228] It's still a popular recreational route for cycling, so by traveling up it, I was joining in a fine series of wheelmen and wheelwomen.

I arrived in Bellingham about an hour after full dark, but fortunately by this point I was having better luck with my maps than I had at the beginning of my adventure. I managed to find Tom's apartment without getting too lost in the night. My old buddy greeted me with a friendly bear hug.

I was more tired than hungry so I declined Tom's offer of food—which concerned him slightly. Once while he was backpacking through wilderness miles and miles from any sort of civilization, Tom's entire stock of food was eaten by a bear. In his spare time when he's not doing laboratory work or field research, he volunteers for wilderness rescue. Tom worries about people getting enough to eat.

I did ask Tom for water, since I had drunk the last drops from my canteen about fifteen miles back. I drained two tumblerfuls of water, sank into a chair—and promptly was handed a large box full of bones and fossils.

The routes on my maps marked off around sixty-five miles of distance. I had gotten lost a few times along the way, so I judged that I had covered closer to seventy. This was over three times farther than I had ever traveled by bike before, and moreover I had been awake since four thirty in the morning. I was tired. If most people had handed me a box of rocks instead of a pillow at that point, I might have had sharp words for them. Tom isn't most people, though. He's one of my oldest friends and holds a particularly dear place in my heart. Besides, these weren't just any bones and stones either. These were *stories*.

People who are experts in their field are great fun to hang out with, since their enthusiasm for their topic radiates in such a contagious way. Tom has so many different degrees I have trouble keeping track of them all, but his main focus is bones—how they change and how they fossilize. I wouldn't trade the story time that ensued for any amount of sleep, regardless of how tired I was. This was a history lesson of far greater antiquity than I usually deal with.

Each fragment of ossified matter came wrapped in a narrative: a tale about what sort of animal it had come from, what had happened to it before or after death, and the geography-spanning tale of how Tom had found it. He reported all this data from the stony objects in the box as casually as if he were reading it out of a book—an exceptionally good story book.

Soon I started trying to guess the bones' tales before Tom related them. I picked up one of the longest bones in the box: a smooth, ivory-colored wand.

I held it up against my forearm, comparing its length to the distance from my wrist to elbow.

Tom chuckled. "You're going to have a hard time if you try to find that bone on your own body."

"So it's something humans don't have?" I queried.

"Oh no, we've got them." Tom smirked, leaning back. "We just don't have them in the same place."

That really was a puzzle. I looked down at my own leg, and Tom seemed to grow even more amused. After a while he offered a hint. "It's a finger."

"A finger!" I stared at the bone. I couldn't imagine any creature with finger-bones the length of my forearm. I thought briefly about orangutans, but dismissed the idea immediately. I doubted even the great apes could possibly have finger bones this long. I held it up against my hand, and it stuck out like a pole.

I finally looked at Tom in complete perplexity. "I give up!"

"It's something you would like to shoot out of your window," he hinted.

"A deer?" I asked, shocked. I frequently complain to Tom about the vast herds of wretched ruminants that camp out in my yard and demolish my rosebushes. It makes me nostalgic for my target-shooting days in the University of Washington archery club. (Tom was the president, although with his quirky sense of humor he always preferred the title Supreme Dictator.)

"Deer don't have fingers!" I exclaimed.

"They have all the same bones we do."

I made a mental note that it might finally be time for me to read Darwin's 1859 work *On the Origin of Species*. It was one of the most important books of the Victorian era, so I really should read it eventually. I've tried a number of times, and always got hung up on Darwin's dry-as-mummy-dust writing style. He didn't have nearly the knack for making things interesting as my buddy does.

Tom asked how I had gotten from the highway up to Bellingham, and I told him I had taken Chuckanut Drive. "I thought so." He grinned, a twinkle in his eye. "You mean that little insignificant road next to that huge, cool fossil formation?"

Apparently the Chuckanut formation is the largest sedimentary sandstone formation in North America. Its story stretches back fifty million years to the Eocene era—definitely older history than I'm usually exposed to. Tom showed me some fossils he had found there, then I went back to the guess-the-bone game I had been enjoying so much. The one that really stumped me was a knobbly little bone about half the size of a Pink Pearl eraser. It turned out to be a penguin's foot bone from southern Argentina. Some of my friends are so cool, I wonder why they bother with me.

The history contest I had journeyed to Bellingham to judge went well; it is always a true delight to see young people really engaging with history and getting excited about it. I had allotted more time for the trip than I really needed (four days when it only required three), so I had ample opportunity to loiter around the environs of Tom's laboratory at Western Washington University and enjoy the geological exhibits on perpetual display. When I wasn't thus engaged in history lessons of the modern or prehistoric variety, Tom cooked me everything from homemade pizza to chocolate pancakes so I had plenty of energy to cycle back to Port Townsend.

I found fewer dead animals on my return trip, but the weather was somewhat less idyllic. The skies had been beautifully clear and sunny on my entire ride up to Bellingham; on my way home, gray clouds pelted me with rain all day long. I was very glad that I had brought Gabriel's waxed canvas cape with me, so at least my torso stayed dry. The cape is actually the detachable upper half of an Inverness coat—a copy of an antique garment in our collection. The waxed canvas did an admirable job of keeping everything between my collar and hips dry, but my skirt got so sopping wet that by the time I arrived back in Port Townsend, I could literally wring water out of it. (I spread it over the side of our bathtub and it took days to dry.)

After my experience going northward on the Twin Bridges, I was terrified to cross them again. To my delight, however, I discovered that the southbound bridge over the Swinomish Channel actually has a decent bike lane reasonably segregated from traffic. I resolved that in the future I would always cross the channel on this far safer side of the bridge.

I arrived home wet and cold but very happy, and my dear Gabriel wrapped me up in his arms and told me how proud he was of me. He wiped down my bike for me while I changed into dry clothes and a fresh corset, then served me a special dinner of beans, spring vegetables, and rice. I felt tired but not exhausted—until we climbed the stairs to bed.

"Ugh—quads!" I groaned as my legs wobbled underneath me.

Gabriel squeezed my arm and gave an empathetic chuckle. "Climbing stairs is always the hardest thing after a long ride. I'll rub your legs for you when we get in bed."

While my husband massaged my weary leg muscles, I told him about all my adventures of the long ride: my confusion about directions when I first arrived on Whidbey, the easy ride over Deception Pass and the terrifying one over the northbound half of the Twin Bridges, giving the dead eagle fragment to the very disturbed church secretary . . . Gabriel smiled at all the tales and promised that soon we would go out for a cycle tour together.

Gabriel oiling the Ordinary. Photo courtesy Matt Choi, Mary Studio.

25

Wheeling

"To what does all the above, however crudely and imperfectly expressed, tend? To the acquisition of *confidence*, and confidence in bicycling means success."

—Henry W. Williams, 1883[229]

My first cycle tour drew quite a bit of attention from people who saw me biking along the highway or met me at my destination; a few months after *Victorian Secrets* was released, I received an invitation from Village Books in Bellingham to do an author event there. Gabriel arranged to come with me this time, and in addition to a book signing, we promised the bookstore we would also give a presentation on Victorian bicycles.

Gabriel and I had wanted to do a bike tour together ever since he acquired the high wheeler, and we started hopping with excitement as we counted down the days to the trip. Of course, the more eagerly something is anticipated, the more is likely to go wrong in its execution. Only two weeks before our 130-mile bike ride, Gabriel sprained his foot while jogging. The bruising pattern followed the peroneal brevis tendon up his leg with the sharp distinction of an anatomical drawing. As the date of our planned departure drew near, we waited nervously to see if he would be in a fit state for the epic journey.

The 1887 Singer he would be riding was a worry on par with our concerns about Gabriel's foot. It was a beautiful machine and well-made, but any sort of vehicle is likely to start feeling its age after more than a century. The front wheel was no longer completely straight or round, which created dangerous wobbles at high speed. One of the sixty spokes in the front wheel (each of them about two feet long) was irreparably loose. The crank he had broken in the race had been re-welded but remained a worry, and the connection between the seat and the bike's backbone had already broken and been replaced. All of these issues were complicated by the fact that the suppliers of all of these parts are long gone, so each replacement had to be custom-made. We rather cynically wondered what would break this time—and how catastrophically would it affect the ride?

Foot worries and bike worries—what if one proved up to the challenge, but the other failed along the route? I certainly couldn't pick up Gabriel if anything went wrong. The idea of putting an Ordinary bicycle into a safety bike's panniers is a picture even a comic artist would have difficulty drawing. At least we were reasonably sure my bike and I could make it since the March trip over the same terrain had gone so well.

I was strongly inclined to tell Gabriel to stay home, rest his foot, and enjoy some time off work—but there was a catch. Press releases about the bookstore events had gone out all over Bellingham, the Seattle area, and up into Canada. All this publicity promised we would be showing off an antique high wheeler. The only way to transport the bike was to ride it, and the only one who could do that was Gabriel—if he could.

We set up the same routine for Gabriel's sprained foot that I had used to heal my own a few years earlier when I had broken it: comfrey soaks and massage as soon as the swelling went down. The lymphatic drainage techniques I used on him dramatically reduced the bruising. *Would it be enough?* We wondered—and worried.

As the day drew near, Gabriel insisted he was willing—and able—to ride, so I pushed my worries aside and enjoyed my pride in his gumption and fortitude.

We had given a lot of consideration to our packing list. The bag on the back of the Ordinary is smaller than many women's purses, and Gabriel would barely have enough room for his own food. If he wanted to take off his jacket (which he surely would by midday on a sixty-mile ride in June), the only way to carry it would be to strap it to his bike's handlebars. Carrying the rest of our kit would be entirely up to me—and the load space on my own bike was likewise not very considerable. My bike has two panniers (each about the size of the backpack I'd carried back in elementary school), a rack with some elastic bands, and one tiny bag that fits under the saddle. (If I filled that last bag too full, it would stick up above the saddle—resulting not only in an exceedingly uncomfortable ride, but also in my crushing whatever was inside the poor bag.)

Gabriel was absolutely determined to avoid any anachronistic material whatsoever, even in packaging for our foods. This was easy enough in most things: I was already in the habit of wrapping his daily sandwiches in waxed paper. He had a sort of trail mix made of almonds, hazelnuts, and candied ginger that at first I suggested he twist up in waxed paper as well, but when I saw him looking wistfully at a calico bag I had made to carry my toiletries, it was easy enough for me to sew up a similar little sack out of calico scraps for his mixed nuts. The real problem was water—we only had one metal canteen, and we knew we wouldn't be keeping pace with each other for much of the route.

As a bike shop manager, plastic water bottles seem to follow Gabriel home the way that fleas would trail a veterinarian. We don't like them and we don't really use them, but no matter how many we get rid of, somehow they keep appearing. At trade shows and sales rep visits, these plastic bottles are an easy way for sellers of everything from bikes to bib shorts to get their product name in people's hands.

Cycling sixty miles in June without a drop of water is an ill-advised idea. Since we only had one metal canteen, I suggested to Gabriel that he use one of the magically proliferating plastic bottles. It might not be ideal, but at least it would prevent dehydration. Gabriel, however, would have none of this.

The night before our departure, he picked up a small bottle of Perrier (company established 1899) as his water source for the trip. It only held 250 milliliters (a few drops over one cup), and I asked my husband if he was really sure that he wouldn't rather take one of the plastic bottles.

"Nope!" he insisted, smiling at me. "This is much better!"

"It's kind of small," I pointed out. "Sixty-five miles is a long way." Moreover, the weekend of our trip was predicted to be the hottest of the month.

"It'll be fine!" he insisted. "I'm sure there's a water fountain at Deception Pass where I can fill it."

"Actually, there's not." I knew this rather definitively, since I had looked for one myself. "I checked."

"It'll be fine," Gabriel insisted, waving off my concerns.

The next morning, I hopped out of bed at four a.m. to the raucous jangling of my alarm clock. The first ferry from Port Townsend to Coupeville would be leaving at six thirty, and I wanted to have plenty of time for breakfast and other morning activities before we left. If we missed the first boat, our next opportunity to cross the water wouldn't be until eight a.m.—significantly later than we wanted to get started.

Gabriel wanted a little more sleep, so I bathed using my bowl and pitcher as quietly as possible, then tiptoed downstairs. I made both our lunches, packed a few last-minute items (like my hairbrush), and set the teakettle on the stove. When Gabriel wandered into the kitchen, rubbing his eyes, I was enjoying a large bowlful of local strawberries drowned in thick cream, strong tea, and a fat slice of homemade bread.

We rolled down to the ferry with ample time to spare, marveling at how bright the world was. A few weeks remained until the summer solstice, and yet the six a.m. sky was filled with almost as much light as the eleven a.m. world had been a few months previously. Puget Sound was smooth and glassy in the calm morning air, which had not a hint of wind. Unfortunately, as soon as the boat pulled away from the dock, a problem arose.

"Shoot!" Gabriel said suddenly. "I forgot my water!"

I looked at him, concerned. "That's not good!" I had already been worried about him taking so little liquid with him. Now he would have none whatsoever. "Here—" I curved my ankle around my bike's kickstand and swung it out into position. "You watch the bikes, and I'll see if there's a vending machine or something I can get you a bottle of water from."

"No, no!" Gabriel insistently motioned for me to stay where I was. "They would only have the plastic bottles."

I looked askance at him. "It's better than nothing! You don't want to ride sixty miles with no water!"

"I'm sure there'll be water along the way," he said dismissively.

"Where?" I stared at him, greatly dubious.

He looked out over the Sound. "I'm sure there's a water fountain at the Pass."

"There's not!" I ejaculated, repeating what I had already told him when we'd been planning the trip. "I was just there, remember? There's a Pepsi machine, but it specifically doesn't sell water—I checked!"

"I'll be fine," he insisted with irritating nonchalance. "Don't worry about it."

I was worried about it. Unfortunately, there was nothing I could do at the moment since my husband wouldn't let me buy him the only water available. I distracted myself by reviewing my map collection one last time.

After we landed at the Coupeville ferry terminal on Whidbey, we rode together a few flat miles until our route turned from the main highway onto a historic coastal road. Here the hills would start to truly emphasize the difference in our cycling skills as well as our bikes. We stopped for a brief embrace and to wish each other safe travels, then Gabriel launched into a significantly higher speed than I was capable of.

"See you at Deception Pass!" we called to each other as the distance between us grew wider. "Love you!"

It was a beautiful morning and there was wildlife out in plenty: rabbits and raptors (although luckily for the former, I never saw both at once) and flocks of little black birds whose nests must have been near the sides of the road. They drafted the wake of air from my bike, chattering and scolding me until I had passed far enough to become the concern of a different group of the same species of little birds, then the process would repeat itself afresh.

Passing by Penn Cove, I saw people wearing traditional Salish cedar bark hats and digging for shellfish on the mud flat, just as the local tribes have done for countless centuries. I reflected on how the way that Gabriel and I live makes us notice so clearly all the present's connections to the past. We see all the many *dal segnos*—the places where the music of history comes to a repeat sign and goes back upon its own refrain.

Every individual views the world through their own lens, and as I rode along waxing philosophical, I wondered how my husband was seeing the same scenery. On a purely practical level, I wondered how far ahead of me he was—and how he was coping without water on a day that was growing increasingly warmer.

I interrogated Gabriel later about his half of the trip and learned that while I had been pondering poetic analogies, my partner had been counting dismounts and analyzing gradients with a numerical precision that would bring a happy tear to the eye of any mathematics teacher.

His first dismount (to remove his jacket) was on the uphill portion of a slope with a 14 to 15 percent gradient. When the road grew level enough for riding again, he remounted and continued onward at a cruising speed of approximately fourteen miles per hour . . . (Further digital details omitted. Gabriel has managed to completely internalize the writing style of Victorian cycling magazines, which were written in the same precise, statistical manner so that cyclists could follow the tour routes of other riders. Unfortunately, I fear it might try the patience of modern readers.)

The first cyclist he saw on the road had a bike that was black and red like the Singer—although admittedly with a very different style. Whereas the black of the Singer's frame is offset by red rubber tires, the red of the other cyclist's bike was purely ornamental. Red and black paint covered the frame of a highly modern, carbon-fiber Trek. The other cyclist was clad completely in Lycra, while Gabriel was all in wool. If they had been riding side-by-side, the top of the passing cyclist's helmet might have reached Gabriel's knee, at most.

With a 130-year-old bicycle on a 130-mile trip, there are bound to be some unnerving moments. The first came as Gabriel descended a steep hill passing through a suburban neighborhood. A curve in the road blocked his view of the path ahead, which proved to be a steep downward slope. On a freewheel bike, this would have just meant the delight of sudden, easy coasting, but on a fixed-gear bike like the Ordinary, the situation was downright hazardous. On a fixed-gear, every turn of the wheel mandates a turn of the pedals. If the rider doesn't keep up, the pedals will fly out from under his feet—ripping away all control of the bike. The tilt in the road threw the bike forward at increasingly faster velocity and Gabriel's pumping legs had to keep pace with the breakneck speed while trying to maintain control.

In the golden days of Ordinary bicycles, particularly skilled Wheelmen would coast by taking their feet off the pedals and let those whirring pegs do what they might while the riders hooked their legs up over their handlebars. In cycling magazines of the time, there are even illustrations of riders coasting down gravel roads in the Rocky Mountains this way!

The reason for this position is two-fold: it keeps the rider's feet out of the way of the manically spinning pedals, and it puts him in the optimal position for an emergency dismount if he crashes. Normal mounts and dismounts on a high wheeler are done off the back, over the little wheel. (Most high wheelers have a little step above their smaller wheel to assist the rider.) For technical reasons involving centers of balance, a high wheel bicycle's handlebars are directly over the rider's legs. If the bike suddenly stops, his legs are trapped there. When the most courageous Wheelmen hooked their legs over their handlebars to coast down the Rocky Mountains, they knew that at least if they crashed, in that position they would land on their feet.

Anyone who crashes a bike receives an unpleasant lesson in Newton's first law: "An object in motion tends to remain in motion." Since the rider is, most decidedly, in motion, he will tend to remain in motion—even if his bike comes to an abrupt halt underneath him. This commonly leads to a crash where the rider shoots straight over his handlebars. If he's still holding his grips when this happens (or if his legs are trapped under his handlebars, as they are on an Ordinary), a sort of dual somersault can result, with the bike tumbling over and tackling the crashed rider. This phenomenon has been responsible for a number

Illustration from *The Wheelman*, May 1883.

of fractured clavicles in both historic and modern cycling. A modern road bike weighs an average of around twenty pounds, and it can do plenty of damage in a crash. The Singer weighs forty-seven pounds and would be an even less pleasant wrestling partner.

Gabriel hasn't quite mastered the difficult art of coasting a high wheeler, so when he suddenly found himself descending a steep downhill slope, he had two choices: pedal apace with the speed his bike was gaining, or crash. Fixed-gear bikes aren't like the coaster-brake bikes ridden by children; pedaling backward won't act as a brake. On level ground and a lighter bike, pedaling a fixed-gear backward causes it to move backward—a neat trick, but one that the Singer is far too heavy to accomplish, especially downhill. The bike has so much momentum that even attempting to slow the speed of spin is most likely to just rip the pedals from the rider's control. Gabriel pedaled faster—and faster—

The rim of the bike's front wheel had been bent at some point in its nearly 130-year history, putting the 54-inch wheel out of true. When the intrepid Wheelman exceeded twenty miles per hour, Gabriel started to feel speed wobbles from the uneven wheel. He wished he could have ridden it when it was still new and pristine—and as this thought whizzed through his head, he kept pedaling faster to keep up with the bike's ever-increasing speed.

Finally the road leveled briefly—and then soared skyward in a spirit-crushingly long uphill slope. Gabriel's momentum from the downhill only lasted a short time, and then he was fighting against gravity again. Panting, sweaty, but undaunted, he kept pounding pedals and climbed heavenward. When he reached the summit of the hill, he beamed with pride in himself for making the climb without dismounting—even once! Feeling triumphant, he saw a group of school children waiting for a bus and merrily rang his bell at them. They completely ignored him.

Attempting to avoid the noise and fumes of the highway as much as possible, Gabriel charted his course along roads that sometimes led him in the right direction—and sometimes didn't. At one point partway down what he thought was a road, the path ahead seemed to suddenly disappear. He dismounted to investigate and realized the path he was following went straight down a cliff and into a salt marsh. He turned around and took another route—only to find himself on military property. Gabriel passed through the grounds of a naval air station expecting to be halted and turned back at any moment. Luckily for him, there were no checkpoints on that portion of the road and he managed to pass through to the main highway without incident. As he passed two jets on display outside the grounds of the base, a man in a dump truck who had stopped at a traffic light yelled out his window at him: "I like your bike!" He flashed Gabriel a thumbs-up.

Hills are unavoidable in the Northwest, and the second set of downhill/uphill slopes was even more disconcerting than the first had been. Gabriel was carrying a lot of speed to mount an uphill, and when the road took a sudden turn downward again, the pedals battled against his feet, fighting his cadence. He thought he'd lose his foothold, but he managed to keep control of the bike through to more gradual slopes. Thoroughly jarred, he resolved to be more careful about pacing and kept riding.

When Gabriel was almost to the terrifying Twin Bridges, a state trooper on a motorcycle pulled alongside him and started pacing the Wheel, his mouth set in a firm line and his expression unreadable. The law officer looked the high wheeler up and down.

Ah, man, Gabriel thought. *Is he going to give me a ticket for not wearing a helmet or something?*

The trooper inspected the Ordinary and its rider, from the top of Gabriel's head to where the Wheel glided along the ground. Then he looked Gabriel in the eyes. "That's a most impressive form of transportation, sir!" With that, the trooper sped off.

Relieved, Gabriel chuckled to himself and continued riding.

While Gabriel was thus engaged in battling hills and escaping police censure, I stopped at a grocery store in Oak Harbor, locked up my bike, and ran inside. The June day was heating up quickly, and I was extremely worried about my husband's lack of water.

Given his earlier objections, I didn't even try looking at the water in plastic bottles. Unfortunately, the store's only option for single glass bottles of mineral water was the one-liter size, and I knew this would never fit in Gabriel's bag. They did sell the smaller bottles—but only in party packs. This represented considerable weight (not to mention bulk), but I judged my husband's wellbeing to be worth the haulage. I bought a pack of four Perrier bottles, rushed back outside, and squeezed them into my panniers.

As I approached Deception Pass this time, it practically seemed like home ground since I had been there so recently. I made it to the bridge at eleven a.m. and wasn't at all surprised to find Gabriel had been there waiting for over an hour. He hadn't had a chance to get bored, though. A crowd was gathered around him, and he had been far too busy answering questions about his Ordinary to grow impatient.

I pulled up to the scenic overlook where Gabriel was waiting and proudly presented my very thirsty husband with a pack of four separate bottles of water from my pannier. He packed one in his bag and drank one with lunch. I encouraged him to drink more while he had the chance, but he assured me that this was not necessary, so I drank one bottle with my own lunch and saved the remaining bottle in my pannier. As I rode through the dusty fields of the Skagit Valley later, I would be very glad to have it.

I left my bike with Gabriel and trotted over the bridge's pedestrian walk-way to the restrooms located at the far end for tourist traffic. As I returned, I took a deep breath of the fresh, windy air and looked far down to the waters of Deception Pass. Nearly two hundred feet below me, two harbor seals bobbed casually at the surface of the swift water.

Gabriel and I finished our lunch and let a few curious tourists take our photos, then swung our legs over our trusty steel steeds once more. As our wheels drew apart, we called out the same endearments and benedictions for safe travels we had shared earlier, and this time pledged to meet each other at Tom's apartment in Bellingham.

When I was nearly through the Skagit Valley and approaching Chuckanut Drive, a couple of very nice women in their forties came alongside me on motorized Vespa scooters and paced me a while, chatting. They had overtaken Gabriel when they left Bellingham earlier, and now they were on their way home. Expecting to pass him again, they promised to say hello for me and let him know how far behind him I was. That way he could approximate an expected time for my arrival.

Going up the hills on Chuckanut Drive, I remembered what Tom had told me about the whole mountain being one large fossil formation. I had fun spot-ting fossilized palm fronds in the rock formations, and remembered the tales of Mary Anning searching for pterodactyls. It's good to be reminded to take a *really* long view of history sometimes.

I knew beyond any doubt that by the time I arrived at Tom's apartment, Gabriel would have been there for hours ahead of me. Sure enough, when I came up to the door, my two favorite guys were right inside. My husband put a cold, wet towel in my left hand; my buddy put a large glass of ice water in my right.

I used the towel to scrub the crusted salt off my face from my own dried sweat and dug at the corners of my eyes to excavate the yellow crystals that had accreted there. Then I drained the water cup in a few greedy gulps. With a grin, Tom grabbed the empty cup from me, refilled it, and handed it back. We repeated the process.

While Tom refilled the large cup for me a third time, Gabriel looked at me with some concern. "Oh dear," my husband said, frowning at the bridge of my nose. "Your sunglasses seem to have chafed you really badly!"

"Hmm?" I asked, then realized what he was seeing. "Oh, no—that's just oxidation from the steel." I took off the steel-rimmed 1890s sunglasses and ran my forefinger along the place where they had been resting. A streak of rusty specks came off on my finger.

Tom handed me the water cup again and I promptly drained it once more. I rubbed at my nose with the damp towel that had taken the salt off the rest of my face, and when I looked at the white cloth again, it showed a bright, blood-colored smear of rust. I squinted down at my nose. "Did I get it all?"

"Not all of it." Gabriel took the towel from me and delicately dabbed at my nose. Tom, who had refilled the water cup for me yet again, looked at us with slight curiosity.

"Gabriel gave these to me last year for our steel anniversary," I explained, handing him the sunglasses. (In the vasculum chapter, I mentioned the tenth wedding anniversary is tin; the eleventh is steel.) The nose-bridge between the lenses was actually quite shiny and clean; all the rust from the century they'd been in storage was now on my nose. "They have steel rims, and the oxidation rubs off a bit."

Tom inspected the blue-tinted spectacles, then handed them back. "That makes sense," he said in a tone of scientific assessment. He passed back the cup I was using, which he'd refilled yet again. By this point, my stomach was nearing its holding capacity so I sipped at the liquid a bit more slowly. *Was that my fourth cup, or my fifth?* I wondered curiously.

I looked at Gabriel. When we'd left Deception Pass, we each had one small bottle of sparkling water—but I had also had the canteen, and I'd drained it about five miles before reaching Bellingham. "How did you make out, with so little liquid?"

He grinned and shrugged. "I was pretty thirsty!" he admitted with a smile. "But I got the same treatment you did." He nodded toward Tom, who gave him another glass of water.

Gabriel and I had a very sound night's sleep on the futon in Tom's living room, and the next morning he made French toast. After breakfast, Gabriel and I headed out on our bikes to attract publicity for the day's events at the bookstore.

In the middle of the nineteenth century, modern-day Bellingham was actually three separate villages: Whatcom (a former trading post for the Hudson's Bay Company), Sehome (a coal mining community), and Bellingham (a relatively unimportant village until it was incorporated into the other two). Fairhaven was founded nearby in 1889 (that magic year, again!). Railroad millionaire Nelson Bennett saw the location as the ideal place for train rails to meet up with ships docking in Bellingham Bay, but at the time the property was owned by an old settler named Dan Harris. Bennett offered Harris $50,000 for his land (quite a princely sum), but the old squatter refused to sell. When Bennett doubled the offer to $100,000, Harris "coolly pocketed the check . . . and retired to the life of ease which the fortune assured him." Bennett hired "a small army of men" to clear the land, build docks, open coal mines, and grade the land for railroad lines.[230] Fairhaven incorporated with the three older communities in 1903.[231] Today, the footprint of the old city of Fairhaven takes great pride in being Bellingham's historic district. Village Books, where we'd present, is right in the middle of it.

We touched base with the events coordinator at the bookstore, then loitered outside for a while and chatted with the inevitable crowds gathering around the high wheeler. The Wheel is quite an amazing machine and the size of it is difficult for some people to wrap their minds around the first time they see it. Neither Gabriel nor I are particularly short (he's five ten and I'm five nine), yet in photos the high wheeler can make us look like General Tom Thumb and his wife if there aren't enough other items in the picture to give a proper scale. In person most people comment on how enormous it is—which amuses Gabriel because to him the Ordinary is, well, ordinary. Living with something every day changes a person's perspective on it. One of the key things we endeavor to communicate to people is that things that seem exotic now were once commonplace, and they can be again with a little effort.

Tom soon joined us at the bookstore, and as the scheduled time for the first presentation approached, we all went inside together. We had a good turnout for the bike lecture, and afterward Gabriel demonstrated some high wheeler riding outside in a nearby courtyard. People mostly watched from the sidelines, but at one point a group of children ran alongside him, trying to keep pace with the Wheel. None of them could manage it, but this didn't seem to disappoint them. Gabriel demonstrated mounting the bicycle, a half-coast (pedaling with only one foot, and holding the other off to the side while one pedal spins freely), an ordinary dismount (catching a small step on the backbone of the bike with one foot and swinging the other foot over the bike like dismounting a horse), and an emergency dismount (jumping smoothly over the back of the bike.)

While Gabriel was still showing off the high wheeler, I went inside and changed into my summer dress for the book signing. This was a welcome relief, since my cycling outfit (designed for spring and autumn touring) is quite warm and it was a hot day. Someone else was pounding on the door of the bathroom to get in, and I undressed and re-dressed in such a hurry that I didn't even try to take off my shoes, but instead pulled all my garments over my head. (I reflected that this was a great advantage of a skirt over trousers. Trying to remove trousers by pulling them off over one's head could only end badly.)

As I came out of the bathroom, I wondered why my feet were so hot—then I realized I had forgotten to take off my gaiters! I quickly ameliorated the situation, but I must have looked pretty silly coming out of that restroom: sports gaiters below a frothy lawn dress decorated with twenty-seven yards of lace! It was more or less the Victorian equivalent of sports cleats with a prom dress.

By the time the reading and signing were finished, Gabriel and I were far too hot to change back into our cycling clothes, so we walked with Tom back to his place, wheeling our bikes beside us. As is Tom's custom (remember, he does wilderness rescue), he presented us with as much food as we could eat.

We spent the evening visiting and while we talked I worked on a small project I had brought with me. Prior to the trip, I had read a nineteenth-century magazine article about visiting that said that while staying with a friend or relative, a visitor should create a small bit of handiwork to present to their hosts as a gift when they left—a sweet souvenir of their stay. I felt it was a charming idea, but didn't think the flowers and curls of traditional embroidery would quite fit in with Tom's decor. It might clash with the horse brain in a jar on his shelf.

I had found a piece of cloth pre-printed with realistic pictures of arctic animals—realistic in terms of the pictures of the animals themselves, at least. The overall tableau was one I knew would amuse a professional scientist like Tom. Predators and prey, polar bears, foxes, owls, seals, and rabbits were all snuggled calmly together in a crowded collage on the fabric. The name of the design was Arctic Friends. Anyone with the remotest idea of the dietary needs of the animals involved should have called it Two Milliseconds Before the Bloodbath.

Seated at Tom's desk, I pulled out the fabric, a small embroidery hoop, a needle, and some thread. "So," I commented. "I'm thinking there should be cartoon bubbles on here with the seal telling the rabbit, 'I knew this was a bad idea,' and the rabbit responding, 'Just look big!'"

Tom inspected the fabric and laughed. "Yeah," he agreed. "That's not a good situation for anyone in that picture."

While we chatted throughout the evening, I used an embroidery technique called satin stitching to add the commentary to the picture, then hemmed it and gave it to Tom. He had a good chuckle over it and said he would hang it up in his lab.

Sunday morning, Gabriel and I got an early start. We left at six a.m., full daylight at that time of year. It didn't take Gabriel long to outpace me again, and we had decided that this time we wouldn't bother trying to rendezvous mid-route.

Gabriel's mental tallying of all numeric quantities resumed. He averaged two miles an hour faster for the return trip, his overall total of dismounts was half of that on the trip north . . . (Further digital details omitted.)

After crossing the bridge at Deception Pass, he stopped to take a break and chat with the crowds of tourists who were enjoying the view. While an American family was asking him questions, a Japanese group came up and expressed interest in the machine. Linguistic issues made most of them shy, but the man with the strongest English skills leaped forward to declare, "I must try it!" .

Gabriel explained that the Ordinary was very old and fragile and required a great deal of practice to ride. (A two-hundred foot bridge was not the ideal location for lessons.) The man seemed crestfallen. In compensation, Gabriel spent some extra time demonstrating riding techniques before continuing onward.

Arriving at Coupeville, Gabriel had some extra time before the ferry left. He spent it talking to various people, all of whom were incredulous that he had ridden such an extraordinary bike all the way from Bellingham in a single morning.

He arrived home several hours before I did and set up an incredibly sweet homecoming for me. He had gone to Pippa's Real Tea downtown and asked the owner for my favorite iced tea. He had it brewed and nicely cooled for me by the time I got home.

When I arrived home tired, hot, but happy, I smiled to see my dear husband waiting for me. He had already cleaned the road dust off his high wheeler and returned the machine to its stand in the parlor; as I washed my face, he wiped down my bike for me and arranged it in its customary place in the kitchen. As I sipped the cool, sweet drink he had prepared for me, I regarded my trusty steed of steel and thought of the many miles it had covered. "So," I asked, turning to my husband with a twinkle in my eye. "When's the next cycle tour?"

26

A Typical Day

"The simplest pleasures are the best."
—*Good Housekeeping*, 1889[232]

As I write these words, it has been almost exactly four years since my husband and I moved to Port Townsend. We have just celebrated another Thanksgiving (warmer than the first) and once more there is snow outside our windows. A few years ago, the weather was lovely scenery; now we have a way to put it to use. Last night I set out tin cans filled with water to freeze in the yard overnight so that we could get a bit of free ice for the ice box. The structure of our life is forever teaching us new lessons. Looking around my cherished home, I see ways in which we have enhanced that structure—and of course work that remains to be done.

It was chilly this morning; when I lit the lamp at the side of my bed, I could see my breath rising around me. I kissed Gabriel and told him to stay in bed until I started the process of warming the house; he smiled in the darkness and snuggled deeper into the blankets.

First I lit the Perfection heater, the marvelous old kerosene-burning device that has served us so well since we moved here. Since I'm right-handed, I started lighting it at the eight o'clock position on the circular wick, then drew the match around the wick clockwise so that I wouldn't be reaching through the flame at any point. I fastened the tubular metal top that houses the flame spreader, adjusted the level of the burning glow, and smiled up at the flower-like pattern it cast upon the ceiling. I had brought up a kettle of water to the bedroom after we went to bed last night; once the Perfection heater was burning, I set the copper kettle on its top to warm my wash water.

We've replaced the horribly ugly and inefficient 1970s heater that was in the parlor when we moved here with a beautifully refurbished gas stove from the 1890s. After I lit the Perfection heater in the bedroom, I padded downstairs to light the parlor stove so the lower portion of the house would grow warm as well.

Britons of the nineteenth century referred to the items filling their homes as household gods. The term was sometimes used in jest, or even pejoratively, yet I think it apt. For me it holds no irony. Home is a sacred space; it is only fitting that it should be inhabited by gods and that we should pay them homage. Every morning as I kneel in front of our parlor stove to kindle its flame, then light our lamps with a match from the vesta on my chatelaine, I think of the goddess who lends the match safe its name. It reminds me what a small link I am in a chain of history stretching to ancient Greece and beyond.

Back in the bedroom, the Perfection heater was starting to make headway against the cold. I crossed the room to my marble-topped washstand, which supports the bowl and pitcher I once coveted so avidly. Now they've become a standard part of my daily routine, but I never take them for granted. Every morning I revel in the beauty of the set I wanted for so very long. Familiarity need not equal contempt. On the contrary: familiarity can breed the deepest love, which is the whole point of marriage.

By this point in the narrative, my dear better half was emerging from bed. "Brrr!" Gabriel shivered. "It's going to be a hard workout this morning, with that other room so cold. The past few days my weights have been freezing, literally freezing, when I picked them up!"

I looked at my husband in concern. "You could skip this morning," I suggested.

He shook his head. "Nah. My back's been hurting, and the Sandow routine always makes it feel better."

I kissed him and wished him luck.

He usually puts on a lightweight workout suit for his exercises—a copy of a cyclist's racing outfit from the 1880s. It's made of a stretchy wool jersey no thicker than a T-shirt and fits nearly as tightly as Lycra. Today, though, he kept on the bright red union suit he had slept in.

"Would you like oatmeal or beast cakes for breakfast?" I asked.

His eyes lit up. "Mmm . . . Beast cakes!" he said enthusiastically.

Beast cakes are pancakes made by pouring pure sourdough starter (unstirred) straight onto a hot, greased pan. I keep a sourdough culture perpetually bubbling in the back of the kitchen. It has to be fed once a day to keep the yeast breeding (it consumes a mixture of one part flour to one part water) so when I first started tending it, I told Gabriel I felt like we had a pet again. He started calling it The Beast, and by extension, sourdough bread became beast bread, sourdough pancakes beast cakes, etc.

I grinned at my husband's enthusiasm. "Beast cakes it is!"

He made appreciative sounds as he went into the next room to start his workout.

I poured cold water from my porcelain pitcher into its matching bowl, reflecting idly on the nineteenth-century debate over whether it is healthier to bathe in cold water or warm. (There were devotees on both sides of the issue— Sandow recommended cold.) I don't always warm my wash water in the summer, or even in the late spring or early autumn, but as I shivered this morning and strained my eyes to see the snow outside my window, I reflected that one would have to be an extraordinarily adamant proponent of cold-water bathing to eschew any warmth on a morning such as this. I added enough water from the kettle to make the liquid in the bowl tolerably warm, then performed my morning ablutions.

I dried myself with the towel hanging on a hook behind my washstand, then held my daytime corset over the kerosene heater a moment to warm its metal bones before I put it on. I dressed quickly: pantalets, a shift, a cotton petticoat (easily washed), then a sturdy quilted winter petticoat made of thick felted wool sandwiched between a cozy flannel lining and a brushed cotton shell that outer skirts slip over freely without bunching. Over all these, I slipped a warm woolen tea gown that I made a few years ago by copying an antique one in our collection. There are two completely different styles of tea gowns: one is a frothy affair, usually of silk and lace, for informal entertaining at home. The other is a sturdy housedress, one step up from a nightgown, worn while doing household chores. My tea gowns are the latter sort. (Last night I slept in a flannel one that is another copy of the same antique.) I added sturdy boots that wouldn't mind the snow.

I fixed my hair then, a process that took longer than putting on my various layers but less time than brushing my teeth. I would like to think of that statement putting a happy tear in my dental hygienist's eye, but if I'm perfectly honest, it's more a mark of how quickly I can get dressed than how meticulously I scrub my pearly whites. Modern people often make appalled ejaculations about how long they think it must take to put on Victorian clothing, but it's quick and easy when it's a natural daily routine.

I turned to my first task of the day: making the bed. I stripped off all the coverings we had slept under the cold night before: a wedding ring quilt Gabriel gave me the first Christmas after we were engaged; a green quilt I made him for our second anniversary (the cotton anniversary); a thick, scratchy blanket made out of a huge rectangle of felted wool as thick as my pinky finger and so large it has to be partly folded over itself to fit on the bed; a white cotton coverlet (really intended for summer, but it certainly can't subtract any heat so I added it to the pile); my old soft "blankie" that I've had longer than I can remember; and a flannel sheet. Stripping all these, I disinterred the four hot water bottles we slept with last night and set them and our pillows aside. I picked up one edge of the feather tick, shook it in a slow, waving motion, then went around to the other side of the bed and repeated the process. The mounds of feathers that had molded to our bodies overnight fluffed up into heavenly soft clouds again and I replaced the pillows and blankets.

Once the bed was in order, I blew out the larger of the two oil lamps and lifted the other (my antique finger lamp) to light my way downstairs. Time for beast cakes!

Down in the kitchen, I made a face at the small electric range that was here when we moved in. We've finally saved enough money to buy a real nineteenth-century wood cookstove and we've placed our order. As I watched my breath puff out from my lips early this morning, I thought how wonderful it will be to have yet another source of heat in the house. The building was designed around the assumption of a heat-producing kitchen stove; I can't wait until it has one again. We've been making do with the electric range until we could find and afford the coveted replacement, but the anachronism has always been frustrating. Knowing how soon its time will be at hand, I clucked my tongue at it, telling it soon it would go the way of the electric fridge.

Once my great-grandmother's cast-iron pan was hot, I turned to my sourdough culture. As long as the starter (i.e. the beast) is kept happy, sourdough breads are incredibly easy to make; they are some of the oldest breads known to man. They were popular with gold miners in both the San Francisco Gold Rush of 1849 and the Klondike Gold Rush of the 1890s. Some middle-class families in our period might have looked down a bit on sourdough as being a rough food and slightly beneath them, but we like it. (Even in a single class then, as now, people are different. Diversity again!)

By the time Gabriel finished his workout, washed, dressed, and came downstairs, the first beast cake was nearly ready. As I transferred it to a plate, he finished gathering a few things he'd want for the day, including his corduroy jacket. We quipped that the jacket and the breakfast are appropriate accompaniments to each other, given the historical link between sourdough and miners. The jacket is a replica of an antique I gave Gabriel as an anniversary present last summer. I bought the original from a man who explores old mining camps. He had found it stuffed in the collapsed entrance of an old mine shaft. There had been a fire in the shaft in the late nineteenth century, and in an effort to smother the flames, the miners had shoved everything on hand—including this jacket—into the opening. The back and bottom of the jacket were burned, but the fire took all the oxygen out of the environment before the shaft collapsed and sealed it, so the remaining portions were fairly well preserved. A seamstress in Seattle had been able to reproduce the jacket, and now Gabriel's fond of wearing the copy to work.

After breakfast, my husband left for work and I started making fresh bread. I used my grandmother's tin measuring cups to transfer two and a half cups of flour to a large ceramic bowl. Sourdough starter reacts badly to metal, so I stirred the beast with a wooden spoon, then used a half-pint glass jelly jar to add two and a half cups of leavening to the flour. It was time to "feed the beast," and since I'd used so much of it this morning, I mixed an extra-large portion of feed: two cups of flour and two cups of warm water, which I mix to a smooth paste in a separate bowl before adding it to the original starter—the living beast. I stirred the beast and its feed briskly together with the wooden spoon, then used a damp towel to cover the ceramic bowl where the beast lives, then inverted another bowl on top of it to create a loose seal.

I turned back to my bread in progress and smiled to see air bubbling out of the lively starter as it oozed over the flour. I added a large double pinch of salt and mixed the mass with my hands until it held together, then I turned the dough out onto a large breadboard and kneaded it vigorously. When it felt lively, I let it rest on the breadboard while I washed the dishes, then I buttered a piece of a waxed paper and lined a pie pan with it. (The waxed paper keeps the sourdough from reacting badly with the metal pan. Buttering the waxed paper keeps it from sticking to the bread.)

By now a faint dawn was touching the kitchen with rosy fingers, so I blew out my lamp. I kneaded the dough a few minutes more, patted it into a smooth, round loaf, and placed it on the buttered waxed paper. If I stopped here, the surface tension on the loaf's exterior would keep it from rising to its fullest potential, so I cut a crosshatch pattern on the top of the dough to let it spread out. Then I set the loaf aside in a corner of the kitchen, inverted a bowl over it to keep out dust, and evaluated my further tasks for the day.

The floor was clean enough that I judged sweeping unnecessary, but right inside the kitchen door were a few marks left by snowy shoes, so I wiped these away with a damp cloth.

I remembered that my white undergarments wanted washing and there was no sense in trying to make clothes clean by putting them in a dirty sink, so I scrubbed the kitchen sink with baking soda. I filled the teakettle and put it to heat on the stove, then plugged the sink and adjusted the tap to pour out the hottest water my hands could tolerate. I took a bar of Ivory soap (company established 1878[233]) and rubbed it into the warm water filling the sink until no more soap would dissolve.

I ran upstairs and, noticing that I hadn't emptied my washbowl yet, I took a half a moment to tip its contents into the bathroom toilet and wipe it out. Then I gathered all the whites I wasn't currently wearing: two pairs of pantalets, a shift, and a petticoat. I carried the armful of lacy garments to the kitchen and dropped them in the soapy water, then I rubbed more Ivory soap directly into the fabric. Since I had already saturated the water with as much soap as it could hold, small bits clumped off the bar and clung to the garments or floated up to the surface. However, raising the temperature of the water increases the amount of soap it can hold, and now the kettle was steaming. I poured boiling water over the laundry, stirred it with a wooden spoon, and watched the soap chunks dissolve. I splashed in some bleach, stirred it again, and left the mixture to soak and cool.

I spent several hours writing, then decided it was time for lunch. My laundry was still in the sink, so before I could eat, I had to drain off the soapy gray water, then rinse and wring my whites. I hung them in the downstairs bathroom where they could drip into the tub. (Tomorrow I'll move them upstairs to our antique drying rack, and when I find time, I'll starch and iron them.)

I peered under my mixing bowl at the sourdough loaf I had set up earlier. It had barely risen in the cold kitchen, and I reflected on how nice it will be when the house has a wood-burning stove again. I anticipate a learning curve the size and slope of Mont Ventoux when the stove arrives and is installed, but I long for the challenge.

A bit of yesterday's bread loaf remained, so after I put the kettle on for tea, I reached into the bottom compartment of the ice box. The less an ice box is opened, the longer the ice lasts; since we keep the cheese and butter in the same compartment, I removed them both, took what I wanted, and put them back together. I made sure the latch was well settled, then took a jar of pickles from a different section of the appliance—the one beside the ice instead of underneath it. Cold sinks more easily than it travels sideways and pickles are less sensitive than dairy products.

Halfway through lunch, I saw the kettle was steaming, so I rose from the table to fix my tea. I filled my tiny teapot and its matching cup with water from the teakettle to warm them, then drained the pot and scooped a couple of teaspoons of loose leaves into it. (It only holds two cups of tea—I have larger teapots for when I have company.) I refilled it with boiling water. If I hadn't warmed it first, some of the heat would have been lost to the pottery and the temperature would be too low for optimal brewing.

I flipped over a five-minute sandglass and finished my lunch while the fragrant leaves steeped. When the sands had run from the top teardrop of the timer into its bottom, I emptied the hot water out of my teacup and poured tea from the tiny pot through a miniature strainer to catch the leaves.

I opened the one compartment of the ice box I hadn't accessed earlier: the ice compartment itself, the coldest section of the whole appliance. We were out of cream but the milk was in there, snuggled up against the ice. As I took it out, I smiled at the way the slowly melting ice had contoured to the glass bottle, as well as to Gabriel's wrapped meats, which were also in this section.

I finished my lunch with an apple for dessert, then went back to work. It was midday and the natural light was as bright as it would get this time of year, so I fetched down the reservoir from the kerosene heater. I knew it wanted refilling and the level of oil is easier to see by day than by lamplight. I set the reservoir in the sink, pulled the plug at its top, slipped a funnel into the opening, and filled it from a five-gallon jug of kerosene. I didn't think I had spilled any, but I used a dry rag to wipe the outside of the reservoir anyway and also wiped the outside of the jug. I put the extra kerosene away, then took out another clean rag.

I turned the heater's flame spreader counterclockwise to disengage it from the grooves that hold it in place, then lifted it free of the reservoir. I held it over the garbage can, scrubbed it vigorously to remove soot, then angled it toward the light from the window. Sometimes stubborn flakes of carbon cling to the underside of the flame spreader or clog the holes that let in air to the fire, so I scrub the apparatus with an old toothbrush to remove them. Today, though, it was clean enough to render this unnecessary.

I reassembled the heater, then went around the house checking the lamps. None of them wanted filling today, but I trimmed their wicks and washed the glass chimney of my little fingerlamp. (It was the only one showing marks of soot.)

I had some errands to run, so, after washing my hands, I changed into clothes more suitable for an outing. I stripped off my tea gown, but left all my undergarments in place. In fact, I added one underskirt—a striped silk petticoat I don't wear doing housework because I don't want to risk dirtying it. Striped silk petticoats were all the rage at the end of the nineteenth century. Their crisp rustling was considered supremely erotic; the brief flash of color within a woman's skirts as she moved was a flirting scintillation whispering of deeper silken textures. The one I put on is a copy of an antique from our collection. I put on my favorite plaid dress, then one of my antique fur coats and a matching bonnet, and went out.

The cold was keeping most people indoors today, and for once I received more compliments than venomous attacks. It was a small blessing, but one takes what one can get.

An overwhelming majority of people assume that interacting with nineteenth-century artifacts and technology is the hard part of what Gabriel and I do. This assumption is as far from the truth as Earth is from the Andromeda Galaxy. We love the gentle light of oil lamps, the meditative awareness we have of the function of all the objects in our life, the myriad insights every new/old item we add to our lives gives us. These are immense joys, the dearest parts of life to us. The hard part is dealing with other people's reactions. We live in a society that prides itself on diversity, yet has ironically narrow definitions of which types of diversity it will tolerate.

People who would never dream of pulling their eyes into slants to make faces at Asians will point at me and give voice to the most ridiculous stereotypes imaginable of the nineteenth century. No politically correct American would dream of fondling a Muslim woman through her hijab, yet they'll stride up and start groping my waist. I've even been in situations where people started screaming (literally screaming) at me for removing their hands from my body. People can display an appalling lack of compunction when encountering a lifestyle outside their narrow frame of tolerance. With the exception of a glancing reference to some of the hate mail we've received, I've refrained in this text from mentioning the vitriol we're subjected to on a constant basis. This has primarily been a story of our home, our sanctuary from a hostile world. Here I tend our household gods and look for the angels in the details. The Victorians were fond of saying that home is our heaven; I will not allow the demons of ignorance to invade this sacred space.

I walked to the grocery store for cream, then to the hardware store for lamp oil, and back home. I transferred the cream from its fragile cardboard carton to a glass bottle and smiled at a remembered comment Gabriel had once made watching me do this: He said I looked like a milk counterfeiter. I set the bottle on the ice in the ice box, put away the lamp oil, then went into the parlor and relit the gas.

I had a little time for sewing, and I wanted to do it while I still had some daylight. Dark colors get higher sunlight priority than light ones because light colors reflect lamplight better. I finished some dark mending before I took up a cream-colored flannel shift I've been making. After a while, the mailman delivered an antique book I had sent away for, along with a nineteenth-century magazine clipping destined to be an illustration in the book you're reading now.

When I started to lose the light (which happens early at this time of year), I set my needlework aside. I'd had my sewing fun for the day and it was time to get back to work. I lit both the lamps in the parlor and focused their light on a chair by a gas heater, where I wrote until late in the evening.

When the clock's hands drew close to the time for Gabriel to return home, I lit our kerosene railroad lantern and hung it outside the door. The bread dough had risen, so I preheated the oven and put it in to bake. When, through the bay view window, I saw my husband arrive home, I set my writing aside. I went out on the porch and held aloft the lantern to welcome him home.

While Gabriel set down his bag and took off his jacket, I lit the kitchen lamp as well as my little fingerlamp (which had migrated downstairs earlier in the day) and extinguished the lights in the parlor. We warmed up some Thanksgiving leftovers for dinner and savored them with hot bread fresh out of the oven. There was still some pumpkin pie left from the holiday, so I poured some thick cream into a bowl and whipped it to stiff peaks with an antique rotary beater.

While we ate, we chatted about the day and then settled into our books. I read a reprinted *Good Housekeeping* from 1890 while Gabriel perused a likewise reprinted copy of *The Wheelman* magazine. We shared choice passages from each and discussed them.

When we finished eating, I fetched the hot water bottles from upstairs and treated them the same as my teapot earlier: filled each with hot water to warm the receptacle, emptied them, then refilled them so they would stay warm as long as possible. I wiped stray drips from their exteriors, put them in their cloth covers, and handed them to Gabriel. He turned off the gas in the parlor while I emptied the ice box's drip tray, then I carried my fingerlamp to light our way upstairs. I set the little lamp on its perch on one side of my vanity dresser, then lit the lamp on the other side while Gabriel tucked the hot water bottles into bed.

While Gabriel wound his watch, I let down my hair and brushed it, then we both undressed for bed. My sleeping corset (one that started as a day-time corset but was demoted to nightwear when it showed significant signs of wear) was lying over my cedar chest where I'd set it to air earlier in the day. I held it over the heater to warm its metal bones before I switched out of my day corset, then snuggled into my flannel tea gown.

We left the heater burning while Gabriel read to me from an M. E. Braddon novel. I watched the play of firelight on the ceiling as we discussed whether the heroine had *really* killed the moping side character. When we grew sleepy, I wound the mechanical alarm clock and snuffed the heater, and Gabriel blew out his lamp. In the dark, we whispered reflections on how far we had come in four short years, as well as plans for new adventures. The stove will be coming soon, and our explorations of the power of Victorian bicycles have just begun. We talked of cycling tours to flower festivals in different counties and to ghost towns. "But first," I reminded Gabriel, "I want to go to Canada with them!"

"Oh, yes!" With my cheek against my husband's, Gabriel's smile was something I felt more than saw in the darkness. "This coming spring. Imagine how appropriate they'll be in Victoria! It'll be such a fun ride up there—and there's the long ferry ride to get to the island."

"I wonder how the customs people will react to the high wheeler!"

Gabriel laughed. "We'll see!"

We snuggled close and drifted to sleep, dreaming of our continuing adventures.

Epilogue

When I penned the closing words of the last chapter, I thought they would be the end of the book. I had already read through the manuscript more times than could be counted, but I read through it again twice more to add a few things, subtract others, and make a list of the words that I clearly cannot spell. (My New Year's resolution is to have the list mastered by next Christmas.) I thought the manuscript was ready to send to my editor, all neat and tidy. Life is an ongoing story, though, and just as I thought I was done with this volume, something happened that begged to be added: The refurbished 1890s kitchen stove arrived. We assembled it last night, all cast iron and nickel plate, and I can still hardly believe that it's real—and really mine.

The previous owners of our house chopped off the original chimney below the roofline sometime in the twentieth century and filled the entire chimney with broken bricks and sand. (Yes, sand.) Before I can even start learning to use our beautiful new stove, Gabriel will have to install a chimney for it—yet another adventure and set of learning experiences. I've already told my friends that when we have the chimney set up, they'll be invited to a stove warming party. I've gotten pretty good at making some of Mrs. Beeton's recipes, but as I learn the quirks of the new/old stove, I'll doubtless be asking my guests, "Do you want the food that's half-burnt, the one that's half-raw, or the one that's a cinder?" Every adventure begins with a few stumbles.

The next year will doubtless bring many more challenges, but the synchronicity of the stove's arrival and the end of this volume allows me to twist time a little. Most books take about a year between the submission of the manuscript and the setting of the volume upon bookstore shelves. As I contemplate where my story will go from here, for once I look into the future instead of the past.

When the printed version of this book arrives, I see myself sitting in front of that beautiful stove, with a merry fire warming the kitchen. I shall look back on the experiences—still unknown—that will have passed since I penned these words and, smiling, cut a slice of bread pudding baked on the sort of stove Mrs. Beeton intended. I shall pour a cup of tea, crack the spine of a freshly printed book, and once more connect the past with the present.

Acknowledgments

A little health, a little wealth,
A little house and freedom;
A few good friends for certain ends,
And little use to need them.[234]

I've certainly needed my friends for this project! Special thanks go to:

Nicole Frail, my wonderful, hardworking editor, for all her insights and advice and for showing such confidence in me.

Joanna Burke, for helping us find the home of our dreams, and Carolyn Frame for negotiating financing in spite of the tightest market crunch in decades.

The Paul Azoulay collection for permission to reprint their lovely photograph of a woman wearing a chatelaine.

Cathy—a gem of a geologist! For "introducing" me to Mary Anning, and for all her encouragement and support.

Tom Evans, for being my go-to guy for any and all science questions, telling us the best places and methods for fossil hunting, letting me invite myself into his home on multiple occasions and cooking more food for me than I knew what to do with, being a kind and loyal friend, and for making the world a significantly more awesome place.

Meredith Everett, for educating me about the difference between wolf spiders and European giant house spiders; for tea, friendship, mutual giggling, and for knitting the socks that kept my feet warm while I worked on a significant portion of this book. I'm sorry our mushroom hunt didn't make it into the text this time, but the chanterelles were delicious and I'm sure they'll appear in a future book.

J. S., our mentor in Victorian bicycles. His authority in the subject is one to which we can only aspire and we are forever grateful for all his help.

Francis Gace, for his beautiful paintings. See: francisgacestudio.com

Tanya Pilant, for her lovely photograph in the Sequim lavender field. See: www.facebook.com/TanyaPilantPhotography

Elizabeth Ogle, for the fun day of photography and the resulting recreation of Perugini's. See: www.elizabethogle.com

Special thanks to Estar Hyo Gyung Choi and Matt Choi of Mary Studio Photography for taking so many beautiful pictures and generously allowing them to be published. (Thanks also to Estar for her delicious kimchi lessons!) See: www.pinterest.com/Estarhyogyung/mary-studios and www.facebook.com/marynature/timeline

And always, to my most beloved Gabriel, for more than I can ever express.

My darling and me. Image courtesy Estar Hyo Gyung Choi.

End Notes

[1] Written on the front endpaper of James Eagleson's diary commencing July 1, 1884. James Beatty Eagleson Papers. Special Collections, University of Washington.

Introduction
[2] Smil, Vaclav. *Creating the Twentieth Century: Technical Innovations of 1867–1914 and Their Lasting Impact.* New York: Oxford University Press, 2005. p. 5–6.
[3] "Je ne suis pas d'accord avec ce que vous dites, mais je me battrai jusqu'à la mort pour que vous ayez le droit de le dire."

Chapter One
[4] Arnold, Jeanne E., Anthony P. Graesch, Enzo Regazzini, and Elinor Ochs. *Life At Home in the Twenty-First Century: 32 Families Open Their Doors.* UCLA: Cotsen Institute of Archaeology Press, 2012. p. 19.
[5] "Snow and Other Weathers—Seattle and King County." www.historylink.org/index.cfm?DisplayPage=output.cfm&file_id=3681.
[6] Cadbury, Deborah. *Chocolate Wars: The 150-year Rivalry Between the World's Greatest Chocolate Makers.* New York: Public Affairs, 2011.

Chapter Two
[7] Dana, Olive E. "Thanksgiving For Two." *Good Housekeeping,* November 24, 1888. p. 32.
[8] Hale, Sarah Josepha. *Northwood; or, Life North and South: Showing the Character of Both.* New York: 1852. p. 68.
[9] Hale, Sarah Josepha. *Manners; Or, Happy Homes and Good Society All the Year Round.* Boston: J. E. Tilton and Company, 1868. p. 6.
[10] "Battles and Casualties of the Civil War Map." www.washingtonpost.com/wp-srv/lifestyle/special/civil-war-interactive/civil-war-battles-and-casualties-interactive-map.
[11] "Civil War Timeline / Chronology for 1863." blueandgraytrail.com/year/186309.
[12] Baker, Peggy M. "The Godmother of Thanksgiving: The Story of Sarah Josepha Hale." www.pilgrimhallmuseum.org/pdf/Godmother_of_Thanksgiving.pdf.
[13] *New York Citizens to Abraham Lincoln, Saturday, April 8, 1865 (Petition requesting day of thanksgiving).* Letter. From Library of Congress, *The Abraham Lincoln Papers, Series 1, General Correspondance, 1833–1916.* memory.loc.gov/cgi-bin/ampage?collId=mal&fileName=mal1/415/4159500/malpage.db&recNum=0.
[14] Editor's Table. "Our National Thanksgiving Day," *Godey's Lady's Book and Magazine,* Volume LXXXIX, No. 533, November 1874. p. 471.
[15] Baker, ibid.
[16] Adams, William. *Thanksgiving: Memories of the Day: Helps to the Habit.* New York: Scribner, 1873. p. 4–5.
[17] Dana, Olive E. "Thanksgiving For Two." *Good Housekeeping,* November 24, 1888. p. 32.
[18] Hadley, Lizzie M. "Blackberry Pies." *Good Housekeeping,* Volume 9, No. 8, August 17, 1889. p. 179.

Chapter Three
[19] Sturgis, Dinah. "Moving." *Good Housekeeping,* April 13, 1889. p. 281–282.

Chapter Four
[20] Abbott, Lyman. *The Woman's Book.* New York: Charles Scribner's Sons, 1894. p. 354.

[21] Denison, Allen T. and Wallace K. Huntington. *Victorian Architecture of Port Townsend Washington.* Seattle: Hancock House Publishers Inc., 1978. p 12.

[22] "The Mediterranean of the Pacific." *Harper's New Monthly Magazine,* No. CCXLIV, September, 1870. p. 482–483.

[23] "PT. Townsend's Resources." *Morning Leader,* Wednesday, October 2, 1889. p. 1.

[24] Ibid.

[25] "Port Townsend: The Future Metropolis of the Pacific Coast." *Morning Leader,* Wednesday, October 2, 1889. p. 8.

Chapter Five

[26] Rowe, Helena. "Family Fashions And Fancies." *Good Housekeeping,* May 26, 1888. p. 33.

[27] Beeton, Isabella. *The Book of Household Management.* London: Ward, Lock & Bowden, 1893. p. 18.

[28] Webb, Ella Sturtevant. "Where the Screw Was Loose." *Good Housekeeping,* Volume 8, No. 11, March 30, 1889. p. 246.

[29] Morris, William. *Hopes and Fears for Art, Five Lectures Delivered in Birmingham, London and Nottingham, 1878–1881.* London: Ellis & White, 1882. p. 108.

[30] Hill, Thomas E. *Hill's Manual of Social and Business Forms.* Chicago: Hill's Standard Book Company, 1891. p. 173, 176.

[31] Neale, Harriet M. "Home Furnishings and Decoration—II: When Economy Economizes, and When It Does Not. Carpets and Rugs, Window Draperies and Portieres." *Good Housekeeping,* March 16, 1889. p. 228.

[32] McCabe, Lida Rose. *The Woman's Book Volume II.* New York: Charles Scribner's Sons. p. 345.

[33] Hill, Thomas E. *Hill's Manual of Social and Business Forms.* Chicago: Hill's Standard Book Company, 1891. p. 167.

[34] Hill, ibid. p. 111, 167.

[35] "Chicago Tops Bed Bug Cities List For Second Year in a Row." www.orkin.com/press-room/chicago-tops-bed-bug-cities-list-for-second-year-in-a-row.

[36] "Bedbugs! 15 Worst Cities." www.cbsnews.com/pictures/bedbugs-15-worst-cities.

[37] *Montgomery Ward & Co. Catalogue 1895.* New York: Skyhorse Publishing, 2008. p. 16, 621.

[38] Kaufman, Leslie and Klaudia H. Deutsch. "Montgomery Ward to Close Its Doors." *New York Times,* December 29, 2000. www.nytimes.com/2000/12/29/business/montgomery-ward-to-close-its-doors.html.

"Sears History—1886: In the Beginning." www.searsarchives.com/history/history1886.htm.

[39] Harris, Lucy Ronalds. "The Diary of Lucy Ronalds Harris." *The Eldon House Diaries: Five Women's Views of the 19th Century.* Ed. Robin S. Harris and Terry G. Harris. Toronto: The Champlain Society in Co-operation with the Government of Ontario, 1994. p. 423–424.

[40] "Singer: History." www.singerco.com/company/history%20?iframe=true&width=100%25&height=100%25.

[41] Berkley, Maud. *Maud: The Illustrated Diary of a Victorian Woman.* Ed. Flora Fraser. San Francisco: Chronicle Books, 1987. p. 53, 63, 173, 183, 187.

[42] "QFC." www.grocery.com/qfc.

Chapter Six

[43] Beeton, p. 18.

[44] Ogle, Maureen. *All the Modern Conveniences: American Household Plumbing, 1840–1890.* Baltimore: The Johns Hopkins University Press, 1996. p. 4.

[45] Ogle, p. 8.

[46] Ogle, p. 146.

[47] City of Port Townsend. "Basic History." cityofpt.us/collectionsystem.htm.

[48] United Nations General Assembly. *Sixty-fourth session agenda item 48: The human right to water and sanitation.* August 3, 2010. www.un.org/waterforlifedecade/human_right_to_water.shtml.

[49] Washington Suburban Sanitary Commission. *Indoor Water Consumption.* www.wsscwater.com/home/jsp/content/water-usagechart.faces.

[50] Morris, William. *Hopes and Fears for Art.* London: Ellis & White, 1882. p.108.

Chapter Seven
[51] Mallemont, Mons A. *Manual of Ladies' Hairdressing For Students.* Bramcost Publications, 2008. p. 6.
[52] Beirne, Clara Grundy. "The Hair: Some Suggestions As To Its Care and Beauty." *Good Housekeeping,* March 2, 1889. p. 203.
[53] Berkeley, Maude. *Maude: The Illustrated Diary of a Victorian Woman.* Ed. Flora Fraser. San Francisco: Chronicle Books, 1987. p. 39.
[54] Aitken Read, Lucy. *Happy Hair: The Definitive Guide to Giving Up Shampoo.* Lucy Aitken Read, 2014.
[55] "Kirks Natural." www.kirksnatural.com/products/original-bar-soap.

Chapter Eight
[56] Muir, John. *Steep Trails.* New York: Houghton Mifflin Company, 1918. p. 220–221.
[57] "Obituary of Thomas Bracken Sr." Jefferson County Archive B277. This is the main source of information about Thomas Bracken Sr. except where otherwise noted.
[58] University of California Press, 2000.
[59] blog.nmai.si.edu/main/2011/01/introduction-1st-question-american-indian-or-native-american.html.
[60] Walbert, Kathryn. "American Indian vs. Native American: A note on terminology." www.learnnc.org/lp/editions/nc-american-indians/5526.
[61] "Washington History Online." washingtonhistoryonline.org/leschi/indianwars/timelines/feb1856.htm#timeline.
"Chief Patkanim." journals.lib.washington.edu/index.php/WHQ/article/viewFile/6581/5653.
[62] "Indian Wars of 1855–56." washingtonhistoryonline.org/leschi/indianwars_timeline.htm.
International Committee of the Red Cross. *Rule 156: Definition of War Crimes.* www.icrc.org/customary-ihl/eng/docs/v1_cha_chapter44_rule156.
[63] "Census of the Inhabitants in Port Townsend, in the County of Jefferson, Territory of Washington. 1889." 1880 census.
"Obituary of Mary Bracken." Jefferson County Archive Obit. B180.
"Obituary of Charles Bracken." Jefferson County Archive Obit. B347.
[64] 1880 census, 1889 census (ibid.).
"Obituary of Edward Bracken." Jefferson County Archive Obits. 246, 268.
"Obituary of Daniel Bracken." Jefferson County Archive Obit. 296.
N.D. Hill & Son Drugstore Ledger BC-56 p. 714. Jefferson County Archive.
[65] Marriage license of Thomas and Mary Bracken, October 23, 1871. FA Prefontaine officiating. Jefferson County Archive.
[66] 1889 census (ibid.).
"Twelfth Census of the United States. Schedule No. 1—Population. State: Washington. County: Jefferson. 9th June, 1900."
[67] "Obituary of Edward Bracken." Jefferson County Archive Obit. 268.
[68] "City Delinquent Taxes." *The Sunday Leader,* September 1, 1895.
[69] *The Sunday Leader,* ibid.
[70] "September 24, 1895. General Expense Fund." Jefferson County Archive, Record 96.55.265.
[71] N.D. Hill & Son Drugstore Ledger BC-56. p. 854. Jefferson County Archive.
[72] "Historic Property Inventory Report for George Swan Rental House."
[73] N.D. Hill & Son Drugstore Ledger BC-56. p. 513. Jefferson County Archive.

Chapter Nine
[74] Wilkie Collins originally wrote *The Frozen Deep* as a stage play in 1856. Many of Victorian England's literary lions knew each other, and the first performance of this play took place at Charles Dickens's house. Dickens himself played the lead role, and other characters were portrayed by Collins and by Mark Lemon (the editor of the satirical magazine *Punch*) and their friends. The story was published

in book form in 1874. The exchange quoted here is found on pages 14–15 of the 1875 edition of the book. Collins, Wilkie. *The Frozen Deep*. Boston: William F. Gill & Co., 1875. p. 14.

[75] "Six People Still Alive Who Were Born in the 19th Century." *USA Today*.www.usatoday.com/story/news/world/2014/09/05/six-people-still-alive-who-were-born-in-the-19th-century/15122367.

[76] Biggs, Matthew, Jekka McVicar, and Bob Flowerdew. *Vegetables, Herbs & Fruit: An Illustrated Encyclopedia*. San Diego, California: Laurel Glen Publishing, 2002. p. 349.

[77] Wilmer, W. H. "Effects of Carbon Monoxide Upon the Eye." *American Journal of Ophthalmology*, Volume 4, No. 2, February, 1921. p. 73–90. This story was also reported in the radio program *This American Life*, October 27, 2006, Episode 319, "And The Call Was Coming From the Basement."

Chapter Ten

[78] Sawyer, Anna. "The Etiquette of Correspondence: Note and Letter Writing." *Good Housekeeping*, Volume 8, No. 10, March 16, 1889. p 221.

[79] Bore, Henry. *The Story of the Invention of Steel Pens with a Description of the Manufacturing Processes by Which they are Produced*. New York: Ivison, Blakeman & Company, 1890. p. 13.

[80] Bore, ibid. pp. 3–4.

[81] "1670 Inks Collection." *Fountain Pen Inks and Fine Writing Accessories*. www.jherbin.com.

[82] Harrison, Constance Cary. *The Woman's Book Volume I*. New York: Charles Scribner's Sons, 1894. p. 161–162.

[83] Sawyer, ibid.

[84] Clark, Georgina G. *A Bottomless Grave and Other Victorian Tales of Terror*. Ed. Hugh Lamb. New York: Dover Publications, 1977. p. 142–154.

[85] Hill, ibid. p. 183.

[86] Brocklehurst, Steve. "Why Are Fountain Pen Sales Rising?" *BBC News Magazine*. www.bbc.com/news/magazine-18071830.

[87] Steinberg, Jonathan. *Fountain Pens: Their History and Art*. New York: Universe Publishing, 2001. p. 18–19.

[88] Steinberg, ibid. p. 19–20.

[89] Steinberg, ibid. p. 24–33.

[90] Arnold, Jeanne E., Anthony P. Graesch, Enzo Ragazzini, and Elinor Ochs. *Life At Home In the Twenty-First Century*. Los Angeles: The Cotsen Institute of Archaelogy Press, 2013. p. 41.

[91] Hill, Thomas E., ibid. p. 78.

[92] United States Postal Service. *Delivery: Monday through Saturday since 1863*. about.usps.com/who-we-are/postal-history/delivery-monday-through-saturday.pdf.

[93] Hill, p. 102, 113.

[94] Anonymous. "Better Mail Service Demanded." *The Morning Leader*, October 2, 1889. p. 4.

Chapter Eleven

[95] Beeton, p. v.

[96] Beeton, p. 1259–1260.

[97] Beeton, p. 355–356.

[98] White, Mrs. William C. "Every Day Cookery: Including Good, Bad and Indifferent." *Good Housekeeping*, August 3, 1889. p. 149.

[99] Weightman, Gavin. *The Frozen Water Trade: A True Story*. Waterville, ME: Thorndike Press, 2002. p. 119–120.

[100] Weightman, ibid. p. 350–351.

[101] "Union Refrigerator Transit Lines Ventilated Refrigerator Car No. 50056." www.whippanyrailwaymuseum.net/exhibits/equipment/rail-equipment/ventilated-refrigerator-car.

[102] Weightman, ibid. p. 350–351.

[103] "Union Refrigerator Transit Lines Ventilated Refrigerator Car No. 50056." www.whippanyrailwaymuseum.net/exhibits/equipment/rail-equipment/ventilated-refrigerator-car.

[104] Miller, Kenneth. "Archaelogists Find Earliest Evidence of Humans Cooking With Fire." *Discover*. discovermagazine.com/2013/may/09-archaeologists-find-earliest-evidence-of-humans-cooking-with-fire.

[105] Beeton, p. 1.

[106] Beeton, p. 37.

[107] Arnold, Jeanne E., Anthony P. Graesch, Enzo Ragazzini, and Elinor Ochs. *Life At Home In the Twenty-First Century.* Los Angeles: The Cotsen Institute of Archaelogy Press, 2013. p. 81.

[108] For more on this, see Rees, Jonathan. "Ice Boxes vs. Refrigerators." histsociety.blogspot.com/2013/12/iceboxes-vs-refrigerators.html.

[109] Gosnell, Mariana. *Ice: The Nature, the History and the Uses of an Astonishing Substance.* Chicago: The University of Chicago Press, 2005. p. 369.

[110] Weightman, Gavin. *The Frozen Water Trade: A True Story.* Waterville, ME: Thorndike Press, 2002. p. 68.

[111] "Whew! Whew! Isn't it hot!" *Port Townsend Leader,* June 12, 1894.

[112] Gosnell, ibid. p. 381–383.

Chapter Twelve

[113] "Pickles and Sauces: The Kitchen Table." *Good Housekeeping,* June, 1893. p. 262.

[114] Kurlansky, Mark. *Salt: A World History.* New York: Walker Publishing Company, 2002. p. 38, 44.

[115] Kurlansky, ibid. p. 38.

Chapter Thirteen

[116] Beeton, Isabella. *The Book of Household Management.* London: Ward, Lock & Bowden, 1893. p. 1081.

[117] Beeton, ibid. p. 1083.

[118] "A Man in the Kitchen: The Difference Between a 'Betty' and the Other Kind." *Good Housekeeping,* February 16, 1889. p. 178.

[119] Ormsbee, Agnes B. "Seven Dollars A Week: How Far It Can be Made to Go At A Pinch." *Good Housekeeping,* August 31, 1889. p. 202.

[120] Beeton, p. 1082.

[121] A Country Parson. "The Kitchen Apron: When it Did Good Service On A Man." *Good Housekeeping,* January 19, 1889. p. 136.

[122] Hardy, Pauline Adelaide. "Bread and People: A Similarity of Character Between Them." *Good Housekeeping,* October 12, 1889. p. 271.

[123] G. M. C. "Buried Bread: How It First Rose And Then Fell, To Rise Again." *Good Housekeeping,* May 24, 1890. p. 36–37.

[124] Beeton, p. 1080.

Chapter Fourteen

[125] "Help For Young Housekeepers: Over the Hill of Difficulty." *Good Housekeeping,* August 17, 1889. p. 169.

[126] Dickens, Charles. "Cookery: The Chestnut Season." *Household Words,* December 24, 1881. p. 176.

[127] V. L. W. "Christmas Candies: Some Good Recipes for Making Them." *Good Housekeeping,* November 24, 1888. p. 39.

[128] "Story Behind the School." www.mhs-pa.org/history/story-behind-the-school.

[129] P. B. *The Western Druggist: A Journal of Pharmacy, Chemistry, and Allied Sciences,* 1892. p. 185.

[130] "Pepys Jr. in Philadelphia." *The Illustrated American,* August 15, 1891. p. 628.

[131] Saxe, D. W. *Saxe's New Guide or Hints to Soda Water Dispensers.* Milwaukee, WI: The Saxe Guide Publishing Co., 1897. p. 10–14.

Chapter Fifteen

[132] Anonymous. "San Francisco Newsletter." *Good Housekeeping,* May 24, 1890. p. 42.

[133] Hisey, G. and K. Hisey. *The Deer Bom: Discussions on Population Growth and Range Expansion of the White-Tail Deer.* Chatfield, MN: Pope and Young Club, 2003.

[134] Stableford, Dylan. "Deer snarl traffic on Golden Gate Bridge." news.yahoo.com/deer-golden-gate-bridge-video-150412230.html.

[135] Sterba, Jim. "If Only Hunters Could Sell Venison: Could loosening rules on deer meat help combat an urban scourge?" *The Wall Street Journal.* online.wsj.com/articles/SB100014240527023044102045 79139424081224050.

[136] Mackinnon, Andy and Jim Pojar. *Plants of the Pacific Northwest Coast.* Canada: B.C. Ministry of Forests and Lone Pine Publishing, 1994. p. 78.

[137] Smith, Jane S. *The Garden of Invention: Luther Burbank and the Business of Breeding Plants.* New York: The Penguin Press, 2009. ("Over Fifty Years of Plant Invention," timeline at front of book.)

[138] Glisan, Rodney. *Journal of Army Life.* San Francisco: A. L. Bancroft and Company, 1874. p. 229.

[139] Mackinnon, ibid. p. 76.

[140] Mackinnon, ibid. p. 53.

Chapter Sixteen

[141] Smith, Alexander. *Dreamthorp: A Book of Essays Written in the Country.* London: George Rutledge & Sons, 1907. p. 346.

[142] Hatt, Michael. "Thoughts and Things: Sculpture and the Victorian Nude." *Exposed: The Victorian Nude.* Ed. Alison Smith. New York: Watson-Guptill Publications, 2002. p. 37.

[143] Smith, Alison. "The Nude in Nineteenth-Century Britain: 'The English Nude.'" *Exposed: The Victorian Nude.* Ed. Alison Smith. New York: Watson-Guptill Publications, 2002. p. 12.

Chapter Seventeen

[144] Ruskin, John. *Pearls for Young Ladies.* New York and Boston: H. M. Caldwell Co., 1878. p. 165.

[145] Fisher-Høyrem, Stefan Tørnquist. *Time Machines: Technology, Temporality, and the Victorian Social Imaginary.* Oxford: Oxford Brooks University, June 2002. p. 87.

[146] *Alexander Graham Bell to Alexander Melville Bell, March 10, 1876.* Letter. From Library of Congress. memory.loc.gov/cgi-bin/query/r?ammem/magbell:@field(DOCID+@lit(magbell00500211)).

[147] Bell, ibid.

[148] "The Telephone." *Scientific American,* Volume 36, No. 13, March 1877. p. 192. archive.org/stream/scientific-american-1877-03-31/scientific-american-v36-n13-1877-03-31_djvu.txt.

[149] Standage, Tom. *The Victorian Internet: The Remarkable Story of the Telegraph and the Nineteenth-Century's On-line Pioneers.* New York: Berkley Books, 1998. p. 80.

[150] Standage, ibid. p. 84, 88, 89.

Chapter Eighteen

[151] Anthony, Geraldine. *A Victim of Circumstances.* New York: Harper & Brothers, 1901. p. 308.

[152] Berkeley, Maude. *Maude: The Illustrated Diary of a Victorian Woman.* Ed. Flora Fraser. San Francisco: Chronicle Books, 1987. p. 92.

[153] *A Midsummer Night's Dream,* Act II, scene I, line 31 (Puck)

[154] Cummins, Genevieve E. and Nerylla D. Taunton. *Chatelaines: Utility to Glorious Extravagance,.* Suffolk, England: Antique Collectors' Club Ltd., 1994. p. 19.

[155] Beirne, Clara Grundy. "The Hair: Some Suggestions As To Its Care and Beauty." *Good Housekeeping,* March 2, 1889. p. 203.

[156] "Flared Jeans—Try The Trend For Fall 2013."hollywoodlife.com/2013/10/04/flare-jeans-fall-2013-trend-flared-leg-denim.

[157] "Bunad—Norwegina Traditional Costumes." mylittlenorway.com/2009/05/bunad-norwegian-traditional-costumes.

"The Norwegian Institute of Bunad and Folk Costume." www.bunadogfolkedrakt.no/filer/TheNational CouncilofFolkCostumesinNorwayx.pdf.

[158] "Goldsmith Sando." www.sando.no/en/category/6/1.html.

Chapter Nineteen

[159] Shenton, Alan. *Pocket Watches: 19th & 20th Century.* Suffolk, England: Antique Collectors' Club Ltd., 1995. p. 18.

[160] Townsend, Colonel George E. *American Railroad Watches*. Michigan: George E. Townsend, 1977. p. 1.

[161] Pope, Nancy. "The Great Kipton Train Wreck." *Smithsonian National Postal Museum Blog*. postalmuseumblog.si.edu/2013/04/the-great-kipton-train-wreck.html.

[162] Townsend, ibid. p. 1.

[163] Fisher-Høyrem, Stefan Tørnquist. *Time Machines: Technology, Temporality, and the Victorian Social Imaginary*. Oxford: Oxford Brooks University, June 2002. p. 102.

[164] "A Brief History of Time Zones—19th century challenges." www.timeanddate.com/time/timezones-history.html.

[165] Shenton, p 71.

[166] Shenton, p. 192.

[167] Shenton, p. 192.

[168] For more about this, see Berkavicius, Rob. "83 jewels too many?" people.timezone.com/library/workbench/workbench0025.

[169] "Ladies' Kid Button, item number 52073." *Montgomery Ward Catalog*. p. 510. "Ladies' Newport Suit, item number 5704." p. 36.

Chapter Twenty

[170] Byron, Lord George Gordon. *Childe Harold's Pilgrimage*. 3rd Ed. Venice: The Armenian Monastery of S. Lazarus, 1889. p. 126.

[171] "Neanderthal." *Encyclopedia Brittanica*. www.britannica.com/EBchecked/topic/407406/Neanderthal.

[172] Vernot, Benjamin and Joshua M. Akey. "Resurrecting Surviving Neandertal Lineages from Modern Human Genomes." www.sciencemag.org/content/343/6174/1017?related-urls=yes&legid=sci;343/6174/1017.

[173] Whittingham, Sarah. *The Victorian Fern Craze*. Great Britain: Shire Library, 2009. p. 11.

[174] For an example of this, see Kemble, Marion. *Art Recreations: Guide to Decorative Art*. Boston: S. W. Tilton and Company, 1884. The chapter on taxidermy starts on page 293, right after the chapter on making wax dolls and flowers.

[175] Brinkley, Douglas. *The Wilderness Warrior: Theodore Roosevelt and the Crusade for America*. New York: HarperCollins, 2009. p. 10.

[176] Blanchard, Emile. "The Children of Arachne." *The Cosmopolitan*, Volume 7, Number 4, August 1889. p. 333.

[177] Master Tinsmith Carl Giordano. His work can be seen at www.cg-tinsmith.com.

[178] Whittingham, p. 19.

[179] Whittingham, ibid. p. 14.

[180] Nicholson, Henry Alleyne. *A Manual of Palaeontology Volume I*. Edinburgh and London: William Blackwood and Sons, 1889. p. 3–4.

[181] "Fay Fuller—First Woman to Summit Mt. Rainier."www.visitrainier.com/pg/personality/1/Fay%20Fuller%20-%20First%20Woman%20to%20Summit%20Mt.%20Rainier.

[182] Pastoureau, Michel. *The Devil's Cloth*. New York: Columbia University Press, 1991. p. 64, 65, 69–72.

[183] Roberts, Cokie. *Ladies of Liberty: The Women Who Shaped Our Nation*. New York: William Morrow, 2008. p. 91, 185.

[184] Byatt, A.S. *Possession*. New York: Vintage International, 1990. p. 291–292.

[185] Davis, Larry E. "Mary Anning: Princess of Paleontology and Geological Lioness." *The Compass: Earth Science Journal of Sigma Gamma Epsilon*, Volume 84, Issue 1. p. 57. digitalcommons.csbsju.edu/cgi/viewcontent.cgi?article=1007&context=compass.

[186] Chambers, William and Robert Chambers. "The Fossil-Finder of Lyme-Regis." *Chambers's Journal of Popular Literature Science and Arts*, January–June 1857. p. 382–384.

[187] Thorne, Isabel. "The Little Fossil-Gatherer." *Chatterbox*, November 2, 1869. p. 386–387.

[188] The Trustees of the Natural History Museum, London. "Mary Anning." www.nhm.ac.uk/nature-online/science-of-natural-history/biographies/mary-anning.

[189] Thorne, p. 386.

[190] Goodhue, Thomas W. *Fossil Hunter: The Life and Times of Mary Anning (1799-1847)*. Bethesda, MD: Academica Press, LLC, 2004. p. 20.

[191] Goodhue, ibid. p. 21.

[192] Goodhue calls Henley "a committed Liberal who supported reform and helped overturn the aristocratic Fane political machine." Ibid. p. 21.

[193] Chambers, William and Robert Chambers. "The Fossil-Finder of Lyme-Regis." *Chambers's Journal of Popular Literature Science and Arts,* January–June 1857. p. 383.

[194] Goodhue, ibid. p. 26, 42.

[195] Goodhue, ibid. p. 33, 34.

[196] Goodhue, ibid. p. 30.

[197] Goodhue, ibid. p. 42.

[198] Goodhue, ibid. p. 41.

[199] Chambers, ibid. p. 383.

[200] Goodhue, ibid. p. 33.

[201] Goodhue, ibid. pp. 23–24.

[202] *Chatterbox*, November 2, 1869, No. 49.

[203] Thorne, ibid. p. 387.

[204] Luke 10:37. *King James Bible.*

[205] Davis, ibid. p. 56.

Figure 1, Goodhue. p. 38. (The original of this painting is in the British Museum of Natural History, London.)

Chapter Twenty-One

[206] Sandow, Eugen. *Strength and How to Obtain It*. London: Gale & Polden, Ltd., 1897. p. 9.

[207] Zweiniger-Bargielowska, Ana. *Managing the Body: Beauty, Health and Fitness in Britain, 1880-1939*. New York: Oxford University Press, 2010. p. 38–39.

[208] H. H. M. "Greek vs. Modern Physical Culture." *Outing and the Wheelman*, December 1883. p. 215.

[209] "Greek vs. Modern Physical Culture." p. 215–216.

Chapter Twenty-Two

[210] Butler, W. H. "Boston to Buffalo, and Beyond." *Outing and the Wheelman*, December 1883. p. 199.

[211] Kron, Karl. "The Environs of Springfield." *Outing and The Wheelman*, December 1883. p. 186.

[212] Hazlett, C. A. "Outing and the Wheelman's 100-Mile Record, 1883." *Outing and the Wheelman*, February 1884. p. 367.

[213] Anonymous. *The Sociable: Or One Thousand and One Home Amusements*. Bedford, MA: Applewood Books.

Chapter Twenty-Three

[214] Comstock, Flora. "Rosalind A-Wheel." *Godey's Magazine*, April 1896, p. 388.

[215] Blackham, George E. "The Other Wheel." *Outing and the Wheelman*, December 1883. p. 207.

[216] Bisland, Mary L. "Woman's Cycle." *Godey's Magazine*, April 1896. p. 385–386.

[217] Bisland, ibid. p. 386–388.

[218] "A Cycle Show in Little." *Godey's Magazine*, April 1896. p. 377.

[219] Bisland, ibid. p. 388.

Chapter Twenty-Four

[220] Bisland, Mary L. "Woman's Cycle." *Godey's Magazine,* April 1896. p. 386.

[221] de Montaigu, Countess Annie. "Fashion, Fact and Fancy." *Godey's Magazine*, April 1896. p. 442.

[222] "Est. 1866: The Story of John Boultbee Brooks." www.brooksengland.com.

[223] "World's Scariest Bridges." *Travel and Leisure.* www.travelandleisure.com/slideshows/worlds-scariest-bridges/13.

[224] Immigration Aid Society of Northwestern Washington. *Northwestern Washington: Its Soil, Climate, Productions and General Resources.* Port Townsend: Puget Sound Argus, 1877. p. 39.

[225] These figures come from a sign at the southern end of the bridge, posted by the Deception Pass Park Foundation.

[226] "Fun Facts About the Statue of Liberty." www.statueofliberty.org/fun_facts.html.

[227] "Swinomish Channel Navigation." www.laconneryachtsales.com/navigation.

[228] Washington State Historical Society, Washington State Department of Transportation, and the Conservation Corps. "Chuckanut Drive." Interpretive sign.

Chapter Twenty-Five
[229] Williams, Henry W. "But Is It Safe?" *The Wheelman,* February 1883. p. 378.

[230] Jones, Edward Gardner. *The Oregonian's Handbook of the Pacific Northwest.* Portland, OR: Press of The Lewis & Dryden Printing Company, 1894. p. 392–401.

[231] Lieb, Emily. "Bellingham—Thumbnail History." www.historylink.org/index.cfm?DisplayPage=output.cfm&file_id=7904.

Chapter Twenty-Six
[232] "Wise Sayings: Impaled By Our Steel Pen and Steal Sheers." *Good Housekeeping,* August 17, 1889. p. 174.

[233] "Ivory Description." www.pg.com/en_CA/product_card/pb_ivory.shtml.

Acknowledgments
[234] Hill, p. 142.

Introduction

The Angels in the Details

All creatures surround themselves with the things that make them most comfortable. In the case of my husband and myself, we just happen to be more comfortable with surroundings more of a nineteenth-century nature than of a twenty-first-century one. In technical terms, our life is a long-term experiential study in temporal diversity of culture and nineteenth-century technology. We study the late Victorian era the way avid linguists study foreign languages: by interacting with our subject as much as possible. There is no passport for traveling through time, but we do our best.

It started with our clothes. When Gabriel gave me a corset on my twenty-ninth birthday, I had no idea how that simple garment would capture my imagination and ultimately lead me into a different world from the one I had been born into—a world of ticking clocks and rustling silk, scented by kerosene and paraffin and inks pressed from the fragrant petals of flowers. It is a world that the modern era is separated from, yet touched by. As historian Vaclav Smil says in *Creating the Twentieth Century*, "[T]he fundamental means to realize nearly all of the 20th-century accomplishments were put in place even before the century began, mostly during the three closing decades of the 19th century and in the years preceding WWI."[2] The nineteenth century birthed the twentieth—and, by extension, the twenty-first.

My husband and I have both always loved history in general and the Victorian era in particular. It often seems to us as though everything worth inventing—everything that made the modern world what it is (for good or ill)—came into being in the last few decades of the nineteenth century. When I

Resources

My husband and I are often asked where we acquire various items. Some of the stories have been told in this book, and a great deal of our antiques come from eBay. Here are some other sources:

BICYCLES
Brooks: www.brooksengland.com. Founded in 1866 (it originally produced horse harnesses and switched to bike gear in 1878), Brooks manufactures high-quality leather bicycle accessories including saddles and bags. My saddle and the bags on both our bikes were made by Brooks.

Copake auction: 266 Route 7A, Copake, New York, 12516. www.copakeauction.com. Every year Copake Auction Inc. holds the biggest auction and swap meet for antique bicycles in the United States.

Gazelle: www.gazellebikes.com. The Gazelle bicycle company was founded in 1892 and is still going strong! My bike is a Gazelle Tour Populair.

Kunst & Leder: www.kunst-und-leder.de. Leather touring bags for bicycles.

Mesicek: www.mesicek.cz. Produces good quality high wheel bicycle replicas.

Victory Bicycles: http://www.victorybicycles.com. Another source for good quality high wheel bicycle replicas.

The Wheelmen: www.thewheelmen.org. A group of modern high wheel bicycle enthusiasts. Information, events calendars, and photographs (both historic and modern).

BOOKS / READING MATERIALS
Antique books: Abebooks: www.abebooks.com.

Digitized nineteenth-century books and magazines that can be downloaded and printed at home: Google Books advanced search: www.google.com/advanced_book_search. This subset of Google Books allows a search by specific date range (for example "Return content published anytime between" January 1885 and September 1886).

Digitized nineteenth-century newspapers (Washington State focus): www.sos.wa.gov/legacy/newspapers.aspx.

Reprinted books, professionally bound: www.skyhorsepublishing.com. Readers who enjoyed *This Victorian Life* might find the following Skyhorse reprints to be of particular interest:

Montgomery Ward & Co. Catalogue and Buyers' Guide (1895)
Sears Roebuck & Co. Consumer's Guide for 1894
1897 Sears Roebuck & Co. Catalogue
The Watch & Clock Makers' Handbook, Dictionary, and Guide by F. J. Britten

CHATELAINES
eBay: www.ebay.com, www.ebay.co.uk. The British version of eBay tends to have a bigger assortment of chatelaines than the American one. eBay is constantly refining their search engines so that international choices can be more readily found from any of their various sites, but if you can't find a desired item from one version of the site, it's always worth doing a quick search through the eBay postings of a different country. (Remember to pay attention to shipping charges.)

Etsy: www.etsy.com. Antique chatelaines as well as new ones made by small-scale artists.

CORSETS
C & S Constructions: www.candsconstructions.com

Orchard Corsets: www.orchardcorset.com

Timeless Trends: www.timeless-trends.com

FABRIC
D.C. Dalgliesh Ltd.: www.dcdalgliesh.co.uk. The last of Scotland's artisan tartan weavers. Ninety percent of small clan tartans are only available from this mill.

The Lining Company: www.theliningcompany.co.uk. Quality linings and trimmings.

ReproductionFabrics.com: www.reproductionfabrics.com. Cotton fabric printed with designs from 1775 to 1950.

William Booth Draper: www.wmboothdraper.com. Fabrics (including cotton, silk, wool, linen and hemp) and notions.

Woven by Water: wovenbywater.com. Cotton fabric woven by a historic water mill. The Quarry Bank Mill was founded in 1784, and is the last remaining water wheel-powered cotton mill (with accompanying mill town) in the world. In addition to yardage, they also sell aprons, shirts, and kitchen linens.

FUR
Moscow Hide & Fur Company: www.hideandfur.com. Furs and feathers, both antique and modern.

HATS
T.P. & H. Trading Co.: www.benderhats.com. Authentically produced nineteenth-century men's hats in a variety of styles.

Randi Jo Hats: www.randijofab.com. Bicycle caps.

MILLINERY SUPPLIES
Timely Tresses: www.timelytresses.com

MISCELLANEOUS
Amazon Drygoods: www.amazondrygoods.com. Paper and celluloid collars, as well as books, notions, and a variety of other accessories.

The Antique Stove Hospital: stovehospital.com. Wood and coal stoves returned to day-one condition.

Carl Giordano: www.cg-tinsmith.com. Giordano is the master tinsmith who made my vasculum. He produces a variety of other eighteenth- and nineteenth-century style tinware as well, including camp kettles and kitchenware.

Darcy Clothing: www.darcyclothing.com. Ready-to-wear men's clothing.

Lacis: lacis.com/catalog/data/AE_PurseFramesMetalFrames.html. Purse frames, including the frames for making chatelaine purses!

Miles Stair: www.milesstair.com. Wicks for lamps and kerosene heaters.

SHOES:
American Duchess: www.american-duchess.com. Historically accurate footwear based on styles from the Renaissance through the 1920s.

WRITING SUPPLIES
J. Herbin: www.jherbin.com. Inks and accessories for fountain pens and straight pens.

Paper companies whose products work well with liquid ink:

Crane & Co.: www.crane.com

Piccadilly: piccadillyinc.com